THIRD WORLDS

In this book Heather Deegan provides a re-examination of the way in which we conceive of and describe the very different regions that we know as the 'Third World'. She asks whether such an umbrella term can have real validity when applied to the Middle East and Africa, arguing that the traditional categorisation of these regions has masked not only their contrasts and contradictions but also their historic and cultural similarities.

Once removed from the category of the Third World, a different picture of these regions emerges. Dr Deegan looks closely at the alternative Islamic development agenda for Africa which in part mirrors that of the World Bank and the IMF. The Islamic agenda contains political, religious, economic, regional and cultural influences. Deegan focuses on each of these themes, examining the relationship between Western patterns of democratisation and Islamic notions of democracy; comparing the policies of Western international aid agencies and their Islamic counterparts – the Islamic Conference Organisation and its funding agency, the Islamic Development Bank; looking at Islamic economics and 'ethico-economics' and their potential for reviving the more impoverished economies of African states; discussing religious devotion and women's worlds; and looking at the influence of political changes in South Africa and the Israel–Palestinian peace negotiations.

What emerges is an original and very revealing view of Third World politics in general and the politics of the Middle East and Africa in particular, which will be invaluable for those with interests either in politics or in development issues.

Heather Deegan is Senior Lecturer in Comparative Politics at Middlesex University.

THIRD WORLDS

The politics of the Middle East and Africa

Heather Deegan

London and New York

First published 1996
by Routledge
11 New Fetter Lane, London EC4P 4EE

Simultaneously published in the USA and Canada
by Routledge
29 West 35th Street, New York, NY 10001

Routledge is an International Thomson Publishing company I(T)P

Typeset in Baskerville by Florencetype Ltd, Stoodleigh, Devon

Printed and bound in Great Britain by
T. J. Press Ltd., Padstow, Cornwall

British Library Cataloguing in Publication Data
A catalogue record for this book is available from the British Library

Library of Congress Cataloguing in Publication Data
A catalogue record for this book has been requested

ISBN 0–415–12218–x (hbk)
ISBN 0–415–12219–8 (pbk)

CONTENTS

v

ILLUSTRATIONS

FIGURES

TABLES

ILLUSTRATIONS

ABBREVIATIONS

ACSAD	Arab Centre for the Study of Dry Regions and Arid Territories
ADB	African Development Bank
AFAA	Association of Faculties of Agriculture in Africa
AFC	Alliance of Forces for Change (Niger)
AMP	African Muslim Party (South Africa)
ANC	African National Congress
ANDP	Alliance for Democracy and Social Progress (Niger)
ARCEDEM	African Regional Centre for Engineering, Design and Manufacturing
CAFRAD	African Centre for Administrative Research and Training for Development
CAMRE	Council for Arab Ministers Responsible for Environment
CDS	Democratic and Social Convention (Niger)
COMCEC	Standing committee for Economic and Commercial Cooperation
COMESA	Common Market for Eastern and Southern African States
COMSA	Commonwealth Observer Mission to South Africa
DLCOEA	Desert Locust Control Organisation for Eastern Africa
ECOMOG	Economic Community of West African States Ceasefire Monitoring Group
ECOWAS	Economic Community of West African States
ERP	ECOWAS recovery Programme
ETUF	Egyptian Trade Union Federation
EU	European Union

EUMOA	Economic and Monetary Union of West Africa
FAO	Food and Agriculture Organization
FUMO	Frelimo and Mozambique United Front
GCC	Gulf Cooperation Council
GDP	Gross Domestic Product
GNP	Gross National Product
GTZ	Gesellschaft Für Technische Zusammenarbeit (German Development Agency)
IBRD	International Bank for Reconstruction and Development
ICIPE	International Centre of Insect Physiology and Ecology
ICO	Islamic Conference Organization
ICRC	International Committee of the Red Cross
ICRISAT	International Crops Research Institute for Semi-Arid Tropics
IDA	International Development Association
IDB	Islamic Development Bank
IDEP	African Institute for Planning and Economic Development
IEC	Independent Electoral Commission
IICs	Islamic Investment Companies
IIRO	International Islamic Relief Organization
IMF	International Monetary Fund
IP	Islamic Party (South Africa)
IPK	Islamic Party of Kenya
ITFO	Foreign (Import) Trade Financing Operations
KANO	Kenya African National Union
LTTFS	Longer-Term Trade Financing Scheme
MIGA	Multilateral Investment Guarantee Agency
MNSD	National Movement for the Society of Development (Niger)
NAM	Non-Aligned Movement
NGO	Non-Governmental Organization
OAU	Organization of African Unity
OAPEC	Organization of Arab Oil Producing and Exporting Countries
OCLALAV	Joint Organisation for the Control of Locusts and Birds
ODA	Official Development Assistance
ODI	Overseas Development Institute

ABBREVIATIONS

OECD	Organization for Economic Cooperation and Development
OICMA	International Organisation for the Control of African Migratory Locust
PANA	Pan-African News Agency
PNDS	Niger Party for Democracy and Progress
PTA	Preferential Trade Area
PTI	Programme of Targeted Interventions
SADC	South African Development Community
SAHPSWU	South African Health and Public Service Workers Union
SALs	Structural Adjustment Loans
SAIRI	Supreme Assembly of the Islamic Revolution in Iraq
SARDC	South African Research and Documentation Centre
SPA	Special Programme of Assistance
UNECA	United Nations Economic Commission for Africa
UNICEF	United Nations Children's Fund
WFP	World Food Programme

INTRODUCTION

The Third World has always been a category of contrasts. Yet academics and practitioners have sought to establish a common set of determinants, e.g. historic, economic, imperialist, which would provide an understanding of, and partly explain the area's apparent endemic political instability. Within this interpretation the relationship between the Middle East and sub-Saharan Africa has been placed in the post-colonial setting of newly independent nations, artificially created by past colonial rivalry and sharing similar political features: military rule, one-party control, authoritarian government and so on. However, tensions arose within that relationship in the 1970s and critics suggested that poor Third World states had become client states of the richer Third World countries. The oil-rich Middle Eastern states distanced themselves from the detritus of economic malfunction and political instability of the poorer African nations, and were capable of creating a new Economic Order funded by petro-dollars.

The international system has changed radically since that debate and in the evolving globalism of the new political environment it is necessary to re-examine the relationship between these two regions. The focus of this study's attention is the alternative Islamic development agenda for Africa which, in part, mirrors that of the World Bank and International Monetary Fund. In a sense, the grouping of the two regions within the umbrella term, the Third World, has masked not only the contrasts and contradictions of the two areas but also their historic and cultural similarities. Islamic influences in sub-Saharan Africa, then, are defined as political, religious, economic, regional and cultural.

This work is divided into main sections: historical, cultural/political, economic/international and conflict, principally to enable readers from different disciplines greater access to the material. Chapter 1 is, of necessity, an historical account of the Islamic/African connection and its purpose is to situate the association over the *'longue durée'*. Chapter 2 considers Islam and democratisation. It does not, however, solely, examine the potential for political upheaval and drift to authoritarian rule, which many believe results from a clash between Islam and democracy. Rather, the chapter considers alternative political agendas, Western patterns of democratisation and Islamic notions of democracy which are currently spoken of by Islamists both in the Middle East and Africa, and their appeal, viability and potential sustainability in various states. The experience of Islamic governments suggests there is not one precise Islamic model to follow so the argument that Islamists are *per se* completely opposed to, say, sharing power with other groups at government level is questionable. There can, of course, be no understanding of the potentiality for democracy without an understanding of the role played by civil society. A constituency within society must support democracy otherwise all attempts at political liberalisation will remain fragile and elements of mass society may emerge. Civil society may foster Islamic and secular groups and parties. A developed civil society should provide a countervailing force to the power of the state, without which, there is little motive for the state to respond to society. But one of the central criticisms of Africa and to a certain extent the states of the Middle East is that civil society can be weak, sometimes linked to the specific regime and often particularistic in cultural or ethnic terms. This topic needs far greater empirical research than this study permits but the debate about Islam and democratisation is a complex one and should be dealt with sensitively. The relationship between secular and Islamic groups may not follow a uniform procedure from country to country; that is, levels of support may differ, aims and objectives may vary and there may be either conflict or co-operation in terms of political expression.

Chapter 3 attempts to disentangle the politics and structures of theocratic and secular states. It also considers certain 'unquantifiable' aspects, such as religious devotion and identity as well as 'hard' facts such as women's healthcare and education. Both the west and the Islamic world have much to say which concerns women's worlds. Chapters 4 and 5 look at regional and international influences, comparing and contrasting the policies of Western international aid agencies with their Islamic counterparts, the Islamic Conference

Organisation and its funding agency, the Islamic Development Bank. Economic pressures are crucial and any development programme contains prognostications on the direction economies should follow. The notion of Islamic economics and 'ethico-economics' is discussed particularly as these subjects are gaining greater attention. Chapter 6 examines the nature of the violence, wars and civil disorder which to some extent have plagued both regions. The political changes in South Africa, the continuing Israeli–Palestinian peace negotiations and the moves towards demilitarisation and demobilisation in some states may point the way to peaceful coexistence. Finally, Chapter 7, acting as a concluding chapter, sets the relationship between the Middle East and sub-Saharan Africa within a wider discourse about perceptions of the Third World.

In her capacity as a member of Chatham House, the author has been invited to certain meetings attended by eminent politicians and academics from both Britain and from overseas, at which matters affecting the Third World were discussed. Some excerpts from speeches made at these meetings have been quoted in the text and are cited as 'meetings' (e.g. Chalker 1985; meeting). In addition, the author has interviewed a number of interested parties about various Third World issues. Exerts from these interviews have also been reproduced here; these are cited as 'interviews' (e.g. El-Affendi 1995; interview).

The author has subscribed to the BBC Summary of World Broadcasts (SWB) and other documents and pamphlets also cited in the text and listed in the references have been obtained from libraries of the School of Oriental and African Studies, University of London, the University of Port Elizabeth and Rhodes University, Grahamstown, South Africa.

Part I
HISTORICAL

1

THE ISLAMIC/AFRICAN CONNECTION

INTRODUCTION

The Iranian revolution of 1979 placed Islam on the international political agenda. Equally, the dissolution of the USSR as a super-power has reinforced the importance of Islam as a major global force. Attention has focused on the potential influence of Islam in Africa, and more recently, central Europe and the successor states of the Soviet empire. The raising of Muslim political consciousness and the moves towards democratisation in the developing world have highlighted the necessity of understanding how long-established cultural and religious affinities affect contemporary relationships between Muslims in the Arab world and those living elsewhere. In the case of Africa, what did and indeed, what does it mean to be an African Muslim? How is the Arab world perceived and is its historic role in Africa as a perpetrator of slave traffic acknowledged? Does Islam mean something very different to African Muslims than to their co-religionists in the Middle East? Has Islam been denied, restricted and controlled by colonial powers and the African secular political leadership which emerged in the post-Independent period who adopted and practised variants of Marxist–Leninist theory? In common with a number of works on contemporary politics of the developing world this chapter considers the historical resonance of the past. It adopts what Fernand Braudel refers to as the *'longue durée'* (Braudel 1969; Bayart 1992; Manor 1991). In other words, in tracing the early spread of Islam in Africa to the years of the post-independence period it seeks to understand the changing relation-ship between Africa and the Middle East. Its purpose, then, is to illuminate the discussion and provide an historical framework for the following chapters in which the recent resurgence of Islamic movements and their political agendas is examined.

THE ARABS IN AFRICA

The association between Islam and Africa has been one of long standing and its development has received considerable scholarly attention. According to one study, the 'origins of present-day African–Arab relations are deeply rooted in the early history of mankind and civilisation'. The major points of contact in the evolution of Africa's Islamic heritage can be found in 'trade, war and proselytism.' (Yousuf 1986 p. 13). Certainly, exposure to Islam varied according to region and accessibility to trade routes with early Muslim settlements in East Africa developing into small dynasties along the coast. The Arab and Islamic presence in North Africa can be traced to the impact of the Arab empire when it extended its conquest in AD 656. Islam became a dominant force in Egypt and Morocco and Islamic states emerged in a number of areas including Ghana and Mali (Salim 1985 p. 130).

Differences in the penetrative effect of Islam partly reflected the degree to which settlement had taken place and the extent to which intermarriage had occurred. Arabs had settled in East and Northeast Africa even before the advent of Islam and established strong trading links with Yemen and Oman. Islamic revivalism occurred in Nigeria in 1804 and the East African Swahili Coast Muslims generally regarded themselves as the rightful protectors of Islam, interpreting and translating the Qu'ran. As trade was a major factor in the dissemination of Islam some analysts have believed that native dwellers 'turned to Islam for two reasons: their rejection of Christian missionaries and their need to ensure trade relations with coastal Arabs' (Yousuf 1986). Slaves and ivory were the most desired commodities and whilst the west coast was the main source of supply for Christian slave traders, the east coast was primarily the area for Arab slave traffic.

THE ISLAMIC–CHRISTIAN DIVIDE

An Islamic–Christian divide existed within the continent and by AD 641 there were three Christian kingdoms south of Egypt. One line of argument suggests that because Christianity has been intimately associated with the West and consequently, with processes of modernisation, education and technology, Islam appeared less attractive. This may have been the case in the post-colonial period but in the early years the vast differences in the scale of religious

8

belief could be attributed to 'differences in the invasive religions themselves' (Turner 1993 p. 33). H.W. Turner maintains that the scriptures of the two faiths and the ways in which they were presented to the peoples of Africa were important determinants of their respective development and maturity. A variety of social forms can be found in both Islamic and Christian movements which usually begin with an individual who may be primarily a founder, a leader, a prophet or a healer. Adherers or followers are attracted but 'this will be short-lived unless (the faith) passes over structured forms that provide organisation, continuity and identity'. As Turner asserts 'if the religion proceeds to embrace the whole life of at least some of its members, with economic, educational and social activities in a village or holy city then it can be called a 'total community' (ibid., p. 32).

Yet standards of Islamisation and the stages and rates of progress can be different from society to society, and according to one specific case 'the ideals of the Islamic state were imperfectly applied in Northern Nigeria' (Philips 1985 (in Philips 1982–85); Jalingo 1985 (in Jalingo 1982–85)). Islam, according to one analyst, has three dimensions: 'the Envisioned Truth; understanding it and applying it'. As such it differs with:

> people, time and place. Islamic thought at a particular point in time and in a particular environment, may tend to justify the acceptance of living reality or call for change. Thus the nature of Islamic thought is determined by the socio-economic environment in which Islamic thinkers exist.
>
> (Musa 1985 p. 67)

This interpretation raises the issue of the Africanisation of religious belief. Africanised religious movements may be either Islamic or Christian but they are distinguished by their concern with being African in form and relevance than with representing the classic orthodoxies of either faith (Turner 1993 p. 30). The degree to which such partly indigenised religious groupings can efficiently reflect or, indeed, replicate the teachings of say, the Shia or Sunni Islamic creeds in the Middle East is open to debate.

One school of enquiry maintains that both Christian and Islamic faiths were imposed on what, hitherto, were regarded as pagan peoples. Certainly, tropical Africa attracted Christian missionaries with evident zeal: 'The heathen was his (the missionary's) target, and of all human groups the Africans were believed to be the most heathen' (Coleman 1970 p. 278). D. M. Wai asserts that the twelve centuries of relations between sub-Saharan Africa and Middle Eastern Arabs were not completely harmonious. The Arabs, he asserts, 'infiltrated Africa, enslaved its peoples, imposed Islam on them and educated them'. The Africans did not infiltrate the Arab region apart from their presence as slaves. Consequently, the outcome has been one of tension between Arabs and Africans who with value systems stemming from very different social and environmental backgrounds, have little in common (Wai 1985 p. 62). These interpretations have been refuted by others who seek to establish a much closer linkage between Arabs and Africans and maintain that 'it is completely erroneous to look at Africa on a linguistic basis as Arab Africa north of the Sahara and purely African in the south' (Musa 1985, p. 61). The two areas of the African continent cannot be distinguished ethnically and culturally.

> Population movements between the regions have been continuous over many centuries and human, linguistic, intellectual, religious, economic and social interaction has persisted. Both Africa north of the Sahara and south of it, together with the Horn of Africa and East Africa, constitute a single cultural region reinforced by Islam and the Arabic language.
>
> (ibid.)

Interestingly, Islam has been regarded as inspiring a 'certain cultural uniformity' on some of the emergent modern states of the western Sudan region but doubts have been raised as to the existence of wider commonalities between Africans and Arabs across the continent (Grove 1978 p. 88). One view suggests that 'it would be more appropriate to admit that the Arabs have a separate identity from the Africans than to rule out any such distinction', and concludes that 'it is not accurate to consider African cultures or the cultural development of African peoples as being identical with Arab culture' (Zebadia 1985 p. 81).

The inescapable fact in this debate is that whichever way the issue is considered the potent religious influences penetrating the African continent during that time came either from the West in the form of Christianity or from the Arabs in the structure of Islam. There appeared to be very little indigenous intellectual or religious aggrandisement from Africa itself. According to one study: 'Writing was introduced (into south of the Sahara) with Islam and Christianity. Before the coming of these universal religions written contracts and codes of law were unknown' (Grove 1978 p. 83). It may also be, as H.W. Turner argues, that the overall tendency of religious faith in the long run is to shift from 'neo-primal (forms of belief) to more orthodox forms as the scriptures of both the major traditions achieve greater influence and as the forces of modernisation reveal the essentially archaic nature of primal religions of all kinds' (Turner 1993 p. 31). The implication of this statement is that a form of religious primitivism existed in Africa upon which a system of conversion was imposed by both Christians and Islamists. In fact, it has been acknowledged that among long-distance traders 'a universal religion, such as Islam, was more satisfying than local deities and cults which were tied to particular regions, clans or even natural objects and phenomena' (Philips 1982–85). Certainly, Islam is regarded as playing a 'major civilising and social role in sub-Saharan Africa', largely because it introduced a monotheistic religion to the Africans 'for the first time in their history' (Zebadia 1985 p. 80). Also the imposition of slavery from the West and East through the conduit of trade suggests that the peoples of the African continent lacked economic parity not only with colonialists from the West but also, with the Arabs. African slaves were considered more trustworthy in the Sultanate of Oman than the native subjects of that particular region (Yousuf 1986 p. 19). The Arabs 'sent caravans far inland' for slaves who were then sold on markets in Zanzibar and exported to Turkey, Arabia, Persia (Iran) and India (Grove 1978 p. 94).

ISLAM AND COLONIALISM

The connection between Islam and Africa raises several interesting points and, according to Louis Brenner poses some difficult questions. In the first place, Islam challenges the Pan-African view of a secular politically unified Africa forged in the post-independent era; secondly, it undermines the Afro-Centrist school of thought which asserts a black cultural identity and history, unassociated with either the West or, indeed, Islam; and thirdly, it attacks the political/economic imperatives of African development rooted in the Marxist tradition (Brenner 1993). One interpretation of the conjuncture between East and West in Africa accuses European aggrandisement and colonialism of attempting to 'sever the links between Arabs and Africans by all possible means' (Zebadia 1985 p. 180). If European expansion is considered from the Portuguese explorations of the fifteenth century, parallels have been drawn between the Portuguese settlements on the west coast to those of the early Arabs traders on the east coast, in that new towns sprang up around trading posts and intermarriage occurred (Grove 1978 p. 90). In tracing a continent's heritage, however, very different influences are brought into play which may not be necessarily homogeneous. As the colonial experience was conducted through the policies and practices of many European powers, each with different approaches to the exercise of government and administration, the patterns of political behaviour exposed to indigenous populations may vary.

Studies of colonialism have at times followed an especially Eurocentric line which tends to undermine pre-colonial influences, placing them as secondary to the fundamental economic, geographic and political changes which occured during the imperialist period (Cammack *et al.* 1991). This approach often amalgamates separate states within Africa with states in other regions of the Third World. Thus grouped, the contemporary political systems of those states are then explained within the common framework of the ill-effects suffered by the years of colonial penetration. Such an interpretation, linked into a particular time scale adopts an economic capitalist deterministic model which sees industrial imperialistic powers wrenching pre-capitalist societies away from their traditional belief and value systems and thrusting them into economic exploitation and dependency on a malevolent developed world.

It is often acknowledged that 'many different socio-political organisations existed in pre-colonial Africa. Urban communities existed in parts of pre-European Africa and particularly in the western Sudan ... indeed by the 11th century Kano (now in northern Nigeria) had already become a prosperous trans-Saharan trading centre' (ibid.). Recent studies, using linguistic evidence, suggest that the peoples of Burundi 'participated in a regional trade system that was much older and broader in scale than has been previously thought', and such practices were well established before the arrival of the Arabs. However, although Burundians participated in 'a multiplicity of exchange relations' with a wide range of goods over considerable distances, when the Arabs arrived, their trading practices were superimposed on existing procedures. Sometimes the traders complemented each other, for example, in the boosting of the metals and salt trade, but at times, they competed, as in the garment trade, to the disadvantage of the indigenous Burundians

12

(Wagner 1993). Although no attempt should be made to undermine the deleterious impact of European colonial rule, it is clear that Arab intrusion into the continent affected the working lives of Africans, dramatically altered their belief systems and committed many people to the slave trade.

Ironically, as David Fieldhouse maintains, the nineteenth century European colonialists, unlike their predecessors, wished to abolish slavery and in 1873 Sultan Barghash was induced to end the slave trade between the African mainland and Zanzibar (Fieldhouse 1973 p. 364). Certainly, Arab complicity in the African slave trade was one of the most abiding sources of contention during the colonial period and in some countries, after independence. It is, therefore, misleading to consider the events of the pre-colonial period to be either unimportant or benign. For most African peoples the years of the slave trade conducted by both Arab and European traders were 'years of turmoil and a constant threat to settled life' (Grove 1978 p. 91).

One body of thought maintains that, 'trade with the Arabs brought medieval West Africa into touch with the world of Islam, and with Islam came Arab culture and civilisation' (Emerson and Kilson 1965 p. 7). Jean-François Bayart asserts that 'trans-regional religious movements, especially of Islam, were powerful means of social rapprochement', in that a process of assimilation between communities occurred (Bayart 1992 p. 177). Certainly, the Islamic states of North Africa have been considered 'more civilised than those of any other part of Africa' (Fieldhouse 1973 p. 105). Yet, Tom Mboya, one-time Kenyan Minister of Planning and Economic Development and founder of the Kenya African National Union believed the histories of Egypt, Liberia, Sudan and Ethiopia to be so different that they did not have the same impact on post-Second World War nationalist aspirations in the rest of Africa as did the independence of Ghana in 1957 (Mboya 1970). We shall be returning to this debate later in the chapter. At this stage, however, it is necessary to understand the role Islam played during the colonial period.

THE COLONIAL 'CARVE-UP'

Thomas Hodgkin in his study of Nigeria maintains that

> the two major empire building movements which marked the beginning and the end of the (nineteenth) century – the Islamic Fulani and the British – have in the intellectual renaissance

13

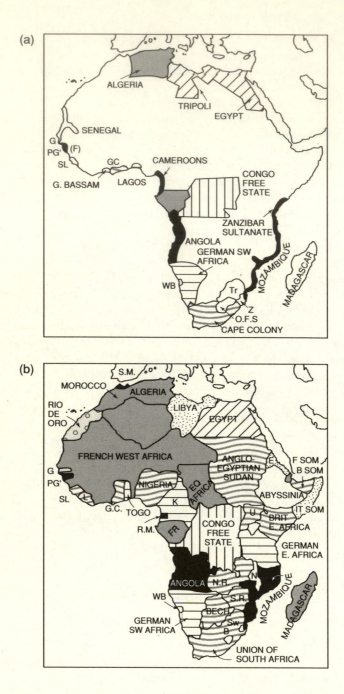

(c)

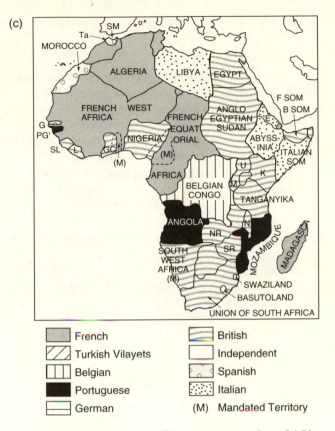

▨ French	▨ British
▨ Turkish Vilayets	☐ Independent
⊞ Belgian	▨ Spanish
■ Portuguese	▨ Italian
☐ German	(M) Mandated Territory

Figure 1.1 Maps showing European penetration of Africa
　　　(a) Africa after the Berlin Conference
　　　(b) Africa after the outbreak of the First World War
　　　(c) Africa at the outbreak of the Second World War

Key maps (a) and (b): B, Basutoland; E, Eritrea; G, Gambia; GC, Gold Coast; K, Kamerun; L, Liberia; N, Nyasaland; NR, Northern Rhodesia; OFS, Orange Free State; PG, Portuguese Guinea; RM, Rio Muni; SL, Sierra Leone; SM, Spanish Morocco; SR, Southern Rhodesia; Sw, Swaziland; T, Tunisia; Tr, Transval; U, Uganda; WB, Walvis Bay; Z, Zululand.

Key map (c): B, Benin; Bu, Burundi; CAE, Central African Empire; D, Djibouti; EG, Equatorial Guinea; GB, Guinea–Bissau; Gh, Ghana, IC, Ivory coast; K, Kenya; Le, Lesotho; M, Malawi; R, Rwanda; S, Senegal; Ta, Tangier; UV, Upper Volta. For other abbreviations see Figure 1.1 (a) and (b).

15

deriving from them as well as in political results, more in common than is usually realised.

(Emerson and Kilson 1965 p. 6)

On the other hand, D.K.Fieldhouse sees the motivation for mid-nineteenth-century colonial extension to be fiscal or political: 'the desire of existing colonies or trading bases to extend the limits of their customs collection to raise more revenues; . . . and in the special case of Senegal, fear of Islamic power inland', together with a desire to increase colonial revenues (Fieldhouse 1973 p. 147). When the imperial powers agreed at the Berlin Conference of 1884 that no new annexations on the African coast were to be recognised as valid unless they were accompanied by effective occupation, it is generally acknowledged that the African continent was, as the phrase goes, 'carved-up' indiscriminately 'with casual disregard for the people whom they thus allocated into one or another colony' (Clapham 1985 p. 17).

As Maps A, B and C (Figure 1.1) indicate the European colonial penetration of Africa was immense and arbitrary. It was both the scale and the territorial rearranging of the continent which separated tribal groupings and also presented a challenge to Arab influences. East Africa, for example, was partitioned into two areas, one initially under German control, Tanganyika and the other land, which included part of Somalia and was later to become known as Kenya, under the British. However, colonial administrations particularly the French and British were aware of the powerful Islamic communities and co-operated with established traditional leaders: e.g. the Fulani Emirs in the northern provinces of the Cameroons and the Muslim brotherhoods of Senegal (Cammack *et al.* 1991 p. 22). Again Arabs and their African offspring occupied high government offices in Tanganyika and Kenya (Khair El-Din Haseeb 1985 p. 132). In some cases it is alleged that Arab commercial activities were actually facilitated by the improved infrastructure and transport systems established under colonial rule. These Arab traders played a secondary role in disseminating Islam through intermarriage with Africans, thus 'Arab communities of pure or mixed descent emerged on a larger scale in the interior away from the coast' (ibid. p. 133).

One central plank of Britain's colonial policy was in certain instances to support the Muslim sects in order to ease British administration and minimise potential resistance (Yousuf 1986 p. 26). In

16

northern Nigeria once initial Islamic resistance was controlled, the British established a system of Emirates based on Islamic law. The policy of promoting friendship and co-operation with dominant Muslim figures enhanced Britain's influence over the whole area (Ismael 1969 p. 150). Accordingly, 'Religious chiefs who favoured colonial rule were put in effective control of such local affairs as education, taxation and the enforcement of Islamic law' (Yousuf 1986 p. 26). Chazan *et al.* point to the Mourides of Senegal who co-operated with colonial authorities and benefited economically from the association (Chazan *et al.* 1988 p. 92). Indeed, in recent studies it is observed that during the colonial years the Muslims of Senegal were 'more concerned for their plantations and their businesses than for Islamic revolution' (Coulon and Cruise O'Brien 1991).

Despite the argument that Arabs mixed with Africans in different ways and understood the injustices they suffered under colonialism, there appears to be a certain ambiguity in the relationship between Muslims and the colonial powers. One view suggests it was European military and technological might which asserted itself over the partitioned colonial territories which ensured that 'the foundations of colonialism in East Africa were laid down and Arab political control was ended once and for all' (Salim 1985). Whilst others assert it was the economic deterioration under colonial rule which ensured the 'colonisers had no choice but to allow Arab commercial activities to continue, which in itself enhanced the Arab presence and its Islamic cultural components (Naim 1985).

So what impact did the 'carve-up' of Africa have on the relationship between Africans and Arabs? In order to answer this question one has to consider either, that Arabs, Africans of Arab descent and Africans share common objectives or, alternatively, to consider their interests to be separate and possibly contradictory. One view in favour of the first proposition suggests that: 'At no point in the long history of Islamic power did a non-African Islamic ruler succeed in controlling the African Muslims.' As such, Islam presented no threat to the interests of Africans as it 'allowed for compromise and harmonious relations with the African way of life, traditions and customs' (Yousuf 1986 p. 28). Looked at this way there can be no distinction between Muslim and non-Muslim Africans. If some powerful Muslim African leaders decided to co-operate with the colonial powers in the administration of truncated territories, it must not be seen to infer a betrayal of the interests of other non-Muslim Africans but should be viewed as the only available option open to subjugated peoples. Colonial rule would neither be in the interests of native Africans nor those of Arab descent as it demarcated territory, imposed administrative structures and introduced a colonial economy which advantaged the European power through fiscal and trading procedures at the cost to the colony itself.

However, if one considers the interests of African Muslims to differ from those of other indigenous Africans, an alternative picture emerges: one of complicity with the colonial power to the disadvantage of the native non-Muslim African population. The old colonial strategy of 'divide and rule', that is the favouring of one community over another, would have no meaning in a society where interests were one and the same. Differences between sections of society, then, were not only clearly perceived by the colonial powers but actually acted upon. In fact, the colonial powers often identified certain groups as 'tribes' and, therefore, were themselves instrumental in creating distinctions between peoples (Chazan *et al.* 1988 p. 103). According to one interpretation 'the role of religion as a symbolic medium of contact and conflict is striking in the colonial history of Africa' (ibid. p. 92). Bayart maintains that the 'two monotheistic religions', that is, Christianity and Islam, have both had 'long experience of accommodation with the State', colonial and otherwise (Bayart 1992 p. 190). Yet, perhaps, the best method of understanding precisely where affinities between different religious groups rested during the colonial years is to examine the period of African independence.

INDEPENDENCE

The catapult into independence of many African states in the 1950s and 1960s raised a new set of dynamics which preoccupied newly emergent nation states. The difficulties were essentially twofold: how to construct national unity and thus integrate peoples within a sovereign state, whilst simultaneously undermining ethnic and religious divisions. As the first election manifesto of Ghana's socialist Convention People's Party under the leadership of Dr Kwame Nkrumah stated:

> The Party System has come to stay. The CPP in accordance with progressive forms of government everywhere, is opposed to the formation of political parties on the basis of racialism,

18

tribalism and religion, and will make use of every legitimate means to combat it. In our country, with its tradition of religious tolerance and respect for all faiths it is highly undesirable that a religious association or denomination should take on itself the character of a political party. If it does so, the public is liable to associate its religious tenets, be they Christian or Muslim, with its political aims, and to withhold from such a religious movement the tolerance which is given to purely religious sects. 'Down with politicians who are exploiting religious fanaticism.'[1]

The Manifesto of the Belgian–Congolese Elite in 1956 also proclaimed the need for national union in which it would be possible for 'pagans, Catholics, Protestants, Salvationists, Mohammedans to agree on a programme of common good' (Okuma 1963). However, while Patrice Lumumba, the President of the Congo, described those Africans of Arab descent to be 'uncles of the Congolese', the situation in the predominantly Muslim northern Nigeria, home to the Hausas and Fulanis, was rather different. These peoples were judged to be anti-Western and 'extremely fanatical about Islamism. They have an open contempt for those who do not share their religious belief' (cf. Okumu 1963; Khair El-Din Haseeb 1985 p. 138; Awolowo 1965). Certainly, the concept of nation-state building through a national consensus escaped the attention of the party, the Northern People's Congress who spoke of 'One North, One People' (Clapham 1985 p. 33).

Racial tensions between Africans and Arabs in Zanzibar became intense in the 1950s and 1960s as the island was proclaimed an independent African state to be merged with Tanganyika (now Tanzania) under the socialist leadership of Julius Nyerere. For Nyerere, 'no under-developed country could afford to be anything but socialist' and for some years Tanzania captured the imagination of many people who considered it to have found the 'African road to socialism' (Emerson and Kilson 1965 p. 163). In a sense, Nyerere pinpointed the difficulties facing newly-independent states:

There are obvious weaknesses on the African continent; we have artificial nations carved out at the Berlin conference in 1884 and today we are struggling to build these nations into stable units of human society. These weaknesses too are being exploited. We are being reminded daily of them. We are told that tribalism will not allow us to build nations; but when we try to take measures to deal with tribalism we are accused of 'dictatorship'.

(ibid.)

French-speaking West and Equatorial Africa had separate political movements. The conference of the Rassemblement Démocratique Africain (RDA) held in 1946 in French Sudan (now the Mali Republic) offered political ideas informed by a Marxist analysis which would be unrestrained by territorial boundaries. The goals of this widely based multi-state association were: 'The emancipation of our different countries from the yoke of colonialism through the affirmation of their political, economic, social and cultural personalities, and the freely agreed union of countries and peoples, founded on the equality of rights and duties' (D'Arboussier 1965). The Kenyan experience, on the other hand, raised the spectre of racial tension when the Kikuyu tribe launched a movement known as the Mau Mau in the early 1950s. The Swahili Arabs, who were linked to the Africans racially and culturally, gave an ambivalent response to the movement. Although, allegedly sympathetic to African aspirations, they were concerned about the threat to their own interests. African leaders responded with recriminations about the Arab role in the slave trade and relationships deteriorated. The country's constitution which followed independence provided for provincial governments to be established with autonomy to be permitted in some areas of policy such as health and education. But after the transitional phase the state became a unitary one under the leadership of Kenya's only political party: KANO (Khair El-Din Haseeb 1985 p. 134). Racial tensions in Uganda, however, were not troubled principally by the growth in the country's nationalism and the transfer of power but rather later when accusations were levelled against Arabs and Arab-Africans of supporting President Idi Amin simply on the grounds that he was a Muslim. Libya and Saudi Arabia also supported his regime, and when he was inevitably overthrown a bloody campaign was fought against his supporters who were forced, to leave the country, with many seeking refugee status is Kenya.

It would appear then, that clear tensions were apparent both at the time of independence and during the years which followed. Whether the interests of Muslim Africans could be identified as being the same as non-Muslim Africans is difficult to answer. The communities were essentially schooled in a very different tradition and at times Islamic Africans were blatantly regarded as backward. Northern Nigeria was readily regarded by some political leaders as 'dragging behind' when it came to 'Western European civilisation', and militating against any quest for national unity (Akintola and Balewa 1965). Yet, the states of the Middle East had also been under colonial control and Gamal Abdel Nasser had exercised a radical anti-colonial revolution in Egypt in 1952 on behalf of Muslim peoples. Nasser was seen in the Middle East as a 'Modernist', cutting a swathe through conservative, traditional Arab opinion and establishing the notion of Pan-Arabism, and as a real and menacing threat to Western imperialism. These actions, however, were not directly reflected in Nigeria, Tanzania, Kenya, etc. where the activities of Muslims were considered a hindrance to progress rather than a vanguard of change. Muslims in the sub-Sahara, then, could only contribute by uniting with other ethnic and religious groups in preserving the integrity of the new nation state. Hence, as emphasised by Ghana's Convention People's Party, any political activity based on tribal, religious or regional differences among the country's population represented a profound source of political instability. The government was committed to 'make use of every legitimate means to combat it' (ibid.).

The key to understanding this apparent contradiction is that, although invoking the spirit of Islam and establishing a Supreme Council for Islamic Affairs as well as a Ministry of Religious Endowments which was responsible for spreading Islam, Nasser conducted the 1952 revolution on the basis of a state-centred, semi-socialist programme rather than on the lines of a strictly religious, Islamic system similar to the models of Saudi Arabia or later, the 1979 Iranian revolution. Certainly before 1952 there seemed little to connect Egyptian nationalist organisations with African nationalist movements, and perhaps this accounts for Tom Mboya's virtual dismissal of the importance of Egypt's revolution to Africa (Fayek 1985). Yet Nasser recognised the relevance of sub-Saharan Africa:

> We cannot, under any conditions, relinquish our responsibility to help spread the light of knowledge and civilisation to the very depth of the virgin jungles of the continent. Africa is now the scene of a strange and stirring turmoil. We cannot stand as mere onlookers, deluding ourselves into believing that we are in no way concerned.
>
> (ibid.)

After 1952 African nationalist leaders were invited to Egypt and solidarity was expressed between Nasser and various African political figures but an element of caution existed regarding the assistance Egypt gave to African Muslims. According to Mohamed Fayek, Egypt resisted any seccessionist movements by sending troops to the Congo in favour of President Lumumba and by supporting the federal government of Nigeria. Also Egypt supported the unification of Zanzibar and Tanganyika which essentially assured the disappearance of an Islamic state. On the one hand, then, Islam was a guiding factor in Egypt's foreign policy with the emergent African nations: providing educational missions, Qu'ranic and Arab language education, scholarships, building schools and mosques and so on, but on the other, Egypt made little attempt to create Islamic blocs or to nurture Muslim groups which might undermine national unity in the newly established African states. Ironically, it was the apparent lack of importance devoted to Islamic theory and practice in the undertaking of Egypt's foreign policy which critics suggested was one of the revolution's major errors and led to opposition from Islamic movements within the country itself (Youssef in Khair El-Din Haseeb 1985).

The intellectual political climate within the nationalist movements in Africa during the last years of the colonial period was dominated by Marxism, variant forms of socialism and certain liberal democratic ideas which had filtered through the administrations of some colonial powers. The path to the future was judged to be secular but most importantly to be driven by European political discourse. Anti-colonialism was to be expressed through the introduction of neo-Marxist–Leninist practices or through the introduction of the political concept of rights and responsibilities. The colonial powers had controlled those African territories during the years of imperialism and it was essentially Western political thought, whether of a liberal democratic or Marxist–Leninist variety which infiltrated the intellectual debate of those newly independent states. The fact that Marxism was a Western concept was masked by the existence of the Cold War and superpower rivalry between the West and the Soviet Union. Despite paying lip-service to Islam, Egypt, in common with numerous African states, chose a quasi-socialist path to demonstrate its anti-colonial struggle.

One observer maintains that the European involvement and the de-colonisation process raised a new difficulty, that of precisely 'what would be the relationship between Islam and the state' (H.S. Yousuf

1986 p. 29). Bayart argues that Islam facilitated a 'disengagement from the state' in that, religious practices transcended the operations of government (Bayart 1992 p. 257). Islam in Egypt represented an area which differed from political idealism but formed part of a religious inheritance. To an extent this was the case in the African states. Islam was perceived by African nationalist leaders as a non-modernising force at that time. If anything, it appeared to harness a country to its pre-colonial past, thereby denying any moves towards progress. All vigour and momentum at the time of independence focused on developing African states, with progress identified as economic growth, social change, national identity, democracy of one form or another, the granting of some political and civil rights and nation-state building. Any religious or ethnic grouping challenging those objectives was perceived to threaten national integration and social advancement. The way forward was secular, statist and, generally, socialist. However, if Islam was not the central political creed of the new African nations then neither was it the focal ideological principle of the Muslim state of Egypt. Islam, then, in the early post-colonial years did not represent the formidable political directive with which it has latterly become identified. Although, it is true to say, as Bayart reminds us, that Islam never was, and indeed, has not become a monolithic religious movement, with Sufi, Mahdist and militant strands all adding 'to the number of divergent social strategies' (ibid. p. 249).

ETHNICITY AND ETHNIC GROUPS

The term ethnicity has been described as 'a subjective perception of common origins, historical memories, ties and aspirations' (Chazan et al. 1988 p. 102). Determinants of these commonalities can be based on residency within a specific geographical region, or common culture and traditions (ibid. p. 103). Equally, religious belief and identification forms part of a mutually shared heritage, which has 'crystallised into specific repertoires' (Bayart 1992 p. 202). However, according to Chazan et al., 'the process of ethnic self-definition occurred in the short time span that it did because of the impact of colonial interventions and the intense competition over power, status, economic resources and social services happening during the late colonial and post-colonial periods (ibid. p. 103). Certainly, there have been examples of colonial authorities distinguishing between peoples by referring to them as separate tribes with one case of Belgian officials identifying people living near the Zaire River as Ngala and later using the term to describe those who had migrated to town (ibid.). Clearly, there was an arbitrary quality in the groupings of people together under colonial rule.

However, in the case of Muslim Africans the sense of separateness was inculcated before the imperial powers arrived in Africa, and during the process of conversion to Islam at the time of early Arab involvement in the continent. It has been maintained that in the period of the initial Arab slave trade, distinctions were made by traders between Muslim and non-Muslim Africans as to who would or would not become a slave. Equally, because of the process of religious dissemination, e.g. via the special Sufi order or through the conduit of trade, Islam has been viewed as the religion of a particular 'segment' of African society, aligning itself with various tribal chiefs for 'the purpose of achieving security and peace, which were necessary for flourishing and prosperous trade' (Khair El-Din Haseeb 1985 p. 63). Allegedly, tribal leaders and chiefs found that Islam provided both a source of material benefit through extended trade, increased political influence and the greater scope of authority beyond existing traditional tribal boundaries. Islam, then, became the religion of the dominant groups within the existing society. Certainly, religious leaders have become immensely important elite figures in states such as Senegal and Mali (*Africa Confidential* 1987). Religious faith and affiliation, however, can carry a different set of features when compared with the generally identified distinctions of tribal ethnicity, in that belief in a deity has a mutable quality. People may not be able to change their tribal inheritance but they can alter their belief patterns. In fact, studies have suggested that a 'gradual process of de-Islamisation lasting several generations' took place when former traders changed their occupations and settled down to farm (Philips 1982–85). Nevertheless, religion becomes important when belief systems remain unchained over a period of time, and a tribe becomes identified as strongly Christian or Islamic.

Chazan *et al.* maintain, that 'an awareness of the (ethnic) group as a distinct entity in relationship to other cultural groups remains a relatively recent phenomenon' (Chazan *et al.* 1988 p. 103). Others perceive European colonisation to have followed from Arab colonisation in that, on the one hand, the Arabs and Muslims civilised and provided culture to the Africans, whilst on the other, they destroyed Africa's states and civilisations such as, the overrunning of the state of Ghana by Murabiteen and of the state of Songhi by

Sa'adyeen' (Trimingham 1970 pp. 144–154). During Africa's struggle for independence and the transfer of power it was clear that certain tribal groups were identified by other tribes as Islamic. Islamic religious identity had been superimposed on ethnic group-ings from the time of Arab incursions into the continent and might not, therefore, be adequately described as a 'recent phenomenon'. The fact that peoples continued to adhere and follow Islamic teach-ings suggests a strong identification with a cultural heritage and not necessarily a passing attachment to religious faith determined by the ebbs and flows of material fortune. It is, as Bayart reminds us, part of Africa's historicity (Bayart 1992 p. 202). In other words, the continuity of religious faith has to be viewed over the '*longue durée*'.

Chazan *et al.* argue that:

> What colonial administrators previously grouped together as 'tribal' identities for administrative purposes became the basis for urban-led demands in the post independence period. As such, the ethnic group has become a useful instrument for mobilising and aggregating interests in competition with other ethnic, occupational and business interest groups for state-controlled political and economic resources.
>
> (Chazan *et al.* 1988 pp. 105–106)

Yet Africa's Islamic heritage has given rise to the emergence of a number of specific organisations: the Uganda Muslim Supreme Council, la Fédération des Associations Islamiques du Sénégal, l'Association Islamique du Niger, l'Union Musulmane du Togo and so on. It would certainly seem that African Islamist groups are asserting their demands for power and status. The degree to which those desires are informed by a strong Islamic heritage and cultural commonalities, or by reasons of contemporary socio-economic imperative and demands for access to resources courtesy of the Organisation of Islamic Conference will be issues pursued further in the following chapter. At this stage we must reassess the important historical factors which serve to combine the past with the present and influence the contemporary debate.

CONCLUSION

The Islamic/African connection is perversely both easy to chart but more difficult to assess. The interaction between Islam and Africa began with the intrusion of Arabs and the process of religious

25

conversion; a process reflective of the dominant/dominated relation-ship which was to become such an unhappy component of the continent's historical development. The role of the Arabs in the history of Africa, then, is hardly auspicious, and much as some writers wish to regard the Arab slave trade as 'a social issue which should not be viewed outside its historical context' (Khair El-Din Haseeb 1985 p. 65) there is clear sensitivity and uneasiness about past injustices inflicted on African peoples. This is not to diminish in any way the impact and effects of European colonial rule, for in a curious way it tended to forge a closer link between the Arabs and Africans, especially during the post-independent period as both regions fought the struggle against imperialism. Yet the years of colonial rule indicate that divisions did exist between Muslim Africans, powerful in their communities, favoured and patronised by some colonialists and other non-Muslim Africans, exploited, deeply resenting the yoke of colonial control, and forging nation-alist aspirations.

Religion *per se* was a contradictory element within African society, with Christianity extricably linked to the imperatives of God but also severely handicapped by its association with the West and colo-nialism. In a sense, the Islamization of a society has been seen to follow a similar pattern with the roles of force and conquest being emphasised, through the exercise of the Jihad, the holy war. The compulsion of conversion has worried many observers of the patterns of religious dissemination in the African continent together with the abiding assumption that belief systems operating within Africa were primitive and primal (Philips 1982–85). Both Islam and Christianity contribute to the cultural inheritance of Africa and have reflected modes and methods of political expression. However, and this is in many ways a fundamental and potentially treacherous point, the nature of Islam has been judged to have changed (Ayubi 1991). We may not, in fact, be speaking of the same entity when we refer to Islam of the past and the contemporary politically charged force which is encapsulated in the Islamic revivalism of the past decade. However, in order for that revival to take place and to carry Islamists in Africa with it suggests that a strong sense of affiliation and identification must exist among African Muslims. Nevertheless, the Egyptian revolution in 1952, an event which by modern standards would be seen as a dramatic enhancer of Muslim political consciousness and capable of producing a wider resonance within the larger continent, was barely perceived as Islamic by

26

Africans. So, in a sense, there is a danger in looking back and attempting to make comparisons simply because African and Islamic political aspirations have moved on.

Having said that, however, in certain parts of Africa, the Sudan, for example, there does seem to have been, as J.-F. Bayart points out, a form of drifting back to a pre-colonial period in terms of 'intracontinental and intercontinental interaction' (Bayart 1992). In other words, if European colonialism attempted to banish or undermine Africa's Islamic heritage, these apparently repressed forces are now resurfacing. These tendencies support the *longue durée* school of analysis in that certain influences must form part of a nation's distinct historicity if they are to reappear at a later stage and in a different form. At this point, however, it is necessary to carry the questions raised in the introduction and the issues contained in the current debate over to following chapters which examine the present relationship between Africa and the dynamics of Islam.

NOTES

1 This statement was contained in the 1954 Election Manifesto of the Convention People's Party, entitled 'Forward with the Common People'.

Part II

CULTURAL/
POLITICAL

2

ISLAM AND DEMOCRATISATION

INTRODUCTION

Thirty years ago I. M. Lewis believed that secular party politics in sub-Saharan Africa would become increasingly efficacious in spite of the continuing growth of Islam in the region. Post-colonial secular politics would effectively put a brake on any 'new expansion of Muslim influence and Pan-Islamic solidarity' because such forms of political discourse were 'more important in the modern world than common religious interest' (Lewis 1966 p. 91). Party politics, however, proved a disappointment and led to predictions that Africa's democratisation trend of the 1980s/1990s would largely follow the dismal pattern of the multi-party experiments of the early independence period in the 1950s and 1960s: election results would be disputed, conflicts would emerge and old ruling parties would continue to dominate. A democratic spirit might continue to exist but 'the daunting economic and financial problems which African governments face' would ultimately contribute to a return of the 'authoritarian strain in African politics' (Tordoff 1993 p. 57). The attempted secularisation of political culture in sub-Saharan Africa mainly ignored or was largely irrelevant to Islamists as it pitched notions of modernity against traditional cultural and socio-religious values.

Islam in Africa is now a major political force. Yet, so too are the thrusts towards multi-partyism inspired either by conditionality arrangements of international donors or by the momentous political changes in South Africa. We need, then, to consider the extent to which Islam intertwines with the new processes of political contestation, and to examine whether it does so in ways which do not replicate the experiences of the past. In looking at the connection between Islam and democratisation then, the chapter examines

31

alternative political agendas, that is, Western patterns of multi-party pluralism and Islamic notions of democracy and their respective appeal, viability and potential sustainability in various African states.

MOVES TOWARDS POLITICAL CHANGE IN 1990s

In 1991 both the Organisation of African Unity (OAU) and the Non-Aligned Movement (NAM) referred to the need for African states to democratise and take seriously 'the expansion of liberalism' and the adoption of multi-party politics (SWB ME/1174 11 September 1991). One year later at the 1992 OAU summit meeting, the Secretary General called on African leaders 'to exchange views on how to manage the democratisation process in a peaceful manner and with minimum turbulence' (SWB ME/1416 25 June 1992). These pronouncements coincided with statements issued by United Nations Secretary-General Boutros Boutros-Ghali. In a major speech at the end of 1992 on the topic of a 'New Agenda for Africa' he identified certain key democratising features to be: 'a participatory government, a free press, the creation of a national police force, the upholding of the rule of law, and credible legal, financial and administrative institutions' (UN *Focus on the New Agenda for Africa* 1993). Equally, the World Bank in its publication *Governance and Development* referred to the need for 'good governance' and better economic and social policy performance in the developing world (World Bank *Governance and Development* 1992). By 1994 the OAU's support for democracy was reasserted and defined: 'a democratic state of law depends not only on the definition of rules to settle disputes among political parties but primarily on the creation of freedom and constitutional guarantees for all citizens, on the participation of civil society in the shaping of government policies and in the discussion of the most appropriate ways of jointly finding fairer solutions to political, economic and social problems' (SWB AL/2024 17 June 1994). In 1995 Dr Salim Ahmed Salim declared the OAU to be 'fully committed to democratisation' (Salim 1995; meeting).

The reintroduction of elections and the organisation of numerous parties in various African states have demanded radical constitutional reform. In Malawi, for example, a Constitution Amendment Bill had to be introduced in 1993 which incorporated a bill of rights and repealed the institution of the life presidency. The bill eliminated the requirement that a Presidential candidate had to be a member of the Malawi Congress Party and repealed the powers conferred on the president to nominate members of parliament to the National Assembly exclusively from the Malawi Congress Party. The voting age was also reduced from 21 to 18 years (SWB AL/1850 19 November 1993). Yet, perhaps it is the profound constitutional and political change in South Africa that has focused attention more fully on democratic procedures and practices. South Africa's new Constitution negotiated by a multi-party negotiating process, passed in Parliament on 28 January 1994 and effective from 27 April 1994 laid down a clause on Fundamental Rights:

> The Constitution enshrines equality of languages and religions ... Rights to life, dignity, freedom of belief and expression and other liberal values, along with labour rights, rights to education and equality of opportunity, specifically for all races and both genders. These aspects along with common citizenship, reverse fundamentally the precepts of apartheid.
>
> See Appendix 1 (South Africa's Elections and New Constitution 26 April 1994)

The South African elections held in April 1994 under global scrutiny demonstrated the moving spectacle of people exercising their right to vote in multi-party elections for the first time. Certainly, as President Mandela stated at the OAU Summit in 1994, the removal of apartheid radically changed the political environment of South Africa and enabled the country to focus attention on its contribution to 'the new African renaissance' (SWB AL/2023 9 May 1994). With South Africa held up as a true example of democracy, equality and justice for all, Mandela confronted the other states of the continent: 'where there is something wrong in the manner in which we govern ourselves, the fault is not in the stars but in ourselves' (ibid.). The objective of Africa as a whole is to emancipate all people from the 'scourges of poverty, disease, ignorance and backwardness', in order that they may move towards the great issues of the moment: 'peace, stability, democracy, human rights, co-operation and development' (ibid.).

These political changes have given rise to optimistic African press reports asserting the unlikelihood of African states returning to single-party regimes or military dictatorships on scales experienced up to 1990 (*Africa Events* March 1994; *African Business* April 1994). Yet, some countries have been less enthusiastic about political pluralism. President Yoweri Museveni of Uganda announced that African societies were 'still largely dominated by the peasantry and therefore classless and backward'. Although multi-partyism was fashionable it was 'not an opportune moment for the reintroduction of political parties in the process of development' (SWB ME/1658 8 April 1993). African societies which were still organised along classless lines would be divided on sectarian lines by political parties. The National Resistance Movement advised the people of Uganda that it was possible to have a more appropriate form of democracy organised on a no-party basis while the state continued to encourage harmony and unity (ibid.). Paradoxically, two years later, the National Resistance Movement pronounced its intention to 'restore full political rights to the people of Uganda to form and belong to political parties' (SWB AL/2183 29 March 1995).

The interpretation of democracy as being distanced from participation and representation and excluding the right of people to choose between different parties at periodic elections has evaporated. Under single-party regimes, predominantly rural populations are politically powerless and marginalised. Only through a process of electoral enfranchisement and choice can rural populations exercise a degree of political participation. Yet the Western conception of liberal democracy, the rule of law, tolerance of opposition groups, freedoms of speech, association and assembly, national integration and sovereignty have often been judged unsuitable and largely unsustainable in African states. The lack of social cohesion is considered a central reason why earlier attempts at democratisation failed. These views rest on assumptions that democracy has a range of pre-conditions or determinants without which it will not function.

INTERPRETATIONS OF DEMOCRACY

From the Ancient Greek notion of direct democracy within a city state, to utilitarian models of representative democracy, to Joseph Schumpeter's 'competitive theory of democracy' and the pluralism and polyarchy of Robert A. Dahl, interpretations of democracy have been many and varied. In fact, Dahl maintains that it is precisely this evolution of democratic ideas that has produced 'a jumble of theory and practices that are often deeply inconsistent' (Dahl 1989 p. 2). Dahl's intention is 'to set out an interpretation of democratic theory and practice, including the limits and possibilities of democracy, that is relevant to the kind of world in which we live or are likely to live in the foreseeable future' (ibid.).

The divide between 'normative' and 'empirical' accounts of democracy has essentially further muddled the debate. Normative accounts stress the notion of a 'good' society which looks to human capabilities, potentialities and aspirations. Whilst empirical approaches emphasise the applicability and efficacy of political practices in the real world. In a major work on democracy, Diamond, Linz and Lipset, separated the political arena from other spheres in order 'to insist that issues of so-called economic and social democracy be separated from the question of governmental structure' (Diamond *et al.* 1988). The inescapable issue of how democracy is understood in the post-Cold War period is associated with the degree and depth of electoral enfranchisement afforded to all peoples, in other words, the democratic universality of electoral choice irrespective of a nation's global positioning: Eastern Europe, Central Asia, the Middle East, Africa and so on.

According to Dahl, democracy, or 'polyarchy' requires certain essential conditions: First, extensive competition among individuals, organised groups, and political parties for government positions; second, political participation in the selection of candidates and potential leaders through regular and fair elections; third, a level of civil and political liberties which provides a framework for society, and permits citizens to express themselves without fear of punishment (Dahl 1989 p. 221). These conditions are far wider than simple electoralism. People are granted rights and responsibilities, accorded freedoms and duties to exercise in a legitimate manner and within encoded parameters. Mass action and mobilisation and violent outbursts would be symptoms of societal disorder (Kornhauser 1957). A pluralist society represents competition between diverse groups but although diversity and opposition are highlighted and groups are permitted to disagree on particular issues, there must exist an overriding commitment from all groups, to the rules of society. In the phrase of Almond and Verba 'a meaningfully structured cleavage in society' must exist to give adequate choice to the electorate (Almond and Verba 1963 p. 358). In essence, 'consensus and cleavage' politics is essential, but more crucially, there should not be too much of either: too much consensus leads to 'a community in which politics is of no real importance to the community' and choice means little; too much cleavage renders a democratic society 'in danger of its existence' (Berelson *et al.* 1954).

Competing interests should not, therefore, be extremist and potentially threatening to the structures of the state and the political system as a whole. Liberal democracy tolerates and contains opposition and competition between groups but its weakest flank, and indeed, that which carries the potential seeds of its own destruction, is its difficulty in dealing with extremism. Repressive action taken against groups which threaten or oppose the structures of the state undermine the phalanx of liberal democracy and notions of tolerance and opposition. These contradictions inherent within liberal democracy render it vulnerable as a political model in a number of states which tend towards excessive polarisation.

Diamond, Linz and Lipset look at the degree to which nations 'permit independent and critical political expression and organisation', as a measure of liberal democratic procedures. (Diamond *et al.* 1988). Clearly, the 'space' between legitimate individual and group action and the response of the state is important and, indeed, measureable, but in the final analysis there exists no space between extremism and a liberal democratic state. The issue is one of perception and interpretation. Essentially, judgements are made by government leaders as to the potential threat of various groups be they labour groups, religious groups, terrorist groups or political groups. In other words, certain aspects of civil society, religious groups, say, act not as the necessary adjunct to a liberal democratic state but rather may be regarded as a possible source of threat and instability.

POLITICAL PROGESS

At the time of the emergence of the old Colonial territories into newly independent nation states in the 1950s and 1960s there was much talk of nation-state building and the concept of political development. Lucien Pye wrote in 1965:

> When attention was first fixed on the problem of economic growth and the need to transform stagnant economies into dynamic ones with self-sustaining growth, the economists were quick to point out that political and social conditions could play a decisive role in impeding or facilitating advance in per capita income, and thus it was appropriate to conceive of political development as the state of the polity which might facilitate economic growth.

> (Pye 1966 p. 83)

Political development became identified with the establishment of public institutions, citizenship, electoral processes and 'the balancing of popular sentiment with public order' (ibid. p. 87). As Lucien Pye maintained at the time: 'Certainly implicit in many people's view is the assumption that the only form of political development worthy of the name is the building of democracies' (ibid.). There can be little doubt that the Modernisation School, as it became known, looked to rationalisation, national integration, democratisation and participation as being hallmarks of development, and objectives for newly independent states to achieve. Frederick Frey suggested that the 'most common notion of political development is that of a movement towards democracy' (Frey 1963 p. 301).

When post-colonial states experienced their first multi-party elections, concepts of pluralism and democracy were as popular amongst theorists in the West as they are in the 1990s: concepts of change and improvement, of progress and 'development', of rationalisation and participation still exist. Notions of political development following procedures and stages remain but now emphasis is placed on 'governance', economic privatisation, greater efficiency, and electoralism. The debate about political development and the appropriateness of democracy did not go away in the 1970s and 1980s, it simply receded. During those decades attention focused on explaining away the drift to authoritarian government in Africa, the Middle East and elsewhere. Analysts then argued that inequitable economic relations with the capitalist West, new forms of neo-colonialism or corrupt individual leaders syphoning resources overseas for their own benefit were the main causes of political debility in the developing world. With the rapidly changing global situation at the end of 1980s, the end of the Cold War and dissolution of the Soviet Union and Communist Bloc and with it Soviet models of development, notions of democratisation and rationalisation simply resurfaced; only this time they appeared in the West and the East. Liberal democracy became the 'end of history' and the stated objective of a host of countries (Fukuyama 1992).

Renewed interest in pluralist, competitive democracy has not, however, minimised or, indeed, obscured the fact that it is enormously difficult to either attain or sustain in certain countries. Consequently, the debate must return to established arguments. One central feature of a functioning democracy presented in the classic study by Almond and Verba in 1963, was the establishment of a supportive 'civic culture' (Almond and Verba 1963). More recently

37

the existence of a 'civil society' has come to be seen as an essential precondition or determinant of sustainable democracy (Woods 1992).

CIVIL SOCIETY

The intention of Almond and Verba was to establish in their comparative study the extent to which 'a pattern of political attitudes and an underlying set of social attitudes' was supportive of a 'stable democratic process'. (Almond and Verba 1963 p. 35). The cleavage within society would be managed and balanced by a civic culture which combined levels of citizen activity with passivity, tradition with modernity. Political parties, interest groups, voluntary associations and a neutral media could contribute to a 'pluralistic culture based on communication and persuasion, a culture of consensus and diversity, a culture that permitted change but moderated it' (ibid. p. 6). Central to Almond and Verba's theme was an understanding that the 'democratic model of the participatory state required more than universal suffrage, the political party and the elective legislature'. It needed a compatible cultural base:

> The working principles of the democratic polity and its civic culture – the ways in which political elites make decisions, their norms and attitudes, as well as the norms and attitudes of the ordinary citizen, his relation to government and to his fellow citizens – are subtler cultural components.
>
> (ibid. p. 3)

State and institutional structures, then, cannnot enforce or ensure democracy. Democracy is concerned with the relationship between the citizenry and the political elite: the degree of trust and identity between the leadership and the people, the level of independence afforded to the individual, the limits to the encroachment of power over the population. Civil society is both necessary and important. It can provide a ballast against the power of the state and permit the existence of channels of public expression in order that society's wishes can be articulated. A civic culture can thus emerge in this enlarged polity which is supportive of democratic practices. Without a civil society there is no motive for state actors to recognise the demands of society and all the temptations of arbitrary rule can become a reality. Civil society is also seen as a way of 'securing substantive political rights and freedoms, essential for a functioning democracy, in an arena outside of state control' (Williams and Young 1993). The activities of groups and organisations such as trade unions, business associations, pressure groups, educational establishments, various voluntary societies, women's groups, religious groups operating with a free press are critical factors in sustaining democratic accountability. In other words, civil society operates in the space between the state and the people.

In the 1990s interest focused on the role and importance of civil society in fostering democratic practices and in creating a demarcation line between what Habermas calls 'a public and a private sphere' (Habermas 1989). The distinction between these two arenas is decisive: the 'private' arena is that of economic and familial relations while the 'public' is that of the development of a 'public opinion' which increasingly demands its voice is heard by the state. With the broadening and deepening of the space between state activity and that of the individual, increasing roles would be available for groups, especially economic groups, who could forge greater productive and economic benefits for the nation as a whole.

The one crucial difficulty with this analysis is whether it is transferable to states in the developing world. There have always existed risks in attempting to transplant Western democratic concepts and institutions to former colonies. These dangers applied as much to the ill-suited Soviet model of development with its rigid pursuit of industrialisation under a proletarian vanguard as to multi-party adversarial politics based on the Westminster model or the highly centralised French system. One of the central criticisms of Africa, however, and to a certain extent the states of the Middle East is that civil society can be weak, sometimes linked to the specific regime and often particularistic in cultural or ethnic terms. Williams and Young state: 'When many Western theorists and social scientists contemplate non-Western social orders they find as it were "not-civil-society" (or certainly something different which is usually not to their liking' (Williams and Young 1993 p. 5). Geertz considered this problem in 1963 when he questioned whether or not the conflict between a nation's primordial sentiments and civil sentiments could be avoided. Essentially, which was more important to an individual: 'The long-standing ties of blood, race, language, locality, religion or tradition, or the relatively new and less familiar attachment to the impersonal legal order of the state' (Geertz 1967). These views have been echoed in the 1990s. Goran Hyden sees the peasantry as an obstacle to development, whilst Woods asserts that African society,

locked into competing ethnic and cultural inhibitors, fails to replicate the dynamic forces which were at play in industrialising Europe
(Hyden 1983; Woods 1992). The director of the London-based
charity, Oxfam, admitted that 'ethnicity was a major problem for
aid agencies', and could affect democratisation programmes (Bryer
1993; meeting). All the hallmarks of traditional society which
were so clearly identified in 1958 and from which populations were
expected to escape via modernity, appear to be re-emerging nearly
four decades later. People were continuing to be separated 'by
kinship into communities isolated from each other and from a
centre' (Lerner 1958 p. 48).

Attempts to strengthen civil society in the developing world were
announced by Baroness Chalker, Britain's Minister for Overseas
Development in the mid-1990s. Aid would be provided through
channels other than government, usually NGOs (non-government
organisations). Assistance would be given to community organisations representing the interests of their members. Organisations
working for the rights of the poor, of women and of other disadvantaged groups were regarded as particularly important. The state
should begin to distance itself from certain economic and social
functions in favour of NGOs. The independent media would be
promoted as would training projects organised to increase gender
awareness. Projects specifically for women would be financed.
Recognising that the immediate benefits of such policies would be
modest, Chalker stressed that in the longer term they would prove
crucial to the 'sustainability of democracy, accountability and toleration' (Chalker 1994; meeting).

Western donors are busy determining the progress of civil society
in the Third World but as, Van Hoek & Bossuyt argue, 'There is
no universal model for the institutional set-up likely to facilitate a
more fruitful cooperation between state and civil society' (van Hoek
& Bossuyt 1993). Both admit, however, that nurturing the emergence
of an organisational base of civil society is a 'major task ahead' but
envisage possible lines of action including: 'technical assistance for
institutional reform, and help in drafting legislation and effective
decentralisation' (ibid.).

POLITICAL PARTIES

Political parties have become a ubiquitous feature of the liberal
democratic process and their roles have been analysed by using a

variety of functional categories. LaPalombara and Weiner defined some basic characteristics a party should display: organisational continuity, in that we should expect a party to survive over time and linked national and local organisations pursuing a determination to 'capture and hold decision-making power alone or in coalition,' by striving for popular support (LaPalombara and Weiner 1966 p. 6). Although parties are often associated with ideological principles it is not necessarily an essential attribute and they may emphasise their pragmatism or technical skills. Parties in liberal democracies provide an integrative purpose by bringing people into the political process through channels of communication between society and the occupants of political roles. By bringing people together and articulating certain moral or social values or a concept of the national community they increase the legitimacy of the political system and thereby reduce the likelihood of violent outbursts.

Political parties are also the main mechanisms of political recruitment in that candidates are selected and prepared for public office. They aggregate interests by expressing and unifying demands into coherent policy proposals. In a sense, they ensure that social cleavages are represented in the political arena and by so doing they provide the basis for institutional cohesion. The political party, then, has been regarded as the 'critical force for modernisation' which could assist in the construction of new political institutions (Apter 1967 p179; Huntington 1967 p. 212).

Yet perceptions of political parties in the Third World have gone through several phases. The expectation that parties would resemble, in both form and function, their Western counterparts evaporated in the 1970s and 1980s. The belief that they would provide an increasingly educated, discerning public with electoral choice and structures of accountability largely evaporated under the weight of empirical evidence. In large swathes of Africa and the Middle East, the early multi-party experiment gave way to one-party systems or the obliquely termed 'no-party' state, only to be followed by a virtual eclipse by the ensuing military leaders (Hess and Loewenberg 1966). At one point it was argued that political parties had little, if any, significance in the nations of sub-Saharan Africa or parts of the Middle East (Tordoff 1993 pp. 120–121). On other occasions political parties were regarded as responsible for 'dangerous forms of clientelism in the mobilisation of ethnic identies', which occurred because of the 'competition for power among indigenous parties' (Clapham 1985 pp. 57/58).

41

The Arab Socialist Ba'th Party, the organisation which paradoxically still serves to link and separate Iraq and Syria was established in 1953, the result of a merger between the Arab Socialist Party and the Arab Renaissance Party. The Party's political stance emphasised social and economic reform; greater Arab unity through a form of Pan-Arabism and the recognition of the relationship between Islam and Arabism. Essentially, it was a quasi-Marxist socialist party committed to a nationalised, redistributive economic system based on the principle of 'socialist nationalism' but which was to be strongly associated with an Arab identity. Class antagonism would replace previous social animosities between Arab peoples based on regionalism, sectarianism or tribalism; elements which had rendered Arab society vulnerable to imperialism and exploitation. The party was to be built up in a 'firm, positive and homogeneous fashion' (Official Ba'th Party document: *Analysis of Sectarianism, Regionalism and Tribalism*, April 1966). In fact, the process of purging the party of undesirable allegiances was seen to be an act of purification; a sign that the 'era of weakness and irresolution' was over. Strength was synonymous with the 'exercise of maximum levels of supervision, guidance and control in calling people to account' (ibid.).

The inevitability of factionalism in an ideologically based movement would always threaten and ultimately, in 1964, the breach between theoretical assumptions and practical application resulted in a party split and the development of two very different strands of Ba'thism, one in Syria, the other in Iraq. Whereas the Ba'th Party in Iraq, unlike its Syrian counterpart, pays less regard to a 'socialist' ideology, it retains a firm belief in the notion of pan-Arabism. Although other parties are permitted in Syria, Article 7 of the constitution places the Ba'th Party as the 'leading party of society and state' (Deegan 1993 p. 63). The Ba'th Party in Iraq under the stewardship of Saddam Hussein retains its pre-eminent position. In both the Syrian and Iraqi varients of the party there exists a process of clientelism and strong ethnic identity but in terms of organisational strength and military cohesion the parties have no counterparts in sub-Saharan Africa.

AFRICAN POLITICAL PARTIES

Political parties, then, can either have no power or they can have too much; they can be overridden by military regimes or they can abuse their influence by exacerbating ethnic tensions and favouring certain groups over others; they can be incompetent and incoherent or they can dominate the political arena for generations by creating authoritarian procedures. By the mid-1980s some analysts were speculating that definitions of political parties had been 'too rigid' and determined by a Eurocentric understanding of what a political party should be (Randall 1988). Question marks were hanging over the role and function of political parties in the developing world when the issue of democratisation first began to be raised and gather attention in the 1980s. If multi-party pluralistic forms of political expression were to return to Third World nations, then political parties would have to play a key role in forging these processes. Some political parties had not disappeared and had roots stretching back to the nationalist movements of the colonial period: Kenya Africa National Union (KANU), Union Progressiste Sénégalaise (Senegal), United National Independence Party (UNIP) Zambia and the Malawi Congress Party (Malawi).

The character of the political parties which exist in the 1990s: their structures, leadership, social bases, objectives and interaction with other parties is not completely clear. In Kenya, for example, in 1993 the KANO Maendeleo ya Wanawake (Women's Progress Movement) disassociated from the political party KANO, with the stated intention of working 'above party politics in the era of multi-partyism', thereby enhancing its role in the decision-making process (SWB ME/1619 22 February 1993). Equally, in 1993 the Lesotho Prime Minister, Dr Ntsu Mokhehle's address following the victory of the Basotholand Congress Party (BCP) in the first election to be held in 23 years, readily recognised the need for 'continual coop-eration and consultation with other political parties.' A large propor-tion of the electorate had voted for other parties including the Basotho National Party (BNP). Dr Mokhehle invited the opposition party leaders to accept the BCP's offer of genuine participation in the reconstruction of the economy and 'in the sustenance of democracy' (SWB ME/1656 6 April 1993). These statements were especially important as suspicions existed that a BCP government would 'retaliate' against opposition parties and effectively purge the bureacracy and military of any supporters. Structures of African parties have tended to be hierarchical with rather narrow social bases, often based on tribal or ethnic affiliations, with the role of the leadership exceptionally important.

However, if democratisation was to have any real meaning and substance in Equatorial Guinea, it was asserted that essential points

Table 2.1 Niger, legislative election results, 14 February 1993

National Movement for the Society of Development (MNSD) (former sole party)	28 seats
Democratic and Social Convention (CDS)	13 seats
Alliance for Democracy and Social Progress (ANDP)	11 seats
Niger Party for Democracy and Progress (PNDS)	10 seats
Other 5 parties	6 seats

agreed between the government and 10 legalised opposition parties had to be observed. These items included the access of opposition parties to state media, freedom to engage in political activities, equal rights for all parties, and state funding of political parties (SWB ME/1616 18 February 1993). Political activities inevitably bring the parties into direct contact with the population and the legislative elections in Niger held in February 1993 resulted in a wide degree of choice for the electorate (see Table 2.1). Opposition parties united under the umbrella title of Alliance of Forces for Change (AFC), not including the previous ruling single party MNSD, and declared that it was satisfied with its comfortable majority of seats in the National Assembly (SWB ME/1616 ii 18 February 1993).

Despite calls from former President Banda of Malawi to retain the one-party system of government under the control of the Malawi Congress Party on the grounds that the country had 'developed beyond recognition', the electorate, when voting in May 1994, decided in favour of multi-party democracy (SWB ME/1609 10 February 1993; SWB AL/2025 A/4 18 June 1994). However, in Nigeria attempts at democratisation have been difficult. After the elections of 1993 were ignored by the ruling military regime, threats were made to arrest pro-democracy groups, particularly the National Democratic Coalition (Nadeco). The Nigerian newspaper, *Sun Ray*, expressed concern that leaders of Nadeco should not be arrested simply on the grounds of 'mere opposition to the government's views' (SWB AL/2024 17 June 1994). The agitation and outcry about these debilitating attempts at democracy led the Minister of Information and Culture to announce the establishment of a Constitutional Conference with the objective of providing a framework for: guaranteeing freedom and equality, equity and justice and even-handed opportunities for social, political, education and enjoyment; establishing a government reflecting the general consensus; preserving the unity and territorial integrity of the Nigerian state and to promoting good governance, accountability and probity in public affairs. The Constitutional Conference hoped to construct a method of forming parties which would lead to the 'ultimate recognition of political parties formed by the people', and it eventually decided that the principle of a 'rotational presidency' between the south and north of the country should be enshrined in the constition (SWB AL/2120 7 October 1994; *Africa Events* March 1994). This would mean that the presidency would rotate between an Islamic north and a predominantly Christian south.

Table 2.2 shows the results of the parliamentary elections held in Mozambique in October 1994. Of the 14 parties participating, Frelimo gained 44.33 per cent of the vote, Renamo, 37.78 per cent and the UD (Democratic Union) 5.15 per cent. All other parties individually received less than 2 per cent of the total vote but collectively their percentage of the vote was quite high, 12.74 per cent. Six million people registered for the elections which represented 81 per cent of all eligible voters. Eighty-eight per cent of those voters cast their vote. Renamo had threatened not to participate but eventually decided against such a policy on the stated grounds of preserving 'political and social stability' within the country (SWB AL/2163 26 November 1994). The elections were declared 'free and fair' by the international observers from the European Union and United Nations although the Southern Africa Research and Documentation Centre (SARDC) expressed concern that in some parts of the country voters had to cast their ballots in 'an atmosphere of fear that war might resume if a certain party were not happy with the outcome of the elections' (SWB AL/2145 5 November 1994). The Renamo leader, Afonso Dhlakama accepted the election results despite its 'irregularities', and denied that the party had introduced armed men into a province with the intention of preventing voting (SWB AL/2155 17 November 1994).

Table 2.2 Mozambique parliamentary elections, October 1994 (%)

Frelimo (Mozambique Liberation Front)	44.33
Renamo (Mozambique National Resistance)	37.78
UD (Democratic Union)	5.15
All other parties	12.74
TOTAL	100.00

Two months after Mozambique's internationally funded multi-party elections several political parties cannot account for the funds given to them for the polls. Only the ruling Frelimo and the Mozambique United Front (FUMO) have presented accounts of expenditure. Another potentially worrying development is the decision by seven opposition parties to form an extraparliamentary political force called the United Salvation Front which intends to influence the Assembly of the republic on social, political and economic issues (SWB AL/2039 5 July 1994; SWB AL/2189 30 December 1994).

SOUTH AFRICA: PARTIES AND ELECTIONS

The elections held in South Africa between the 26 and 28 April 1994 have highlighted the possibility of a democratic future for the whole continent. More than 22 million South Africans were eligible to vote, 17 million of them blacks who had never voted before. The electoral procedure was made as accessible as possible. Anyone over the age of 18 was permitted to vote and the Electoral Commission widely distributed one-time-only identity cards to any South African with a birth certificate, marriage certificate or other credible proof of residence. On one occasion it was reported that the issuing of identification cards was hampered in some areas where literacy levels among blacks were low, by 'the difficulty of reading fingerprints from rural blacks who had laboured so hard they had literally worn their fingers smooth' (*International Herald Tribune* 29 April 1994). As there was no list of voters, poll officials prevented repeat voting by marking documents and fingertips with invisible ink which showed up under ultra violet light. Each voter cast two ballots, one for the National Assembly and one for a provincial legislature. Voters selected parties, not specific candidates and parties filled the seats they won from a list of names submitted in advance. As part of a campaign to persuade voters that their choice was private, the electoral law banned exit polls.

One factor of tremendous importance in democratisation processes is the degree of organisation and management needed simply in order for people to be able to vote. Some of the major problems in a number of countries, for example, Guinea-Bissau and Mozambique in 1994 were the absence of necessary voting material in many polling stations, delays in the registration procedure and deficiencies in the voter education campaign. In Guinea-Bissau,

46

accusations were made of electoral irregularities including an incident in which a member of the ruling party, PAIGC, was 'taking people's hands and teaching them how to vote and who to vote for' (SWB AL/2040 A/14 6 July 1994; South African Broadcasting Corporation Radio; SWB AL/2039 5 July 1994). These difficulties were compounded by travelling problems, inadequate vehicles, bad roads and weather conditions. The absence of voting material in many polling stations, the fact that 20 ballot boxes allegedly went missing and the failure of the government to pay $US 124,000 to a computer firm who was compiling data for the polls all contributed to administrative problems (SWB AL/2207 21 January 1995).

Such difficulties were overcome in the South African elections under the adjudication of an Independent Electoral Commission (IEC). In the run-up to the elections the IEC's programme was to provide greater access to the electorate. At the same time voter education was co-ordinated and directed towards those sectors of the community which needed it most. Over 500 voting stations had to be identified, staffed, equipped and secured in KwaZulu. Over 200,000 officials drawn from the community at large were trained. The IEC was given a mandate to prepare within four months for elections in which there were no voters' rolls and in which an estimated total electorate of 22.7 million, around 16.3 million black Africans were voting for the first time. The IEC chairman announced that viewed in the context of historical animosities, campaigning for the elections was 'relatively free' (SWB AL/1991 7 May 1994).

The total cost of organising the IEC was 984.3 million RM (approx. $US 394 million) but the wider costs involved in the democratisation process were 3826.3 million RM (approx. $US 1530 million) as shown in Table 2.4. Large contributions were made by overseas countries: the United States offered $US 600 million of aid over 3 years, the UK promised £60 million over the same period and gave £3 million to support the elections (Chalker 1994; meeting) Over 5,000 international observers were deployed in South Africa for the elections, including 1778 from the United Nations, 312 from the Economic Union and 60 from the Commonwealth countries and others from the Organization of African Unity (OAU) and non-governmental organisations.

The allocation of seats in the new South African electoral system is based on a proportional representation system which allocates a total of 400 seats in the National Assembly to those six parties which gained the greatest share of the vote (see Table 2.3).

Table 2.3 South African Elections. The National Assembly,
26–28 April 1994

Party	% of total vote	Seats
The African National Congress (ANC)	62.65	252
National Party (NP)	20.39	82
Inkatha Freedom Party (IFP)	10.54	43
Freedom Front (FF)	2.17	9
Democratic Party (DP)	1.73	7
Pan-Africanist Congress (PAC)	1.25	5
Total		400 seats

Source: Star International Weekly, Johannesburg, 5–10 May 1994

Table 2.4 The Cost of South African Elections

	S. African Rands (millions)
Independent Electoral Commission	948.3
Independent Broadcasting Authority	24.0
Defence Forces	1,486.2
Assembly Points	223.1
Inauguration	18.0
Allowances for members of service departments during election	526.0
National Peace Keeping Force	384.0
Transitional Executive Council	15.9
Peace Secretariat	54.1
National Peace Accord	30.0
Parliament	66.0
Advances to Provincial Governments	236.2
Total Expenditure	4,012.3
Less Incidental savings	186.0
Grand Total	3,826.3

Source: Star International Weekly, Johannesburg. May 1994
Note: 2.5 Rands = $US 1

A total of nineteen parties stood in the elections but the extent of support for the ANC was, perhaps, inevitable as it provided the focus for the struggle for democracy under the leadership of Nelson Mandela. In a sense, the ANC is similar to a number of post-independent parties and movements forged under years of oppression and gaining wide-ranging support. Yet, exercising national leadership in government is very different from uniting peoples and factions for a common cause. Parties have to project genuinely national economic and social policies, and avoid running the risk of inculcating false expectations from the population. Some analysts argue that the elections were a reflection of ethnic identity rather than political conviction (Welsh 1994). David Welsh described the elections as 'a rite of passage' as power was transferred from the NP to the ANC (ibid.). But both President Mandela and former leader F. W. de Klerk recognised that a process of reconciliation had to commence before any elections actually took place. (*Star International Weekly* 5–10 May 1994). All parties had agreed to share power in a government of national unity so that a party winning only 5 per cent of the vote was guaranteed a seat in the cabinet. A form of consociationalism, then, was guaranteed for the period 1994–99. As Stanley Uys states: 'The new pattern of political relationships will still be race-based, but it is an immense improvement on long years of white domination' (Uys 1994). A country's history is of fundamental importance in understanding any moves towards democratisation and perhaps the relativist approach of comparing country with country is misleading. Ali Oumlil of the Jordanian-based Arab Thought Forum maintains: 'The road to democracy is a long one; there are countries that have taken steps towards democracy. But there are others where democracy is not even an issue.

Table 2.5 Elections 1994–95

Angola	Kenya
Benin	Lebanon
Botswana	Lesotho
Burundi	Madagascar
Cape Verde	Malawi
Chad	Mali
Comoros	Mauritania
Congo	Mauritius
Cote D'Ivoire	Mozambique
Egypt	Niger
Guinea	Nigeria*
Gabon	Sao Tome and Principe
Gambia	Senegal
Guinea-Bissau	South Africa
Jordan	Yemen
	Zimbabwe

Source: Keesings Record of World Events (1994/1995) CIRCA Cambridge.
Note: * annulled

Democracy is a difficult process, but we must walk its path' (Oumlil 1994; meeting).

ISLAMIC FACTORS

One of the central difficulties confronting the creation and legitimacy of political parties in a number of African states has been the role played by Islam. The Islamic Conference Organisation (ICO), particularly active in the early 1980s following the Islamic revolution in Iran, declared in 1989 that as Muslims in Africa shared a common colonial heritage there was a need for unity between all Muslims (SWB ME/1155 17 August 1991). In Nigeria, with its large Muslim population (50 per cent of the total population are Muslim) reports have indicated that conflicts between Christians and Muslims have 'claimed at least 3,000 lives between 1987 and 1993' (*Guardian* 14 April 1993). Certainly, by 1992 relations between Islamic groups and Christian missionary organisations were reportedly, 'much more tense than 10 years ago' (O'Toole 1994; interview). Islamic political parties are restricted under the proviso that parties must have a base in 19 states (Connolly 1994; interview). Tanzania, which has a Muslim population of between 30–40 per cent, is committed to keeping Islam out of politics but it is not easy, as Tanzanian Islamists seek the establishment of an Iranian-style government and Zanzibar declared unilaterally its membership of the ICO in 1993. Tanzanian government officials have spoken of the need for the country to retain its secular polity and to adopt an attitude of toleration and respect for the rule of law (SWB ME/1661 13 April 1993).

In Kenya, the influential leader of the banned Islamic Party of Kenya (IPK), Sheikh Khalid Balala, threatened to declare a 'jihad' against the government of President Daniel arap Moi, unless the regime stopped 'playing with Islam' (SWB ME/1659 9 April 1993). The situation was exacerbated by the moves towards democratisation within the country. The IPK was unable to contest Kenya's first multi-party elections for 26 years in December 1992 because the government refused to register it as a political party on the grounds that it was a religious-based organisation. However, the IPK formed an alliance with another political organisation, FORD-Kenya, and won two parliamentary seats for the party in the mainly Muslim port city of Mombasa (ibid.). On Balala's arrest, rioting and strikes took place until he was released. These actions created tension and unease on a multi-racial level, with calls for Black Muslims to 'take up arms against their Arab counterparts' (*Africa Events* May 1994). Clashes between soldiers and Islamic 'fundamentalists' were reported in Niger in June 1994 and the President declared that some Niger citizens had 'extremist tendencies' (SWB AL/2021 14 June 1994). Clearly, moves towards democratisation and the return of elections after many years has awakened an Islamic consciousness in a number of African states.

Although the degree of external support for Islam and the form and nature of theocratic states will be considered further in subsequent chapters, at this stage it is necessary to consider the relationship between Islam and democratisation processes. Although accusations have been made that religion is being used as a political base, the attraction and political potential of Islamic parties must be acknowledged. Equally if political liberalisation is to be considered meaningful, it should be concerned with reflecting all shades of opinion. As Almond and Coleman pointed out in their study of the late 1950s, 'religious affiliation has been the basis of political party organisation'. They considered the appearance of Muslim parties in southern Ghana and the development of Protestant and Catholic political parties in Uganda. Where religious and tribal cleavages coincided, they believed, 'the religious factor may in time become even more pronounced in provoking political separatist movements' (Almond and Coleman 1960 p. 279). Some break-away factions from political organisations, e.g. the United Liberation Movement for Democracy in Liberia have declared their intention to create an Islamic state (SWB AL/2011 1 June 1994).

In the case of South Africa, according to the General Secretary of the Muslim Youth Movement, 'Sections of the Muslim community are moving into the future quite positively' (Na'een Jeenah, *Africa South & East* April 1993). Yet the community represents only 2 per cent of the country's population and it is culturally mixed: Indian, Malaysian, Javanese and African. Black South Africans, who have been converting slowly to Islam since the 1970s, are to be the group which will feel 'the most prominent thrust of Islam in the future' (ibid.). In the 1980s, Africans began to see the 'liberatory potential of Islam' and it is hoped that as Africa opens up to South Africa, greater links can be established with Islamic communities in other countries (ibid.). Fifty per cent of the Muslim Youth Movement are Black South African. Before the country's elections a Muslim Forum on Election was formed in order that discussion could take place regarding the endorsement of particular parties. In the elections Muslim groups fielded two parties, the African Muslim Party (AMP) and the Islamic Party (IP). Both parties gained under 1 per cent of the vote in the Western Cape region and only the AMP gained a total of 0.8 per cent of the vote in the districts of Kwazulu/Natal and Pretoria–Witwatersrand–Vereeniging. The Cape-based group, the 'Call of Islam' intended to vote for the ANC on the grounds that they had been 'close to African National Congress forces' (ibid.; SWB AL/1992; ALSI/3 9 May 1994). According to Na'een Jeenah: 'Muslims will not vote in any kind of a bloc. They will vote with their historical alliances and in terms of their personal interests' (ibid.).

ISLAMIC DEMOCRACY

One of the central fears about the increasing influence of Islam is the perceived absolutist and potentially undemocratic nature of its political objectives. Since the 1991 Gulf War different statements have emerged from Islamic quarters. 'Islam', declared Dr Usman Bugaje, Secretary-General of the Islam in Africa Organisation based in Nigeria, 'has a great capacity for tolerance' (*Africa Events* May 1994 p. 28). Yet the renewed importance of religion in the polities of countries in the Middle East and Africa has inevitably given rise to a number of studies examining the relationship between Islam and democracy. Some analysts have pointed to a basic incompatibility between what might be regarded as secular democracy and God's law. Islam, it has been argued, has a totality of view, exclusive of other beliefs, which militates against full participation in multi-party politics (Choueiri 1990). According to Akbar Ahmed the central difference between the West and Islam is rooted in their 'two opposed philosophies: one based in secular materialism, the other in faith' (Ahmed Akbar 1992 p. 264). Nevertheless, others have maintained that it is possible to be both a Muslim and a democrat (Choudhury 1990). The notion of consultation is an important feature of Islam embraced within the institution of *shura*. A *shura* is a consultative council elected by the people: 'The *shura* will assist the Amir (leader). It is obligatory for the Amir to administer the country with the advice of his *shura*. The Amir can retain office only so long as he enjoys the confidence of the people, and must resign when he loses this confidence. Every citizen has the right to criticise the Amir and his government, and all reasonable means for the expression of public opinion should be available' (ibid.). According to Na'een Jeenah, democracy cannot be viewed in a narrow context where people 'simply vote for a government every half a decade. Consultation must take place right down to the local level and on day-to-day issues. For Jeenah it is the 'distorted one-in-four years attitude that makes many Muslims suspicious of the value of the common western understanding of democracy' (Jeenah, *Africa South and East* April 1993).

Raghid El-Solh believes Islamists divide into three groups over the question of democracy: first, those who reject democracy completely and equate it with apostasy; second, those who believe that Islam is inherently democratic, articulated in its notions of *shura* (consultancy); third, those Islamists who 'advocate the appropriation of other societies' concepts of political theories and practices to apply them to Islamic society' (El-Solh 1993). Dr Hasan Turabi, leader of Sudan's National Islamic Front has no hesitation in assimilating the concept of democracy into Islam but he argues that *al-shura* is superior to Western democracy (ibid.). By dividing *shura* into different types, that which is binding (those inclusive of all people and those inclusive of people qualified to act on behalf of Muslims in appointing and deposing the rule) and the forms which are non-binding (those comprised of specialist groups and those providing an arena for public expression), Turabi distinguishes between a more egalitarian form of direct, participatory democracy and a rather less democratic representative version (El-Solh 1993). Islamic democracy is preferable to Western democracy because it is not a separate political practice but permeates all spheres of human existence. Politics is linked to morality and is based on *ijma* (consensus) rather than the rule of the majority. The fact that it is the divine which is sovereign and, therefore, unchallengeable is not seen as a restriction on the freedom of people because they all believe in the principles and details of *sharia* law (ibid.).

Muhammad al-Ghazali and Muhammad Amara argue that whilst adhering to the central principles of the Qur'an it may be possible to learn from the past and to develop and modernise approaches so they may be 'compatible with new circumstances of life' (El-Sohl 1993). Al-Ghazali asserts: 'Western democracy has generally laid down proper principles for political life. We need to take much from these states in order to fill shortcomings due to the paralysis which has afflicted our jurisprudence for many centuries' (cited in El-Sohl 1993). A form of representative democracy would be appropriate in an Islamic state as greater public freedom provided the opportunity for strong religious movements to emerge. El-Sohl (1993) argues interestingly that the differences in attitudes towards democracy between organisations such as the Egyptian Muslim Brotherhood and the Sudanese Islamic National Front lies in the extent to which they have been affected by highly centralised forms of government: 'Those Islamists who suffered under a non-democratic system of government are likely to be more appreciative of the merits of democracy than those who largely escaped such pressures' (ibid.). Conversely, Turabi recognises the benefits to Islamic groups of operating in countries enjoying greater freedoms: 'More democracy will allow the Muslim masses to play an increased role in public life and assert their true sentiment of solidarity.' Once an Islamic state has been declared, however, no political parties would need to exist (*Light and Hope for Sudan* 1995).

Adherents of Sayyid Qutb's strict interpretation of the Qur'an believe that rulers must rule according to what God has revealed and their subjects must accept that rule. There must be no wish to have any law other than that which God has legislated (Haddad 1983). In examining the relationship between Islam and what he calls 'secular humanism', that is liberal democratic views and values of democracy and free speech, the Syrian intellectual Sadik Al-Azm arrives at two conclusions. First, if Islam is regarded as a set of archaic beliefs containing a timeless Islamic essence acting as an 'archetypical constant, continually receding and re-emerging over time', any appropriation of seemingly secular ideas would be wrong. On the other hand, if Islam is not regarded as a static, coherent set of values but as a 'dynamic force' which has constantly renewed itself historically at different periods and over varied geographical areas, then it is possible for contemporary Islam to adopt aspects of secularism (Sadik Al-Azm 1995; meeting). It must be remembered that Islam is not a monolithic force and conflicts and divisions have been a continual feature of the historical progression of the religion.

Islamists have found themselves in something of a dilemma about particating in elections. In 1992, Sheikh Fadlallah, spiritual guide to Lebanon's Shi'ite community announced:

A turning point has been reached in political practice. Certain currents used to call for revolution as the shortest path to power. Now the tendency among Islamic movements in the world is to take advantage of all democratic means available, which will mean participation in elections and politics.

(SWB ME/1274 10 January 1992)

Indeed, the Supreme Assembly of the Islamic Revolution in Iraq (SAIRI), the main Iraqi oppositionist Shi'a organisation, outlined a new programme following the Gulf War of 1991:

1 Respect for Islamic doctine, law education;
2 Respect for ideological freedom, political pluralism and popular opinion;
3 Respect for national social pluralism.

(SWB ME/1314 26 February 1992)

Nevertheless, despite these declarations secular governments have often been unnerved, not necessarily by Islamic parties participating in electoral politics, rather by the prospect of a repressive Islamic state being instituted after the election. In other words, it is feared that Islamic parties might play party politics only to gain power and then subsequently undermine it. Islam has its own perceptions of democratic behaviour enshrined within the concept of *shura*. In some instances, 'Islamic democracy' with its emphasis on discussion and controlled levels of participation within an authoritarian state appears similar to the old one-party socialist model of 'democracy', neither of which can be directly compared with liberal democracy. However, Islamic parties have agreed to govern in association with other secular parties. Jordan's first multi-party parliamentary elections since 1956 were held in November 1993. The parties competing included the Muslim Brotherhood and the Islamic Action Front who collectively won 16 of the 70 seats (*The Star*, Amman, 18 November 1993). The 69 per cent turnout was hailed as a sign of Jordan's growing political maturity and democratic development. The elections that voted in 80 deputies who will serve until 1998 was referred to in the Jordanian press as 'a victory for moderation' (ibid.). Yet, the elections must be viewed in the light of developments which took place before they were held. The amendment to the electoral law, introducing one person, one vote ended the bloc voting system and meant that a voter could only vote for one candidate. What the new electoral system effectively meant was, for the most part, that voters would only vote for candidates with whom they identified ideologically, or on the basis of religion, kinship or clan affiliation. In a sense, it could be that a form of primordialism was at play with most deputies winning seats not necessarily because of their party affiliation and political programmes but rather on account of tribal or sectarian affiliation. Nevertheless, the Jordanian elections have resulted in a form of shared democracy which might be a more appropriate way forward in multi-cultural and multi-religious countries. Furthermore, they also indicate that when given the opportunity in open elections, a sizeable number of Muslims vote for non-Islamic candidates. The Secretary-General of the Jordanian-based Arab Thought Forum, a non-governmental organisation promoting 'enlightened Arab thought', believes that democratisation needs some form of 'national consensus' on basic issues, among which should be the need for 'democratic choice' (Oumlil 1994; meeting).

CONSOCIATIONAL DEMOCRACY

In the mid-1990s numerous media reports from Africa pointed to examples of opposition parties uniting in democratising states in order to strengthen and articulate their views. In Kenya, for example, opposition parties united to form the United National Democratic Alliance, UNDA, with the intention of fielding a common candidate in the elections. One of the main reasons for this move, said the Chairwoman of the UNDA, was the fact that the disunity of the opposition in 1992 had led to 'the elections being characterised by votings along tribal lines'. Equally, in Zambia, seven parties united to form the Zambia Opposition Front with the intention of 'co-ordinating the parties' acitivities at grass-roots level' (SWB/AL/2016 7 June 1994; SWB AL/2022 15 June 1994). In the Congo six opposition parties formed an alliance, the United Democratic Forces, and in Niger, a group of opposition parties re-affirmed their 'strong and united desire' that elections should take place under the supervision of international observers who would give the process 'the much needed guarantee of credibility' (SWB AL/2194 6 January 1995).

In nations with deep social cleavages and political or religious differences pluralist democracy may be threatened by excessive levels of opposition. The objective of consociational democracy, then, is to unite disparate groupings within society by enabling politicians representing sectional interests to govern at national level in a coalition with the leaders of other parties and groups. Thus, by modifying the oppositionist tendencies inherent in the multi-party model of liberal democracy, 'fragmented but stable democracies' can be achieved (Lijphart 1977 p. 1). The development of the consociational model of democracy provides a varient of liberal democracy. Through a system of proportional representation it is possible for all leaders of various groups to be represented at the decision-making level. Such a system operates in the Lebanon on a 1:1 ratio between Christian and Muslim communities. Of course, like most political systems, consociationalism has its critics. One major criticism has been levelled at the way in which an 'elite cartel' can emerge. The cartel then becomes adept at representing the 'particularistic interest of individuals, families and clans' as well as facilitating an efficient vehicle for 'patron–clientelism' based on the exchange of favours for votes (Poole 1991). Consociational democracy is not chiefly concerned with an ideal of equal power or citizen participation beyond the vote and there can be no doubt that elite structures exist. But the important factor is that there is not just one ruling political elite, as is the case in one-party states, or competing elites jockeying for power which is the situation in competitive pluralist states. Numerous elites form and unite at governmental level in order to represent the interests of their communities.

The consociational model is inclusive of societal, ethnic, cultural and religious differences rather than exclusive. In a sense, it is this aspect which attracts greater criticism, that is, the virtual immobilisation of the governmental body which, without consensus, can lead to a situation of policy stagnation and inefficiency. Nevertheless, whilst the adversarial system is seen to be efficient in the short term, it is likely to break down in the long run, there causing animosity and suspicion amongst those sections of society excluded from office. The consociational model on the other hand, even with all its deficiencies may create a climate more conducive to the persistence of a system of democracy. With uncertainty surrounding the possible ulterior motives and ambitions of Islamic parties, it might be that a consociational arrangement offers a process of controlled democratic participation and the prospect of stability. Appropriate mechanisms could be developed to control ethnic tension. The answer to the problem of ethnicity, then, should not lie in banning political parties but rather in 'adopting a constitutional framework which involves careful, legal definition of criteria for recognising genuine national political parties'. Such an institutional safeguard against ethnic competition might require 'a multi-ethnic composition as a condition for recognition as a national party' (van Hoek and Bossuyt 1993). Certainly, suppressing political parties is not the answer according to the president of Uganda's Democratic Party and only serves to 'mask differences, encourage factionalism and dangerous clandestine activities' (SWB AL/2183 20 December 1994).

Nevertheless, in any society there must exist some level of agreement about the direction and objectives of the state, otherwise government will become dysfunctional and drift into what Samuel Huntington once described as 'political decay' (Huntington 1967). Without a clear understanding of national integration societies would be riven by 'parochial loyalties' which would undermine the political structures: conflicts would begin to multiply, procedures for their settlement would sometimes be arbitrary and inappropriate. Political organisations in some African states recognise the need to work together for 'the sake of national unity'. In Malawi a memorandum of understanding was signed in 1994 between the Alliance for Democracy (Aford) and the Malawi Congress Party in an attempt to unite peoples. The Aford president, Chakufwa Chihana, stated that the parties' decision to form a union was not 'intended to derail democratic change', but simply a recognition that the 'country should not be divided just because someone wants to be a leader' (SWB AL/2028 22 June 1994). A number of African leaders maintain that political pluralism will enhance ethnic division. President Museveni speaking at a seminar organised by the German Friedrich Ebert Foundation, claimed there was no 'healthy basis for multi-parties given the backward and pre-industrial structure of African societies'. All shades of political opinion should work together 'in peace and harmony' in order to modernise societies (SWB AL/2179 15 December 1994). Equally, President Daniel arap Moi of Kenya has been an outspoken critic of pluralism maintaining that multi-partyism will inevitably divide people on ethnic lines: 'The current clamouring over democracy has sapped and divided the continent' (SWB AL/2233 21 February 1995). Although both leaders may feel uneasy about their own positions in an increasingly democratising era, there can be no doubt that a fundamental question remains and was posed in a study for the African Development Bank: 'To what extent is democracy a viable form of government in a continent which suffers conditions of pervasive economy decay' (van Hoek and Bossuyt 1993). The World Bank and IMF structural adjustment programmes demand economic changes which carry high levels of social costs as well as conditional democratisation programmes. A study of political liberalisation and economic reform by the Overseas Development Institute (ODI) concluded that 'neither authoritarian rule nor continued political liberalisation offers an assured framework for economic reform' (Overseas Development Institute 1994). The ODI found that national elections and the freedom to form different parties provided only a first, partial step towards political liberalisation and often the single governing party had been replaced by fragmented party systems. There had been few pre-election debates about economic policy and opposition parties had failed to offer any alternative economic or development agendas (ibid.). In a sense, though, this lack of debate is a symptom of the pervasive fear of political division and loss of control, which has given rise to the cultural deterministic view that 'Africa is not ripe for democracy' (Van Hoek and Bossuyt 1993). In Benin, no issues at all were debated in public in pre-electoral and electoral campaign periods as the government banned all political transmissions and radio programmes with 'a political slant' on the grounds they might not be in the 'national interest' (SWB AL/2207 21 January 1995). It is readily admitted that in terms of 'softening the all-embracing grip of the central state and in greater press freedom, the process of political liberalistion still has a long way to go' (van Hoek and Bossuyt). In any case, in countries such as Chad with 52 legalised opposition parties any cohesive alternative political and economic agenda might be difficult to achieve. However, it must be noted here, although it is discussed in a later chapter, that Islamic groups do present different economic programmes.

DIFFERENT POLITICAL AGENDAS

National integration is still important in sub-Saharan Africa. Problems of violence and a drift to civil war often results when national unity is not fully achieved. In this context, the contradiction between some Islamic groups and their objectives and the demands of Western-determined liberal democracy is stark when played out in African states. The situation also raises the question of the extent to which external political agendas are being foisted on African nations: one from the West in the form of pluralist democracy, the other from the Middle East in the shape of an Islamic quest for the establishment of a theocratic state. Are either types of political expression appropriate for Africa? One senior Christian working in a missionary group based in Nigeria believes there exists: 'Something endemic in African culture, at basic level, which is uneasy with Islam' (Connolly 1994; interview). Equally, certain elements within Africa are uncomfortable with liberal democracy. Again in the case of Nigeria's military government, who espouse a commitment to democracy and readily recite that it is built on the rule of law and socio-political order, they are nevertheless reluctant to relinquish office when elections take place and are openly accused of seeking to 'perpetuate themselves in government' (SWB AL/2028 22 June 1994).

Both Western ideas of democracy and Islamic notions of *sharia* and *shura* have been imposed on Africa through conquest and control although both the West and the Middle East maintain, respectively, that the demands come from Africa. Dr Usman Bugaje, the Secretary-General of the organisation Islam in Africa, believes that Africa 'craves for Islam' as a part of its quest for 'cultural freedom' and its search for 'an alternative world view which can stand up to a challenge the West' (*Africa Events* May 1994). Statements by the United Nations Secretary-General Boutros Boutros-Ghali, point to Africa's need for democracy which will provide: 'an informed body of citizens able to communicate with each other and with other governments and to interact with the outside world' (UN Focus on the New Agenda for Africa 1993). In a way, both these interpretations are accurate simply because both Western and Islamic influences on the continent have been so profound and are part of Africa's historical and cultural development.

Cultural diversity within Africa results in part from external influences in the form of language, political ideas, religious faith and so on. All countries over time are exposed to the cultural domination of other powers and often the gradual assimilation of those cultural features. However, the factor which is significant in the case of Africa as a region of the Third World is the fact that the Middle East, also regarded as part of the Third World, has had and, indeed, continues to have a dominant influence over the political direction of a number of states. Clearly, it is not only the West who pursues a policy of cultural aggrandisement towards Africa. Other member states of the Third World do so too. The question must be posed: is there an African political alternative? One leading Christian maintains that democratisation in Africa is very difficult with one central problem being the continuation of a social structure which looks to chiefs and elders for guidance and authority (Walsh 1994; interview). When these structures are replicated at national level authoritarian practices of government emerge which are at variance with liberal democratic sentiments. William Tordoff makes the same observation. (Tordoff 1993).

It may be the case that Islamic ideas of democratic participation in the context of the *shura* find a greater resonance in African states simply on the grounds of similarity with past patterns of political expression. After all the secular one-party socialist model, the 'charismatic' leader and the military ruler, whether revolutionary or otherwise, all added up to pretty much the same experience: authoritarian government with very little opportunity for citizen participation. An Islamic model of political behaviour may actually be viewed as preferable to those practices. However, this is not primarily the point. The issue here is the extent to which the countries within Africa choose their own political structures. This question goes further than simply a debate between Islam and democratisation, it goes to the very core of external control and influence, to cultural assimilation and identity and to funding and access to resources. Van Hoek and Bossuyt refer to the relative 'absence of a genuinely African discourse on democracy and its related search for institutional arrangements which are rooted in African culture and society and relevant to present day realities' (van Hoek and Bossuyt 1993). But if an assimilated African culture is partly an Islamic culture then logically Islamic political practices may emerge. Certainly Islamic modes of political and social behaviour are seen as more adaptable and transferable mainly because Islam has been embedded in parts of African society for hundreds of years. As Callaway and Creevey state in their study of women and Islam in West Africa: 'Islam continued to spread and reach ever larger numbers of people, just by virtue of being there longer' (Callaway and Creevey 1994 p. 24).

CONCLUSION

In any analysis of democratisation it is, of course, impossible to ignore the impact of the South African elections on the wider continent. As one commentator asserted after the results were known:

The rest of Africa has metaphorically winced, groaned, gagged and screamed along with us for they have a special interest in the outcome of our democratic process, for two reasons. First, they have a particular concern with seeing apartheid ended and second, they have great expectations for themselves from the new South Africa.'

(*The Star International Weekly*, 5–10 May 1994, Johannesburg)

The success of democracy in South Africa may boost democratic processes in Africa more generally by demonstrating 'reconciliation by example' (ibid.). However, the Secretary-General of the Commonwealth, Chief Anyaoku, stressed the need for democracy to be perceived not as 'a common format' but rather in terms of its 'essential ingredients'. The exact procedures for democracy would then vary from country to country (Ake 1990). Kuwait's Minister of Information Sheikh Al-Saud Al-Sabah highlights Chief Anyaoku's views when defending his country's decision to bar women from voting: 'The problem we have had is that people in the West believe that what they have should also be applied here, and this does not take into account the differences in our cultures. Our concept and our understanding of democracy is different from theirs' (Al Saud Al-Sabah 1995). To many observers in the west, Kuwait could not remotely be described as a 'democratic' state largely because of its limited electoral franchise; its 'second-class' citizens who have no vote at all; the continuing pre-eminence of the Al-Sabah family and its propensity to imprison leaders of opposition parties (Deegan 1993).

Essentially there is no global definition of democracy's 'essential ingredients'. While Zimbabwe's president, Robert Mugabe speaks of the need for his party, ZANU-PF, to redefine its 'democratic socialist ideology in a manner consistent with our culture and historical experience', the World Bank, IMF and European donor countries link the process of democratisation with pluralism and regular elections. (SWB AL/2109 24 September 1994; Chalker 1995; meeting). References to a country's culture are meaningless unless the full nuances of such a term are defined. When the Kuwaiti Information Minister refers to the main pillars of democracy as 'freedom and people's rights', the words appear in a vacuum devoid of clarity (Al Saud Al-Sabah 1995). It may be that democracy requires 'a blend between tradition and modernity, between indigenous culture and relevant foreign experiences' (van Hoek and

Bossuyt 1993). But such a custom-made democracy may not, in fact, be regarded as such by Western or Middle Eastern donor states.

Certainly, democracy should have a wider resonance within society, increased levels of political participation and a process of legitimate sanction against ruling elites. Equally, it seems that all people need to articulate their views through a procedure of electoral choice. But what if multi-party political systems fail to function in some poor states? In certain nations, the number of eligible voters registering to vote has declined following the initial flurry of activity and excitement of the first multi-party elections. Only 10 per cent of Burkina Faso's electorate turned out to vote in municipal elections in February 1995; a fact which was immediately attributed to a combination of apathy and a paucity of new ideas by aspiring candidates (SWB AL/2227 14 February 1995). It may also be an uncomfortable fact that municipal elections held little relevance for the predominantly rural, Muslim population of Burkina Faso. Is their 'apathy' culturally determined or simply conditioned by the fact that the electorate saw no immediate benefits of voting for a variety of candidates? Or another sign, perhaps, that democracy does not emerge from multi-party politics alone. When a senior Sudanese official was asked whether he envisaged the whole of the African continent becoming Islamic, he thought for a moment, then replied: 'Maybe, not in the forseeable future', before adding, 'But don't forget. The greatest threat to Western interests is the introduction of democratic practices in Africa. Islamists will win' (El Affendi, 25 January 1995; interview).

3

THEOCRATIC/SECULAR STATES AND SOCIETIES

This chapter considers the degree to which a distinction can be drawn between a secular government and a theocratic government in terms of political structures and inputs. To what extent does Islam provide a coherent political programme which differs radically from secular government strategies and policies? Is there an overlap between Arab and African 'worlds'? Certain 'unquantifiable' aspects such as cultural identity and religious devotion will be considered together with 'hard' facts, that is, levels of education; welfare provision and the availability of healthcare; labour; women and their access to education and work. State structures and decision-making processes may reveal whether or not a state, of either a theocratic or secular disposition, is remote and heavy-handed in its political practices and the extent to which societal and cultural affinities/ differences between peoples are acknowledged. Before determining precisely what a theocratic state upholds it is necessary to look at the nature of religious belief itself.

RELIGIOUS BELIEF

The African Synod in Rome, alarmed by the ethnic conflict in Rwanda, met in 1994. One particularly important speech was made by Nigerian Bishop Obiefuna of Nigeria: 'For the typical African when it comes to the crunch it is not the Christian concept of the Church as a family which prevails but rather the adage that blood is thicker than water. And by water here one can include the waters of baptism' (*The Tablet* 18 June 1994). Ties of kinship were placed above religious doctrine and patterns of behaviour were dictated by ethnic identity and familial imperative rather than the demands of faith. In a sense, this interpretation raises both notions of rationality and an understanding of the extent to which religious belief pervades a society. Religious belief has been regarded as non-rational: 'The theology and ethics of Christianity, if surrendered to the analysis of reason and interpreted by advancing knowledge, will vanish' (Kierkegaard 1974). Alternatively, religion may be viewed as an essentially spiritual and natural part of humankind (Clarke 1891). Bryan Turner refers to the 'sociologists of religion' regularly speaking of the crisis of meaning in contemporary society and Max Weber spoke of the increasing need for an 'ethical interpretation of the "meaning" of the distribution of fortunes' among people with the 'growing rationality of conceptions of the world' (Turner 1994 p. 90). Yet it is important to distinguish the theoretical embellishment of 'meaning' which, perhaps invites a reflection on individual behaviour and an ethical imperative which demands observance. Most religions have moral doctrines and codes of conduct which their followers are expected to observe (Arkoun 1994 p. 115).

Thomas Cleary maintains that Islamic faith has grown from 'observation, reflection and contemplation', with the Qur'an offering an 'harmonious interplay of faith and reason' (Cleary 1993 p. vii). In the pursuit of a 'divine reality', however, the monotheistic religions, e.g. Islam, Judaism, Christianity, tend to think of themselves as 'best', meaning they alone are more 'true'. Thereby, claims can be made that animist religions are 'false' (Cohn-Sherbok 1994; meeting). The Qur'an views Judaism and Christianity differently from 'paganism' in that Jews and Christians are considered peoples of the Book (*ahl al-kitab*). Revelation reached those religions through recognised and venerated prophets such as Abraham and Moses (Arkoun 1994 p. 71). The Qur'an appears after the Hebrew bible, the Talmud and the New Testament and by integrating those moments of revelation, it presents itself as the 'final act in the exhibition of the heavenly Book' (ibid.). Equally the Jews and Christians refused to recognise Muhammad as a prophet which contributed to the separation of the faiths. However, verses appear in the Qur'an defining the legal status of Jews and Christians, the *dhimmi* (protected peoples): 'Those who among the people of the Book do not profess the religion of Truth, fight them until they personally pay the *juzya* (tax on non-Muslims) acknowledging their inferiority' (ibid. p. 72). These verses if given a literal interpretation raise many difficulties in contemporary societies and this is one reason why Arkoun calls for the 'urgent need for a modern rereading of these sacred texts that takes account of historical context and doctrinal struggles aggravated by the appearance of the Qur'an at the beginning of the seventh century' (ibid.).

The beliefs of a number of religions, then, rest on 'exclusivist assumptions', which mean that other religious groups are excluded from the truth which is, and can only be, within say, Christianity, or Islam, or Judaism. The traditional flanks of these faiths subscribe to exclusivist ideas (Cohn-Sherbok; meeting). Rabbi Professor Dan Cohn-Sherbok believes that religions can also be 'inclusivist' in the sense that there is an acknowledgement that other faiths may have been exposed in a limited way to god. However, even within inclusivism, god is believed to have revealed himself (sic) more fully to only one religion. Therefore, one faith still regards itself as 'more true' even though other faiths are recognised and respected (ibid.). Cohn-Sherbok proposes a different model of faith: pluralism, which places the 'Divine', which may not necessarily be god, at the centre of faith. As religion is a human construction which attempts to understand or make sense of the Divine, no religion is best and we cannot know that any religion is more 'true' because we are limited by our human capabilities. We are limited by the 'World As It Is' and 'The World As Perceived' and we cannot bridge the two, despite religious traditions which attempt to do so (ibid.). We are confined to the 'World As Perceived' because Divine reality is ultimately unknown. The pre-eminence of one religion cannot be right as all religions are 'constructs of humanness'. However, particular religions, especially monotheistic ones, in their quest to understand Divine reality and identify with a 'knowable deity', construct doctrines which may not be deliberately false but nevertheless cannot be proved. It is the unknowable quality about an infinite being which makes all religions limited (ibid.). The fact that people often become comfortable in a religious tradition tends to support Cohn-Sherbok's assertion that 'humans must find what is spiritually meaningful for themselves' (ibid.). Ernest Gellner believes that the strength of Islam rests not only in its commitment to 'a firmly delineated divine message' which provides a firm social framework, but to the fact that it does not 'sacrilize' daily life: 'Islam may be socially demanding but it does not abolish the dualism, which saves the sacred from being compromised by the profane' (Gellner 1994 pp. xiii-xiv).

Gellner distinguishes between 'High' and 'Low' Islam which he believes has at times generated conflict, but mostly has 'interpenetrated and tolerated each other in peaceful detente' (ibid.

p. xi). The 'High' culture of Islam developed from its scriptural, scholastic, puritanical, urban, merchant background, whereas its Low or folkish culture is expressed in communities and brotherhoods springing up around Islamic saints (Gellner 1993). The High form presented a normative image of the religion which societies would endeavour to, but sometimes fail, to uphold. The impact of Modernity, however, forges a strong link between the exacting fundamentalism of High Islamic culture and the popular appeal of Low culture to an increasingly literate urbanising society (ibid.). The division between High and Low Islam enables it to be a more adaptable and accommodating religion in regions such as Africa. The fact that Islam retains some of the rites and beliefs characteristic of earlier Arab religions, eg. the rites of pilgrimage to Mecca and certain myths, despite its condemnation of the pre-Islamic Arab past as the age of darkness, further enhances its ability to permeate traditional religious societies.

At the societal level religious continuity is dependent on the extent to which generational belief patterns are handed down. Milton Yinger maintains that stable societies pass on to each generation, as a process of acculturation, patterns of ritual and belief (Yinger 1970 p. 155). Religion serves as an important and meaningful connection between generations. Rites and doctrines are viewed as providing religion with appropriate methods of dealing with the needs of individuals confronting the problems of everyday life. Emile Durkheim believed that religious phenomena were naturally arranged in two fundamental categories: beliefs and rites (Durkheim 1976). For Durkheim, all known religious beliefs, whether simple or complex, presented common characteristics of myths and dogmas, articulated through ceremonies, sacrifices, prayers and chants (ibid. p. 42). The objective of religion, he argued, was to raise humans above themselves and to instruct them to lead better lives than they would otherwise follow if left to their own individual whims (ibid. p. 414). The belief in ultimate salvation strengthened individuals as their quest for religious certainty often reflected the uneasiness and isolation experienced by the solitary individual. Durkheim believed religion to be a necessary and vital force in maintaining social stability and an indispensable means of social constraint. The reason for this, he believed, rested on the fact that religion was a 'social act', in which rites and ceremonies assumed social significance. These processes symbolically tied individuals to their kinship community (ibid.).

67

Durkheim's views might not be immediately identifiable in many African countries wrought with religious and ethnic rivalry but in a sense this was the point Bishop Obeifuna was making. Far from providing social stability and cohesion within different communities religiosity can be overridden when kinship affinities came to the fore. In any case, as Ernest Gellner asserts 'Islam is trans-ethnic and trans-social: it does not equate faith with the beliefs of any one community or society' (Gellner 1993 p. 101). Attachment to a religious belief may not necessarily be an organic process closely and strongly intertwined with society. Christian mission groups working in a variety of African states report the decline of any deep attachments to Christianity among various tribal groupings especially when those societies are confronted by economic and social difficulties (Connolly 1994; interview; O'Toole 1994; interview; O'Leary 1994; interview). Interaction between religion and society may not necessarily be strong, but it depends on the nature of the religion and the type of society. Religious belief and practice tend to vary with the size and mobility of a society. As societies urbanise or industrialise, as different class structures emerge and are exposed to changing value systems, the relationship between religion and society alters.

PROTESTANTISM

Max Weber maintained that a dynamic religion could actually cause society and its economic structures to change radically. In Max Weber's view the energetic spirit of modern capitalism was powerfully influenced by the values of Protestantism. Economic rationalism, Weber believed, derived from the religious revolution of the sixteenth century. The term, economic rationalism, used by Weber, described an economic system based not on custom or tradition, but 'on the deliberate and systematic adjustment of economic means to the attainment of the objective of pecuniary profit' (Weber 1974 p. 43). Far from there being an 'inevitable conflict between money making and piety' the two were united under the 'Protestant Ethic' (ibid.). Therefore, thrift, hard work, prudence, and the pursuit of profit became not merely economic ends, but spiritual ends too. Calvinism, the 'ascetic' form of Protestanism, was responsible, Weber argued, for religious rationalism in the context of spiritual values and objectives (ibid. p. 123). Protestantism differed markedly from Roman Catholicism and those following religious orders who were obliged to adhere to vows of obedience, poverty and chastity. Within Catholicism, the Church could mediate to the believer through a Papal intermediary and the sacraments, especially penance. Calvinism had no such mediator between the believer and God which contributed to a strong sense of individualism and a consciousness that the power of God worked through the person. The individual, therefore, had to fulfil 'God's Will' not through a life of contemplative prayer but through diligence, self-discipline and work. This activity provided, Weber argued, the religious basis of capitalism (ibid. p. 157). Within the sociology of religion, then, 'Calvinistic Protestantism transformed Western culture towards an anti-magical, disciplined life-world' (Turner 1994 p. 11).

For Bryan Turner, the Protestant ethic argument raises two major issues. First, rationality is tied to modernity, in that in order for a society to become modern it had to 'undergo and embrace the disciplines of goal-directed rational conduct'. Second, a clear division was drawn between a progressive Christian West and a retarding Islamic Orient (ibid.). Modernism can be identified as 'an industrial society based upon a continuous, cumulative expansion of scientific knowledge' (Bromley 1994 p. 27). Friedrich Engels writing near the end of the nineteenth century stated: 'Muslim risings, notably in Africa, make a remarkable constrast (with Christendom). Islam suits Orientals, especially the Arabs, that is to say, on the one hand townsmen practising commerce and industry, on the other hand, nomadic Beduin.' Although periodic clashes occurred, economic conditions remained intact and nothing changed.

> By contrast, for the popular risings in the Christian West the religious camouflage is only the banner and mask for an attack on a crumbling social order: in the end, that order is overturned, a new one merges, there is progress, the world moves on.
>
> (Engels, *Die Neue Zeit* (1894/95) in Gellner 1993 p. 46)

Far from providing an impetus for future change and development, Islamic society followed a cyclical process of movement from 'central authority supported by tribal federation, through urban impiety and degeneracy to the crisis which renews the impulse of tribal revolt and thus instantiates a new central authority' (Bromley 1994 p. 26).

Like Weber, Karl Marx, considered religion to be closely associated with the economic structure of society, but in a different way (MacIntyre 1971). Whereas Max Weber looked at the influence of religious ideas on the economic system, Karl Marx regarded religion as merely a by-product of economic conditions. According to Marx, religion performed two functions in society. First, it buttressed and protected the established order; second, it compensated the oppressed by promising them a reward in heaven. Religion distracted people from effectively engaging in revolutionary activity. Under a radically altered social system people would have no need of any religious consolations and inevitably religion would 'disappear of its own accord without persecution' (ibid. p. 80). Historical materialism rendered 'other worldly' religion redundant. Where it continued to flourish it did so not because of intellectual conviction but because of social needs (ibid. p. 83). Once the social factors which produced those needs were removed by the transformation of the structure of society, religion would become functionless (ibid. p. 85). In other words, social and economic factors, rather than a sense of spirituality, were the determinants of religion.

Both Weber and Marx regarded 'Oriental' societies as economically stagnant. Marx viewed the absence of social classes, class conflict and any mechanism of social change as resulting in the region having 'no history at all, at least no known history' (Turner 1994 p. 41). Thus a contrast was drawn between a dynamic, modernising West and a retarded and static Orient. The recent focus of attention on postmodernism and Orientalism has renewed interest in the distinctions between monotheistic religions: Christianity, Islam and Judaism. Instead of delineating their differences and one religion's pre-eminence over another Bryan Turner wishes to emphasise those 'points of contact and sameness which unite Christian, Jewish and Islamic traditions into merely variations on a religious theme' (ibid. p. 50). Studies of the distinctions between religions in terms of the attitudes of believers revealed that whereas Mormons and Protestants had very different attitudes, Christian and Muslim villagers had few significant differences (cf. Vogt and O'Dea 1953 pp. 645–654; Fetter 1964 pp. 48–59). Christian and Muslim villagers held similar attitudes towards village life, farming, national leadership, education and the value of co-operation. Those comparable in education, income and length of residence in a locality held 'strikingly similar attitudes, despite their religious differences'. Conclusions suggested that 'differences in religion, insofar as they affect orientations and philosophies toward life in general, tend to be overridden and rendered insignificant by the wider impact of Arab culture generally and the historical–economic–geographical concomitants of rural Lebanese life in particular' (Fetter 1964). These interpretations support Ibn Khaldun's views that political, social and civic virtues are fostered by tribal life rather than religion (Gellner 1993 p. 17).

RELIGIOUS CULTS AND MAGIC

The spread of Christian and Islamic religions in Africa must be seen in the context of conversion. Both Christian and Islamic groups continue to speak of religious conversion as the means of disseminating their respective faiths (Connolly 1994; Turabi 1993). Yet religious conversion has encountered resistance in a number of African states. The Goemai people of Nigeria were particularly resistant to attempts by Muslim groups and Christian missionaries to convert them to Islam or Catholicism. According to Jarlath Walsh, Director of the Institute of Pastoral Affairs in Nigeria, the reason for the Goemai's steadfastness rested upon their satisfaction with the traditional religion of their forefathers. Consequently, they 'saw no need to abandon it and follow religions they did not know' (Walsh 1994; interview). The Goemai religion was founded on the desire to protect the lives and welfare of the people. Two deities, 'Karem' and Matkarem' (male and female, respectively) were believed by the people to be responsible for most events of human concern and rituals were performed to appease these gods. Christianity was seen to be concerned not with life on earth but in an afterlife in a world beyond. Therefore, for the people of Goemai 'new religions had little meaning' (ibid.). Interestingly, Christian missions operating in Nigeria, reported in 1994, that the Ibo ethnic group, who had formerly largely converted to Christianity, were becoming 'more occultist', performing magical rituals, and searching for an 'authentic spiritual identity in keeping with their culture' (ibid.; Connolly 1994; interview).

Max Weber believed that as religious and ethical reflections on the world became increasingly rationalised 'primitive and magical notions' would be eliminated (Weber in Gerth and Wright Mills 1948 p. 275). According to another interpretation magical ritual is sustained by belief and emotion and may be practised by pre-logical people with no true knowledge of the world around them; people who are quite unable to distinguish between a natural cause and a

71

magical one (Yinger 1970 p. 73). The recourse to magic practices may also demonstrate that societies are struggling to deal with contemporary problems in a traditional form. Bayart maintains that the popularity of religious cultism may result from the powerful impact Islam and Christianity had on the African state. In a sense, it is an attempt by Africans to reclaim their cultural heritage (Bayart 1992 pp. 187–189). Magical ceremony, witchcraft and occultist activity does represent an important aspect of Africa's historicity. Despite suggestions that such practices are both irrational and unscientific they nevertheless continue to have a legitimacy in African society. Mission groups reported in 1994 that Christian belief was declining in Africa and increasing numbers of priests and religious figures were, in fact, also dabbling in occultist ritual. Such practices were regarded as 'truly African' (Connolly 1994; interview; Walsh 1994; interview). These developments are in sharp contradiction to the great upsurge of Christian church membership throughout the 1950s and 1960s, the years of post-colonial independence. According to one senior religious figure, Africans at that time seemed almost ashamed of their own roots, including their traditional religions (ibid.). People in their thousands abandoned their old religions for the various denominations of Christian faith.

RELIGION AND THE STATE

The provision of educational and healthcare facilities may have induced Africans to convert to Christianity in general terms. However, the figures for the Nigerian Diocese of Jos displayed in

Table 3.1 Statistics for Catholic Church 1948–78. Prefectures/Diocese of Jos, Nigeria

Year	Number of Catholics	Schools		Medical	
		Prim.	Sec.	Clinics	Hospitals
1938	3,653	44	–	2	–
1948	13,825	97	–	18	4
1955	27,581	121	–	18	1
1961	50,110	124	4	17	2
1978	150,000	–	4	–	–

Source: Society of African Missions, Etats, the Society for the Propagation of Faith, Rome, 1980.

Table 3.1 suggests no obvious correlation: conversions increased despite a marginal increase in educational provision and between 1948 and 1961 an actual decline in the number of clinics and hospitals. In the Jos Diocese attempts by the St Louis Sisters to educate young girls were initially resisted on the grounds that this withdrew labour on the land. Yet when bride price values increased for girls with an education, parents began to send their daughters to school. When the mission primary school opened in January 1955, a class for girls was established (St Louis Sisters 1978).

As Bayart suggests, Christian conversion may have resulted from the strong association between the church and state. He points to the example of Rwanda where the Catholic Archbishop of Kigali sat on the central committee of the party until 1985. Bayart draws the conclusion that to a large extent, the regime in Rwanda was an extension of the church (Bayart 1992 p. 189). Islamic and Christian groups, although rivals, would always gain access and, at times be, co-opted into the state bureaucracy or elite. Certain procedures would then become established: mosques or churches would be constructed and there would be a dispensation of resources. As we have seen in previous chapters, some religious groups formed political parties and continue to do so. Senior personnel from Mission organisations readily admit that 'religious standpoints often mask economic and political interests' (O'Leary 1994; interview; Connolly 1994; interview).

It may be that colonialism, far from instituting religious imperatives, actually secularised 'values, human relations and institutions' in the newly independent states (Coleman 1960). James Coleman points out ironically: 'One of the most powerful of the forces furthering the process of secularisation has been the Christian missionary.' He explains that by becoming a Christian an individual had the opportunity of attending school and gaining an educational standard that would lead to employment, probably of a clerical nature, in the bureaucracy. The political institutions of colonialism and the structures of indirect rule were thoroughly secular in that the ultimate source of legitimacy was not the Church but the Colonial authority (ibid.). Equally, modernisation theories prevalent at the time emphasised progess and development rather than religious faith. Certainly, some colonial administrators were regarded as overtly indifferent to Christian missionary work and in some instances, were accused of idealising Muslim and traditional culture.[1] Equally although Catholicism became the 'moral rhetoric of the

French civilising mission' in Senegal, care was taken not to interfere with French relations with the Islamic marabouts (Callaway and Creevey 1994 p. 26).

Nevertheless, the Annual Reports of the Society of African Missions during the 1950s pinpoint three fundamental reasons why children were being increasingly released from their farming duties and sent to school. First, the children who were sent to school took up jobs which not only brought them money but also gave them a high social status at the completion of their various courses. Second, government offices and firms were in great need of trained clerks and staff and these could only come from schools. Ability to speak and write English could result in gaining an individual the job of interpreter. Third, a government job carried an aura of responsibility together with respectability and power and enhanced a person's position in the home village (Annual Reports from the Diocese of Jos 1955–1957). In a sense, we are returning to the perceived beneficial and functional aspects of religion rather than spiritual fulfilment. As one African writer asserts and as the peoples of Goemai emphasised: 'New ideas, including Christianity, are acceptable only when Africans see they are obviously useful . . . to anything beyond that they are not receptive' (Ekechi 1971). The upsurge in Christianity in the early years of independence and the more recent drift back to traditional religious practices in Africa may result less from a general decline in spirituality and rather more from the inability of Christian churches to deal with increasing levels of socio-economic deprivation. In a study of the popularity of evangelical charismatic Christianity in South Africa, perceived social and economic oppression were motivating factors (Thompson 1995).

It is also alleged that the central concern of religious groups, Christian and Islamic, is gaining access to 'power, money and resources' and it is within this arena that they compete (O'Leary 1994; interview) Rwanda and neighbouring Burundi both have Catholic populations of around 70 per cent. During the Rwandan conflict of 1994 the Catholic Church came directly under attack, with priests and sisters becoming targets, and some Christian missionaries questioning whether they could ever return to the country. Yet Rwanda is not the only country suffering religious tension. In Chad, the organisation the Union for Renewal and Democracy reported that acts of religious hatred, first perpetrated in 1979, were occurring again in the 1990s. Attacks were led by the regular army against civilian populations under the pretext of 'religious cleansing'

(SWB ME/1612 13 February 1993). Leaflets distributed by one Islamic group call for the Christian–animist ethnic group, the Sara community, who live in a predominantly Arab–Islamic region and work as teachers and state officials to either leave the country or convert to Islam (SWB AL/2146 7 November 1994). Accusations were made that Catholic and Protestant places of worship were desecrated by Muslims intent on a process of religious purification. In Uganda, a Catholic priest and nuns were kidnapped by National Resistance Army soldiers (SWB AL/2074 15 August 1994). Whilst in Mauritania, Islamic rebels reportedly killed Catholic priests along with government officials (SWB AL/2112 28 September 1994).

These forms of religious clashes have been attributed to the sometimes covert political role Christian leaders play within states under the cover of formalised religion (El-Affendi 1995; interview). There might, at first sight, exist an apparent contradiction between religious belief and the adoption of violent action. Yet conflict and domination have been justified and enshrined in both the Christian Crusades and the Islamic jihad. Max Weber referred to Islam's early period as 'a religion of world conquering warriors, a knight order of disciplined crusaders' (Weber in Gerth and Wright Mills 1948 p. 269). Although there are continuing calls for religious and political tolerance, Christian and Islamic relations within an unsympathetic state can often be tense and uneasy (Kukah 1993). The state may dispense largesse to certain religious denominations but it may also censor others. The Catholic Church has complained of its churches being attacked and destroyed if any criticism is voiced against the powerful Islamic leadership in northern Nigeria (Walsh 1994; interview). To an extent, religion in Africa and the Middle East has been politicised largely because of the paucity of channels through which to articulate opposition and the general authoritarian or paternalistic political structures which exist. Yet when we speak of theocratic structures and states certain specific images come to mind: Islamic codes of social conduct, discipline, dress and behaviour and the institution of the *sharia* based on Islamic law. We are unlikely to call say, Rwanda, a theocratic state, simply because 70 per cent of its population is Catholic and a Bishop sat on the central committee of the only political party. Equally, we would not refer to Nigeria even with its large Muslim population and powerful Islamic leaders as a theocracy. The fact that societies follow specific religions and devotions does not automatically imply the existence of a theocratic state.

THE THEOCRATIC STATE

The 1979 constitution of the the Islamic Republic of Iran asserts that the country embraces the spirituality and ethics of Islam and that such elements should provide the basis for political, social and economic relations. The Shi'a branch of Islam was declared the official religion of the state and supreme power was granted to the pre-eminent Shi'a religious leader, the Wali Faqi. According to Article 94 of the Constitution all legislation passed by the the 270-member Majlis (National Assembly) must be reviewed by the Council for the Protection of the Constitution where it is scrutinised for its Islamic content. Through the introduction of the Islamic legal code, *sharia*, it has been possible rigorously to enforce Islamic ideas through a formal set of procedures and rules which apply to the penal system, judicial interpretation, strict dress and social laws. Hence, the state during the Khomeini period has been able, via these instruments of control to 'forge a superficial homogeneity upon Iranian society' (Wright 1989 p. 24). However, it would be erroneous to consider the Iranian state to be static and unevolving. In a detailed study of the politics of executive power and succession in the post-Khomeini years, the period is referred to as a 'new' regime, the Second Republic (Ehteshami 1994 p. 55).

Seyyed Hossein Nasr maintains that one of the important aspects of Islam in contemporary life is the appearance of movements standing for the re-establishment of the full and complete reign of the *sharia* over the every-day life of Muslims (Seyyed Hossein Nasr 1975 p. 93). The basis for this trend rests on the strong desire among many people for a 'moral revivification and renewal' (ibid.). Yet despite assertions that the 'return to religion' and the 'resurgence of Islam' are the result of the pursuit of ethical and moral restoration, Arkoun suggests that theological research and ethical reflection have 'practically disappeared from the Muslim intellectual domain'. Contemporary Islam, then, is characterised by a 'flight from ethical concern' (M. Arkoun 1994). The attraction of Islam is reinterpreted by Juan Goytisolo: 'La marea humana de fieles postrados en El Cairo o Argel en los aledanos de las mezquitas es menos una expresion de fervor que una manifestacion de protesta' ('The human swathes of the faithful prostrated outside the mosques of Cairo or Algeria are less an expression of fervour than an act of protest') (Goytisolo 1994).[2] Economic and political deprivation have inclined people towards Islam, Goytisolo argues and from the end of the 1970s:

The affirmation of Islam in the political arena conceals and blocks out all spiritual, cultural and historical values. Reference to the *sharia*, the Sunna or to the holy imams (religious leaders) within Iranian Shi'ism becomes an essential element in the legitimisation of all government projects.

(ibid.)

In the process, Islam, conceived as a faith, a deep personal experience or a code of morality, has been replaced by a 'simplifying doctrine which ignores the individual struggle to interpret the text of the Qu'ran, and restricts itself to the condemnation of other regimes as 'unholy' (ibid.). In a sense, these developments represent an impoverishment of the contemplative and religious in favour of an enhancement of the political and social. Nationalist, socialist politics offer little to young people increasingly looking to Islam for political direction and identity (Hammade 1993; interview). Theocratic states, then, confront all the economic, social and political demands which beleaguer secular states.

In the case of Iran, specific identifiable features have lingered on which connect the pre- and post-revolutionary periods. There is, arguably, no difference between SAVAMA, the Islamic Republic's secret police and the former Shah's SAVAK, the State Organisation for Intelligence and Security, on which it was modelled, in that both have instituted close systematic sureillance over the population. According to reports by both Amnesty Internation and the United Nations Human Rights Commission issued in December 1990, 5,000 people were executed in Iran between 1987 and 1990. The reports also point to the fact that prisoners had no recourse to legal counsel or right of appeal (*Keesings Record of World Events*, December 1990 p. 37,929). This purge of oppositionists which included not only left-wing political activists and sympathisers, but also several clergymen was the result of a crack-down on all 'those who have betrayed Islam and the revolution' (*Middle East International*, 6 December 1985). In 1974–75, at the height of the Shah of Iran's oppressive campaign, an Amnesty International report estimated there to be over 25,000 political prisoners within the country and its then Secretary-General asserted: 'The Shah of Iran retains his benevolent image despite the highest rate of death penalties in the world, no valid system of civilian courts and a history of torture which is beyond belief' (Peretz 1983 p. 512). The similarities between the two periods create an impression of the Islamic

CULTURAL/POLITICAL

Republic as being quite as dogmatic and intolerant as any other one-party, authoritarian secular state.

Some analysts, however, do not view the Islamic state as necessarily reactionary but rather as a post-modern phenomenon, thus: 'Islamic fundamentalism reflects the modernist ideas of secularism and a secular state and society, which are felt to have failed in providing an appropriate and moral social order for humans' (Voll 1989 p. 34; Akbar Ahmed 1991; meeting). Gellner, in fact, believes that of the 'three great Western monotheisms, Islam is the one closest to modernity' (Gellner 1993 p. 7). Musing on the possible existence of an historic Muslim rather than Christian Europe he points to Islam's 'modernist' criteria: 'Universalism, scripturalism, spiritual egalitarianism, the extension of full participation in the sacred community and the rational systematisation of social life' (ibid.). But if modernism, by definition, is secular, with the 'grand narratives' of 'exploitative capitalism and bureaucratic socialism imposing a barren sameness on society', Islamic states must be post-modern (B. Turner 1994 p. 11). The apparatus of the modern state can, however, be adapted to conform to religious imperatives. Nevertheless, the nature of the repression required to stem opposition within the polity can be just as barbaric and arbitrary. On one level, since the demise of the Soviet Union, Islam is viewed as an oppositionist force, antipathetic to Western capitalism, able to provide an alternative political framework and identified as post-modern. On another level, however, Islam may in fact present its own 'grand narrative' of 'religious orthodoxy and uniformity' as penetrating and insistent as any 'modernist' rationalism. This debate will be considered more fully in Chapter 7.

The *sharia* encompasses religious duties and obligations together with secular aspects of law, both substantive and procedural, which regulate human acts. Therefore, the individual must obey the law in action and in conscience. In the early days of Islam, *sharia* did not carry the specific meaning of law and Islamic jurists defined it variously as meaning a set of duties or processes (Moinuddin 1987 p. 7). Today the term *sharia* is an all-embracing concept covering the basic tenets of religion and law but there are problems in the precise definition of an 'Islamic State'. According to Hasan Moinuddin, a 'state may be defined as 'Islamic' in which Islam is expressly or implicitly declared to be the religion of the State' (ibid.). Some Islamic states, eg. Iran, declare themselves as such within their constitutions, whilst others, e.g. Saudi Arabia, do not have a

Table 3.2 Agencies of formal power in Iran

Agency	Year founded	Function
Faqih	1979	Spiritual leader
Executive Presidency	1989	Executive leader
Cabinet	1979	Control of Ministries
Assembly of Experts	1979	Nominate and choose the Faqih
Council of Guardians	1980	Ratify Majlis legislation and supervise elections
Majlis	1980	Approve government policy
Expediency Council	1987	Arbitrate between Majlis and CoG
Reconstruction Policy Making Council	1988	Formulate reconstruction policies
Head of Judiciary	1989	Oversees courts
Joint Chiefs of Staff	1991	Co-ordinate defence policy

Source: Ehteshami (1994)

constitution. An approximate definition of an Islamic state would be one which combines an observation of religious duty with the code of law.

Anoushiravan Ehteshami examines the contradictory political requirements demanded of theocratic states such as Iran when maintaining continuity and at the same time managing change through a period of succession (Ehteshami pp. 48–50) (see Table 3.2).

Since Ayatollah Khomeini's death in 1989 the Islamic Republic has progressed from a state whose authority rested in a single person to 'a constitutionally more solid and institutionally based distribution of power' (ibid. p. 2). The doctrine of the 'Velayat-e Faqih' (spiritual leadership) placed the leadership in the hands of Marja 'a-e Taqlid (source of emulation in Shi'ism), the spiritual leader. Under the 1989 revised constitution, the influence of the Faqih within Iran's political system was strengthened: the President is accountable to the populace and the Faqih, the President must submit his resignation to the Faqih and the Faqih is able to appoint a new President (ibid. p. 49). The Faqih's powers are extensive:

1 Supreme commander of the armed forces;
2 Determining general policies;
3 Supervising the general implementation of agreed policies;

4 Ordering referenda;
5 Power to declare war and peace and general troop mobilisation;
6 May appoint or dismiss:
   Members of the Council of Guardians;
   Head of the Judiciary;
   Director of radio and television networks;
   Chief of staff of the armed forces;
7 Impeaching the President for reasons of national interest or a
   vote of no less confidence in the Majlis.

(Ehteshami 1994 p. 49)

The attenna of the Faqih extends through his private office, provincial representatives, representatives in national organisations and as Commander in Chief of the armed forces. According to Ehteshami, 'Ayatollah Khamenei has 22 provincial representatives covering the length and breadth of Iran, thus representing the horizontal extent of his power. They are accountable to his office and report to him directly of developments in the provinces' (ibid. p. 50). All provincial representatives are clerics. The President chooses Ministers and chairs a number of executive committees. The Council of Guardians screens potential parliamentary (Majlis) candidates. In the 1992 elections 30 women candidates were nominated for election in Tehran, and as Table 3.3 displays the percentage of clerics in parliament has declined from 83/82 per cent during the the the period of Ayatollah Khomeini, to 38 per cent and most recently, 22 per cent.

Presidential elections took place in June 1993 with four candidates standing. Rafsanjani won 63 per cent of the vote on a low turnout of 56 per cent. These figures contrast with the 1989 Presidential elections in which Rafsanjani gained 94 per cent of an electoral turnout of 70 per cent (SWB ME/1714.14 June 1993). Ehteshami admits that in charting the changes between Khomeini's Islamic revolutionary period and the second republic particularly in the

Table 3.3 Number of clerics in the Majlis since 1980

	1980–84	1984–88	1988–92	1992–96
Clerics	98	122	71	49
Non-clerics	118	147	189	219
Percentage of clerics	83%	82%	38%	22%

Source Ehteshami (1994)
Note: The term 'Clerics' refers to 'people of the cloth'

spheres of economic liberalisation he has not concentrated 'too extensively' on the regime's repressive nature (Ehteshami 1994 p. 71). Despite regular elections, a division of powers between the executive, the judiciary and the legislature and the existence and observance of the rule of law, the difficulties of Iran's Islamic republic in democratic terms, is the lack of an oppositionist force. As Ehteshami asserts: 'Political persecution and execution of opponents has continued, both at home and abroad. The prospects for a general national consensus remain bleak' (ibid. p. 73).

Yet it would be misleading to believe that only one form of Islamic state exists. Juan Goytisolo qualifies his views:

> Muslim governments can be totalitarian or liberal, adepts of the ideas of social progress or locked into a rigid, anachronistic tradition. The Qu'ran justifies the legitimacy of traditional monarchies, Jordan, or fundamentalist, Saudi Arabia. Some underline community and social aspects, others, respect for the Sunna and quietist values.
>
> (Goytisolo 1994)

Perhaps one of the best ways of gauging the intensity of Islamic religious life within a state is not to divide between so-called fundamentalist and conservative forces – terms, incidentally which result from Western interpretations of Islam – but to consider the extent to which the *sharia* is embraced and applied. These factors may change depending on regional dynamics. Sudan, for example, a country which straddles Egypt in North Africa with sub-Saharan Africa officially announced the implementation of the *sharia* in September 1983. In Saudi Arabia the traditionalist Wahhabi doctrine of Islam is observed, which rejects later interpretative readings of the Qur'an. The reason for Saudi Arabia's interpretation of Islam, which is not shared by other Islamic states, is allegedly the result of two factors: first, the absence of colonialism and second, the strong identification between religion, social convention and public law. The leadership and authority of King Fahd and the Royal Family are inextricably linked with the observance of a particular form of Islam, especially with regard to women (Doumato 1992 p. 34).

Estimates indicate that around 50 million Muslims live in Africa so it is perhaps not surprising that Islamic States have been declared (Mandivenga 1991). The foreign minister of Niger readily admits that an increased interest in Islam has appeared in recent years which was previously absent. But equally he points to the 'anti-Islamic authentic African values' which are resistant to certain aspects of Islam (SWB AL/2250 13 March 1995). In fact, Sudan's 1989 military regime of Lt Gen Omar Hassan al-Bashiri's upholding of *sharia* law has been condemned as largely an act of cynicism and primarily fostered for political and strategic reasons. Critics suggest that an Islamic state was proclaimed for three basic reasons:

> to gain aid from the Muslim countries of the Middle East; to justify harsh treatment of those forced to steal to live; and to unify the northern Sudan Arabs against the Christians and animists of the south in the long-running civil war.
>
> (Haynes 1993 p. 84)

As far back as 1983 Saudi Arabia exerted pressure on Sudan to declare a constitution which would turn Sudan into an Islamic State (Warburg 1991). External influences or inducements on nations to proclaim themselves Islamic are issues discussed in in subsequent chapters.

WOMEN AND ISLAM

Some analysts maintain that one of the receptive features of Islam in the past has been its ability to integrate with traditional African society. Traditional beliefs and practices have, on occasions, been incorporated into Islam: 'Belief in supernatural forces, the wearing of charms, polygamous marriages became part of the way of life of the new Muslims. In this way new adherents did not find it too strange to belong to the new religion' (Omari 1984). In Malawi, the case of the Yao people tends to support the view that Islam adapts itself to local African culture: 'While the *sharia* Law remains important to the Yao as Muslims, in matters concerning marriage, divorce and inheritance, they prefer traditional law and custom' (Mandivenga 1991). Yet the experience of Islam may be different when a state has declared itself to be theocratic. In Sudan, the domination of the *sharia* over the customary and civil legal codes has produced a different environment for women.

Islamisation, Mervat Hatem argues, has been used by political conservatives, to pass laws which are not directly related to Islam. One example is in the area of attempted adultery:

> While Islamic law had purposely required very difficult conditions to prove adultery, a new law took the unusual step of

making the mere presence of any woman with a man to whom she was not married in a public place and/or in a car, an indication of attempted adultery and grounds for incarceration.

(Hatem 1993 p. 32)

An Islamic dress code for women was announced in 1989 in line with a number of other Islamic states. The 1993 *Human Development Report* published by the United Nations Development Programme ranked Sudan at number 158 out of 173 in terms of the Status of Women. Sudanese women in 1993 had a life expectancy of 52 years; suffered a maternal mortality rate of 700 per 100,000 live births; and represented 29 per cent of the total labour force (United Nations Development Programme 1993 p. 151).-(See Tables 3.4 and 3.5.)

Attempts to reconstruct the hitherto undermined Sudanese Women's Union have been discouraged since 1989. Fatma Ahmad Ibrahim, the president of the union told Mervat Hatem that the union's mobilisation attempts were intended 'to focus on the improvement of women's rights in the family and the personal status laws'.[3] However, 'continued Islamisation has discouraged all political efforts to mobilise women around these issues' (ibid.).

Across the countries of the Third World, irrespective of the political complexion of the countries, there has been uneasiness about the rights and responsibilities of women. Are they disproportionately affected by the economic, political and social impact of their surroundings? Tables 3.4 and 3.5 present alarming information on fertility patterns, and educational opportunies are invariably lower than those for males. Yet educating young women quite possibly yields a higher rate of return than any other investment available in the developing world (Summers 1992). By enhancing a woman's contribution to development by permitting her greater earning abilities and educational opportunities outside the home, she is likely to have fewer, yet healthier children. Interestingly, Callaway and Creevey found in their comparative study of women in northern Nigeria and Senegal that in the case of Senegal, Islam had not removed 'women's freedom of movement, their ability to participate in the market, their right to control what they earned and their readiness to speak out for what they wanted' (Callaway and Creevey 1994 p. 27). Women could work in the fields unveiled, whereas, in Islamic northern Nigeria, wife seclusion is traditional and women are largely absent from the markets. Recently, Christian Mission

83

Table 3.4 Gender comparisons

	Health					Education								Employment	
	Life expectancy at birth (years)				Maternal mortality per 100,000 live births, 1988	% of cohort persisting to grade 4				Females per 100 males				Female share of labour force (%)	
	Female		Male			Female		Male		Primary		Secondary[a]			
	1970	1992	1970	1992		1970	1987	1970	1987	1970	1991	1970	1991	1970	1992
Low-income economies	54w	63w	53w	61w	—	—	—	—	—	—	78w	—	65w	36w	35w
Excluding China and India	47w	57w	46w	55w	—	65w	66w	74w	69w	61w	77w	44w	66w	32w	31w
1 Mozambique	42	45	36	43	—	—	—	—	—	46	70	—	61	50	47
2 Ethiopia	44	50	43	47	—	57	56	56	56	46	64	32	67	40	37
3 Tanzania	47	52	44	49	342	82	90	88	89	65	98	38	72	51	47
4 Sierra Leone	36	45	33	41	—	—	—	—	—	67	70	40	56	36	32
5 Nepal	42	53	43	54	833	—	—	—	—	18	47	16	—	35	33
6 Uganda	51	44	49	43	550	—	—	—	—	65	—	31	—	43	41
7 Bhutan	41	49	39	48	1,305	—	—	—	—	5	59	—	41	35	32
8 Burundi	45	50	42	46	—	47	84	45	84	49	84	3	59	50	47
9 Malawi	41	45	40	44	350	55	67	60	72	59	82	17	53	45	41
10 Bangladesh	44	56	46	55	600	—	—	—	—	47	81	36	49	5	8
11 Chad	40	49	37	46	—	—	43	—	43	34	56	—	22	23	21
12 Guinea-Bissau	36	39	35	38	—	65	77	63	81	43	56	9	53	43	40
13 Madagascar	47	53	44	50	333	—	—	—	—	86	97	62	99	42	39
14 Lao PDR	42	53	39	50	561	—	—	—	—	59	77	70	66	46	44
15 Rwanda	46	48	43	45	300	63	75	65	75	79	99	36	56	50	47
16 Niger	40	48	37	44	—	75	93	74	78	53	57	44	42	49	46
17 Burkina Faso	42	50	39	47	810	71	86	68	84	57	62	35	50	48	46
18 India	49	62	50	61	—	42	—	45	—	60	71	33	55	30	25

19 Kenya	52	61	48	57	—	84	78	84	76	71	95	42	78	42	39
20 Mali	39	50	36	47	2,325	52	68	89	75	55	58	29	50	17	16
21 Nigeria	43	54	40	50	800	64	—	66	—	59	76	49	74	37	34
22 Nicaragua	55	69	52	65	300	48	62	45	59	101	104	89	138	20	26
23 Togo	46	57	43	53	—	85	78	88	86	45	65	26	34	39	36
24 Benin	45	52	43	49	161	71	—	75	—	45	51	44	37	48	47
25 Central African Republic	45	49	40	45	—	67	81	67	85	49	63	20	38	49	45
26 Pakistan	47	59	49	59	270	56	44	60	53	36	52	25	41	9	13
27 Ghana	51	58	48	54	1,000	77	—	82	—	75	82	35	63	42	40
28 China	63	71	61	68	115	—	76	—	81	—	86	—	72	42	43
29 Tajikistan	—	72	—	67	39	—	—	—	—	—	—	—	—	—	—
30 Guinea	37	44	36	44	1,247	—	77	—	86	46	46	26	31	42	39
31 Mauritania	41	50	38	46	800	—	83	—	83	39	73	13	45	22	23
32 Sri Lanka	66	74	64	70	80	94	97	73	99	89	93	101	105	25	27
33 Zimbabwe	52	61	49	58	77	74	81	80	81	79	99	63	88	38	34
34 Honduras	55	68	51	64	221	—	—	—	—	79	98	79	—	14	20
35 Lesotho	52	63	48	58	220	87	87	70	76	150	121	111	149	48	43
36 Egypt, Arab Rep.	52	63	50	60	—	85	—	93	—	61	80	48	76	7	10
37 Indonesia	49	62	46	59	450	67	81	89	99	84	93	59	82	30	31
38 Myanmar	53	62	50	58	—	39	—	58	—	89	—	65	—	39	37
39 Somalia	42	50	39	47	—	46	—	51	—	33	—	27	—	41	38
40 Sudan	43	53	41	51	—	—	—	—	—	61	75	40	80	20	22
41 Yemen Rep.	42	53	41	52	330	—	—	—	—	10	31	3	18	8	14
42 Zambia	48	49	45	46	—	—	—	—	—	80	91	49	59	28	30

Source: World Bank (1994) *World Development Report*

Table 3.5 Demography and fertility

	Crude birth rate (per 1,000 population)		Crude death rate (per 1,000 population)		Total fertility rate			Percentage of births in 1992 to women aged		Projected year of reaching NRR of 1[b]	Married women of childbearing age using contraception (%) 1988–1993
	1970	1992	1970	1992	1970	1992	2000[a]	Under 20	Over 35		
Low income economies	39w	28w	14w	10w	6.0w	3.4w	3.1w				
Excluding China and India	45w	37w	19w	12w	6.3w	4.9w	4.4w				
1 Mozambique	48	45	24	21	6.7	6.5[d]	6.9	15	20	2050	–
2 Ethiopia	43	51	20	18	5.8	7.5	7.3	17	13	2050	–
3 Tanzania	49	45	22	15	6.4	6.3	5.8	17	16	2035	10
4 Sierra Leone	49	48	30	22	6.5	6.5[d]	6.5	21	13	2045	–
5 Nepal	46	38	22	13	6.4	5.5[d]	4.8	11	17	2030	–
6 Uganda	50	54	17	22	7.1	7.1	7.1	18	12	2050	6
7 Bhutan	41	39	22	17	5.9	5.9[d]	5.7	9	23	2035	–
8 Burundi	46	45	24	17	6.8	6.8[d]	6.6	7	22	2045	–
9 Malawi	56	47	24	20	7.8	6.7	6.7	17	17	2045	13
10 Bangladesh	48	31	21	11	7.0	4.0	3.1	16	11	2010	40
11 Chad	45	44	26	18	6.0	5.9[d]	6.1	21	14	2040	–
12 Guinea-Bissau	41	46	27	25	5.9	6.0[d]	6.0	21	13	2040	–
13 Madagascar	46	43	20	15	6.6	6.1	5.4	18	15	2035	17
14 Lao PDR	44	44	23	15	6.1	6.7	6.0	7	22	2040	–
15 Rwanda	52	40	18	17	7.8	6.2	4.9	9	19	2025	21
16 Niger	50	52	28	19	7.2	7.4	7.4	22	15	2055	4
17 Burkina Faso	48	48	25	18	6.4	6.9	6.7	16	17	2045	8
18 India	41	29	18	10	5.8	3.7	3.1	12	10	2010	43
19 Kenya	53	37	18	10	8.0	5.4	4.0	16	14	2015	33

20 Mali	51	50	26	18	6.5	7.1d	6.9	20	15	2050	25
21 Nigeria	51	43	21	14	6.9	5.9	5.0	16	13	2035	6
22 Nicaragua	48	35	14	6	6.9	4.4d	3.7	20	10	2020	44
23 Togo	50	45	20	13	6.5	6.5	5.8	15	18	2040	33
24 Benin	50	44	22	15	6.9	6.2d	5.5	16	15	2035	–
25 Central African Republic	37	42	22	18	4.9	5.8d	6.3	20	14	2045	–
26 Pakistan	48	40	19	10	7.0	5.6	4.6	14	14	2030	14
27 Ghana	46	41	16	12	6.7	6.1	5.4	15	18	2035	13
28 China	33	19	8	8	5.8	2.0	1.9	4	5	2030	83
29 Tajikistan	–	36	–	6	5.9	5.1	4.2	6	13	2025	–
30 Guinea	46	48	28	20	6.0	6.5d	6.5	23	12	2045	–
31 Mauritania	47	50	25	18	6.5	6.8	6.6	18	15	2045	–
32 Sri Lanka	29	21	8	6	4.3	2.5	2.1	8	14	2000	–
33 Zimbabwe	53	34	16	8	7.7	4.6	3.5	13	14	2020	43
34 Honduras	49	37	15	7	7.2	4.9	4.0	17	12	2025	47
35 Lesotho	43	33	20	9	5.7	4.8	4.1	8	21	2025	23
36 Egypt, Arab Rep.	40	28	17	9	5.9	3.8	3.0	10	13	2015	47
37 Indonesia	42	25	18	10	5.5	2.9	2.4	12	11	2005	50
38 Myanmar	38	33	15	10	5.9	4.2d	3.5	5	16	2020	–
39 Somalia	50	48	24	17	6.7	6.8d	6.6	20	13	2045	–
40 Sudan	47	42	22	14	6.7	6.1	5.5	13	16	2035	9
41 Yemen, Rep.	53	50	23	15	7.8	7.6	6.9	15	18	2045	10
42 Zambia	49	47	19	17	6.7	6.5	5.8	17	15	2040	15

Source: World Bank (1994) *World Development Report*

groups have reported the existence of geographically differentiated religious status areas within particular African countries. This has meant that in certain areas of Muslim preponderance the local community's access to healthcare and immunisation programmes provided by the World Health Organization have been curtailed. This practice has led to an increase in childhood illnesses at considerable cost to the community and furthering the burden on women (Connolly 1994; interview).

It is estimated that raising the primary school enrolment of girls to equal that of boys in low-income countries would involve educating an extra 25 million girls every year at a total cost of approximately $938 million. But econometric studies find that an extra year of schooling reduces female fertility by approximately 10 per cent (Summers 1992; *West Africa* 7–13 February 1994). In countries such as Chad, girls have less than a one-in-10 chance of attending secondary school and their mothers have, typically, less than one year of education. On average a woman bears six children and faces the tragedy of losing at least one of her children. Where women gain access to educational facilities, good quality health and family planning, birth rates and death rates decline quickly (*West Africa* 7–13 February 1994). The United Nations Population and Development Conference held in Cairo in September 1994 attempted to address some of these wider concerns.

Dr Nafis Sadik, the Secretary-General of the Conference, urged world leaders to undertake 'personal efforts to enhance population policies and to make an emphasis on improving women's conditions and guaranteeing their involvement in these policies' (SWB ME/2095 S1/1 8 September 1994; Nafis Sadik 17 October 1994; meeting). University educated Egyptian women claim there can be 'no return to their grandmother's time' in terms of the availability of educational and vocational opportunities (Hamza 1994; interview) However, the educational levels of rural womenfolk who tend to be more traditional and not so widely exposed to opportunities are reflected in a literacy rate in Egypt of only 38 per cent for young women aged between 15 and 24 years (United Nations Development Programme 1993).

During the Population Conference it was made demonstrably clear that religious leaders, particularly from Islamic and Roman Catholic quarters have much to say which concerns women. United on a platform against abortion, Islamic countries and the Holy See agreed that such policies undermined the family. Pope John Paul II issued a statement calling on young people to 'practise self-control' whilst a group of Islamic countries warned against population control leading to promiscuity. Saudi Arabia issued a statement condemning family planning proposals as a 'violation of the Islamic *sharia*' (SWB ME/2092 8 September 1994; SWB ME/2097 10 September 1994). By the end of the Conference the Holy See agreed to a 'selective endorsement' and Islamic states consented to a partial acceptance of the conference document which called for improved family-planning and health-care facilities. The 15-page programme of action called for the empowerment of women in education, health care and family planning. Nafis Sadik, referring to the 960 million illiterates in the developing world, two-thirds of whom are women, saw the conference as a major breakthrough in placing women so firmly on the international political agenda, irrespective of the regimes under which they lived (Sadik 1994; meeting). It has become clear to a wide number of states, under both secular and non-secular governments that vast increases in population profoundly under-mine a country's development. Greater resources should be devoted to population control and targets from the international commu-nity run up to the year 2015: $US17 billion in the year 2000, rising to $US21.7 billion in 2015. The developing countries, however, are expected to contribute two-thirds of the cost, although sub-Saharan states may only raise around 30–40 per cent of the total cost of providing improved health care and family planning. It is too early to predict the possible success of the Population Conference in reaching its target of population control because ultimately it will depend on the willingness of the nation state to implement programmes. One immediate response in Niger whose population is 98 per cent Muslim, was negative. A meeting held to discuss possible family-planning policies through the use of condoms was undermined by Islamist groups claiming that such policies would only encourage prostitution and debauchery (SWB AL/2162 25 November 1994).

In countries where IMF structural adjustment programmes have been implemented it is stated that programmes have been designed to avoid adverse social consequences. In reality, however, social sectors have been seriously undermined which has affected women, children and the vulnerable poor in rural and urban areas (Smith and Niedermeier 1995). By way of a response the International Islamic Relief Organization (IIRO) in Saudi Arabia held a confer-ence in 1994 on the needs of Muslim women, particularly those who have been uprooted (International Islamic Relief Organization 1994). The conference emphasised several points and issues including: the special status given to women in Islam, especially in regard to her dignity and protection; the Muslim family structure as recognised under *sharia* which requires the solidarity of all family members; sexual assault on women is regarded as a major crime; an appropriate environment for Muslim women should be provided by securing her social and medical needs through female providers and enabling her to maintain her dress codes; to provide education in coherence with Islamic teachings and to ensure her ability to practise her religious rituals without restrictions and constraints (ibid.). By focusing attention on Muslim women it was hoped that the extreme importance of child care in Islam would be emphasised. The IIRO regards itself as a non-governmental organisation (NGO) although it is funded by Saudi Arabia. It is involved in the fields of education, health care, social welfare, urgent relief and development programmes. According to its annual report the IIRO has implemented 354 health projects in 44 countries and provided medical treatment to 3.4 million people. Various clinics have been established including maternity and motherhood centres in Senegal, Sudan and Ethiopia. The Woman and Child Committee of the International Islamic Council for Daw'a and Relief participated in the NGO Forum and the preparatory meeting of the UN Commission on the Status of Women held in New York in 1995. The Women and Child Committee is part of an umbrella organisation representing around 60 different Muslim organisations who are active in 'women's concerns and issues of development and peace' (International Islamic Relief Organization 1995). Nevertheless, if population growth is not held in check through a process of education, health care and contraceptive provision, development projects will continue to be undermined.

In drawing distinctions between secular and theocratic forms of government, it must be made clear that various forms of theocratic state exist both within the Middle East itself and between Arab/African worlds. Having said that, however, there are identifiable currents of political expression which serve to link Islamic governments in Africa with those in the Middle East. The military government in Sudan looks to the Arab world for sustenance and cultural affinity and sees itself as a vanguard for Islamism in the wider continent. The extent to which politico/religious movements impact upon the wider community needs further empirical research and to a degree the fluidity of religious belief straddles the private/public domain. Poverty and disease afflict the lives and life chances of women and children irrespective of whether theocratic or secular governments are in place.

NOTES

1 The British Resident in Nigeria, C. L. Temple was viewed as such. For further details see St Louis Sisters, Shendam, *The Contribution of the Society of African Missions*, Ambassador Publications, Nigeria 1978.

2 Juan Goytisolo: 'Desde el final de los sententa, la afirmacion del islam en terminos politicos encubre hasta solaparlos sus valores espirituales, culturales e historicos. La referencia a la sharia y la Sunna – o a los santos imanes en el chiismo irani – pasa a ser el elemento funademal y legitimizador de todo proyecto de gobierno. En otras palabras, el islam concebido como fe, vivencia intima o etica personal sustituido con una doctrina simplificadora que dscuida el esfuerzo de interpretacion individual del texto coranico y se limita a condenar por 'impios' a los regimenes en el poder. Los gobiernos musulmanes pueden ser totalitarios o liberales, adeptos a las ideas de progreso social o enquistados en una tradicion anacronica y rigida. Mientras el Coran justifica la legitimadad de las monarquias, ya sea en su vertiente abierta (Marruecos, Jordania), ya fundamentalista (Arabia Saudi). Unos subrayaban sus aspectos comunitarios y solidario; otros, el respeto a la Sunna y los valores quietistas.' *El Pais* 28 March 1994. Translated by Peter Bush 1995. Juan Goytisolo has written widely on the Middle East including *Estambul Ottomano*, Barcelona, Planeta 1989.

3 An interview was conducted between Fatam Ahmad Ibrahim and Mervat Hartem, details of which are contained in Mervat Hartem: 'Toward the Development of Post-Islamist and Post Nationalist Feminist Discourses in the Middle East' in Tucker (ed.) *Arab Women*, Indiana University Press, 1933.

PART III

ECONOMIC/
INTERNATIONAL

4

REGIONAL AND INTERNATIONAL INFLUENCES

INTRODUCTION

Regional and international influences are of exceptional importance in the Middle East and Africa in terms of World Bank and International Monetary Fund activity in the regions. However, a new and more exacting relationship developed between the Middle East and Africa during the 1970s which was forged by an association between oil and aid. A different form of economic realism emerged during that period and studies suggested that a powerful system of patron/clientalism developed (LeVine and Luke 1979; Ismael 1986). The global situation has changed radically since that debate and in the present post-Cold War, post-1991 Gulf War international environment the relationship needs to be reconsidered. This chapter looks at the continuing roles played by oil aid, and the impact of Western and Islamic agencies of development.

THE OIL FACTOR

In November 1990, three months after Iraq's invasion of Kuwait, claims were being made that 'as usual, non-oil-producing developing nations have to bear the brunt of escalating oil prices brought on by the continuing Gulf crisis' (*West Africa* November 1990). This declaration was not vastly different from statements made 17 years earlier, in 1974, the time when the first major oil price 'shock' was beginning to be felt:

> The larger cost of maintaining the oil weapon is borne by the poor nations because it is they who have to drain more and more of their foreign exchange reserves to meet the rising costs of oil and imported manufacturing goods. Still it is the developing

countries, particularly in Africa, which have given the greatest moral support to the cause of the Arabs in the Middle East.

(*Africa Contemporary Record* 1974/75 p. A107)

These proclamations reveal a real and distinct differentiation in the Third World. In September 1990, the Middle East crisis, following the invasion of Kuwait by Iraq, was being congratulated for bringing: 'an unexpected bonus for Nigeria and the other oil producers of West Africa', thus facilitating high production levels, buoyant prices and increased government revenues (*West Africa* September 1990 p. 3,430). The relationship, then, between the Middle East, Africa and the price of oil is not an even, homogeneous one and at times can be a sensitive one.

As early as October 1973, when the Arab Oil Producing and Exporting Countries (OAPEC) announced their intention to use oil as a weapon against countries supporting Israel, a promise was made that 'all nations which assisted the Arab cause against Israel would be assured of regular oil supplies and that special consideration would be given to those who suffered as a result of the quadrupling of fuel prices' (*Africa Contemporary Record* 1976/1977 p. A96). This proposal was criticised on two counts: first, it was a means through which Middle Eastern countries acquired African support in exchange for Arab oil, and second, as the President of the Ivory Coast argued in March 1974, if Afro-Arab solidarity were to exist at all, it should go further than 'special oil prices and cash loans being made available to African states' (*Africa Contemporary Record* 1974/1975 p. A106). A more appropriate measure of solidarity would encompass discussion with developed nations as to the prices of raw materials which ultimately would 'do us a greater service than granting us aid or loans' (ibid.). One factor, however, was quite clear. African states were obliged to react to Arab domestic political imperatives. The decision to increase the oil price in 1973 was strongly connected to the Arab/Israeli dispute. The political instability and unresolved grievances in the Middle East created the impetus for changes in oil-pricing policy and consequently aroused much unease in developing nations.

THE ARAB BANK FOR ECONOMIC DEVELOPMENT IN AFRICA (BADEA)

In November 1973, the Organisation for African Unity (OAU) set up a committee of seven members to maintain regular consultations with OAPEC through the League of Arab States (Arab League). In the same month the Arab Bank for Economic Development in Africa (otherwise known as the Banque Arabe pour le Développement Economique en Afrique (BADEA) was established by the Arab League at the Sixth Arab Summit Conference in Algiers. The bank's headquarters were established in Khartoum, Sudan and as a financial institution it was to be funded by the governments of the member states of the League of Arab States. At the end of 1991, the total resources of the Bank amounted to $1579.4 million (BADEA Annual Report 1991).

Although operations did not begin until 1975, the aims of the bank were threefold: to assist in financing economic development in non-Arab African countries; to stimulate the contribution of Arab capital to African development; and to help provide the technical assistance required for the development of Africa (ibid.). The projects financed by the bank were to be of national importance for the beneficiary countries and would usually form part of their economic development plans. Officially stated as part of the purpose and function of the bank was the objective 'to make Arab–African solidarity a concrete reality and to base this cooperative venture on foundations of friendship and equality' (ibid. p. 5). However, the bank's establishment was initially seen as a step towards preserving Arab interests: 'Our Arab brothers mean well but are they also doing well?' questioned the OAU General Secretariat upon learning of the proposal to set up an Afro–Arab Bank (*Africa Contemporary Record* 1974/75 p. A104).

The fact that the African Development Bank, the existing Pan-African financial institution was overlooked, suggested the Middle Eastern states wished to retain administrative and allocative control over the direction of disbursements. The Board of Governors of BADEA, its highest authority, is composed of the finance ministers of the Arab League member states, although it is the Board of Directors which makes recommendations to the Board of Governors regarding policy, supervises the implementation of their decisions and performs all the executive functions of the bank.

The Board of Directors is composed of eleven members and is entrusted with the management of the Banks's affairs. Any member holding 200 shares or more has one seat in the Board of Directors and these are: Algeria, Iraq, Kuwait, Libya, Qatar, Saudi Arabia and the United Arab Emirates. The eleven members of the Bank jointly select four other members to the Board of Directors for a

Table 4.1 Subscription and voting power of BADEA member states

Member states	Subscription Amount ($)	Subscription Shares	Subscription Percentage	Voting power Number of votes	Voting power Percentage
Hashemite Kingdom of Jordan	2129867.93	21.29868	0.203183	221.29868	1.571445
State of the United Arab Emirates	127792075.86	1277.92076	12.190992	1477.92076	10.494733
State of Bahrain	2129867.93	21.29868	0.203183	221.29868	1.571445
Republic of Tunisia	8874449.71	88.74449	0.846597	288.74449	2.050378
People's Democratic Republic of Algeria	42597358.62	425.97358	4.063664	625.97358	4.445046
Kingdom of Saudi Arabia	255584151.70	2555.84152	24.381985	2755.84152	19.569263
Republic of Sudan	2129867.93	21.29868	0.203183	221.29868	1.571445
Arab Republic of Syria	1419911.95	14.19912	0.135456	214.19912	1.521030
Republic of Iraq	149090755.17	1490.90755	14.222824	1690.90755	12.007155
Sultanate of Oman (1)	15619031.50	156.19032	1.490010	3356.19032	2.529311
State of Palestine	2129867.93	21.29868	0.203183	221.29868	1.571445
State of Qatar	85194717.23	851.94717	8.127328	1051.94717	7.469889
State of Kuwait	156190314.94	1561.90315	14.900102	1761.90315	12.511295
Republic of Lebanon	7099559.77	70.99560	0.677278	270.99560	1.924343
Great Arab Libyan People's Socialist Jamahiriya	170389434.47	1703.89434	16.254656	1903.89434	13.519576
Arab Republic of Egypt	2129867.93	21.29868	0.203183	221.29868	1.571445
Kingdom of Morocco	15619031.50	156.19032	1.490010	356.19032	2.529311
Islamic Republic of Mauritania (2)	2129867.93	21.29868	0.203183	221.29868	1.571445
Total	1048250000.00	10482.50000	100.000000	14082.50000	100.000000

Source: Arab Bank for Economic Development (BADEA) 1994

Note: Unpaid amounts:
(1) An amount of 2,000,000.00 dollars
(2) An amount of 432,492.47 dollars

renewable four-year mandate. Currently, they are Jordan, Sudan, Syria and the State of Palestine. Table 4.1 shows the subscriptions and voting power of BADEA member states. The Board of Directors meets every four months or whenever the activities of the Bank may so require. The Chairman of the Board is elected for a two-year renewable term. The Board of Governors is usually composed of the Ministers of Finance of the member states and their deputies and the Director General is appointed for a three-year period renewable for only two sessions.

In 1987 BADEA had approved loans and grants to African states amounting to $US828.8 million. By the end of 1992 the Bank had contributed almost $1.1 billion (BADEA *Annual Report* 1993 p. 16). The distribution of assistance is largely determined by the priorities of the recipient countries although there has been a tendency for a larger proportion of the budget to be allocated to projects for infrastructural development which accounted for 52 per cent of total between 1975–1993 (BADEA *Annual Report* 1993). Table 4.2 illustrates the extent to which BADEA financed African countries between 1975 and 1993. Table 4.3 provides the sectoral and

Table 4.2 BADEA financing in African countries 1975–93 (in $m)

Country	($m)	Country	($m)
Angola	19.2	Lesotho	24.0
Benin	39.6	Liberia	7.0
Botswana	48.2	Madagascar	48.5
Burkina Faso	60.6	Mali	51.3
Burundi	31.6	Mauritius	27.6
Cameroon	29.0	Mozambique	44.6
Cape Verde	30.4	Namibia	0.175
Central African Republic	8.5	Niger	38.7
Chad	26.0	Rwanda	46.5
Comoros Islands	11.2	São Tomé and Principé Islands	10.4
Congo	24.1	Senegal	68.6
Equatorial Guinea	10.1	Seychelles Islands	5.3
Gabon	8.8	Sierra Leone	6.5
Gambia	11.8	Tanzania	12.4
Ghana	68.4	Togo	7.6
Guinea	57.4	Uganda	39.4
Guinea Bissau	22.0	Zaïre	10.0
Ivory Coast	3.3	Zambia	17.9
Kenya	23.7	Zimbabwe	73.5

Source: Adapted from Arab Bank for Economic Development Report 1994

Table 4.3 Sectoral breakdown of BADEA annual commitments 1975–93 ($m)

Year	Infrastructure Amount	(%)	Agriculture Amount	(%)	Industry Amount	(%)	Energy Amount	(%)	Special programme Amount	(%)	Technical Assistance Amount	(%)	Total Amount	(%)
1975–1987	345.281	50.4	181.314	46.5	77.616	11.3	63.704	9.3	14.600	2.1	2.314	0.4	684.829	100
1988	29.500	47.3	22.600	36.2	–	–	–	–	–	–	0.320	0.5	62.420	100
1989	16.300	28.6	31.150	54.6	–	–	10.000	17.5	–	–	0.550	0.9	58.000	100
1990	28.730	43.3	25.610	48.2	–	–	–	–	–	–	1.999	0.3	56.339	100
1991	41.538	62.4	10.400	15.6	3.500	5.2	8.820	13.2	–	–	2.380	3.6	66.638	100
1992	44.160	59.6	27.650	37.3	–	–	–	–	–	–	2.216	3.1	74.026	100
1993	45.594	60.8	19.180	25.6	7.200	9.6	–	–	–	–	2.975	4.0	74.949	100
1975–1993	561.103	52.0	317.904	29.7	88.316	8.2	82.524	7.7	14.600	1.3	12.754	1.1	1077.201	100

Source: Arab Bank for Economic Development (BADEA) 1994

sub-sectoral breakdowns of BADEA commitments between 1975 and 1993. Initiatives were sustained during 1993 with the objective of 'activating Arab–African co-operation and infusing fresh vitality into its structures and organs' (BADEA 1993 *Annual Report*). The impetus for joint action was recognised by both Arab and African partners especially because of international conditions which call for enhanced South–South co-operation and the establishment of regional entities based, primarily, on economic co-operation (ibid. p. 15). At the 1993 OAU Summit African leaders emphasised the need for co-operation 'to explore new avenues and spheres as well as to adopt effective mechanisms for their development' (ibid.). Essentially economic co-operation depended on the availability of resources. The Summit, unanimous over the crucial role to be played by the private sector, passed a resolution calling for 'intensification and coordination of direct contacts between African and Arab institutions such as chambers of commerce, businessmen, and trade unions' (ibid.).

During 1993 several visits were made to African countries and mindful of the problem of arrears delegations from BADEA were sent to: Mozambique, Guinea, Guinea-Bissau, Cape Verde, Chad, Senegal, Rwanda, Burkina Faso, Mali, São Tomé and Principé, Tanzania, Comoros and Niger. The Bank also participated in a number of meetings both on Arab and Islamic sides, as well as at African and international levels. BADEA representatives were present at the following meetings: Arab League Council Session in 1993, the Higher Committee for Coordination between the League of Arab States and the Arab Joint Action Institutions, the Arab Development Finance Institutions, the Arab Fund for Technical Assistance for African Countries, the Board of Governors of the Islamic Development Bank, the OAU Council of Ministers, the African Development Bank, the Association of African Finance Institution, the World Bank and the agencies of the United Nations. The loans and grants approved in 1993 set out in Table 4.4 divide into Project-Aid and Technical Assistance. Yet, in its lending operations BADEA admit that 'aggravating conditions' face the economies of countries which receive aid from the bank. These obstacles include increasing deficit in public budgets and balances of payment, accumulating debt and a shrinking volume of external financial flows, all of which contribute to the reduced number of projects which were viable for BADEA's financing. Technical assistance divides into feasibility studies and institutional support. Since

Table 4.4 Loans and grants approved in 1993 by BADEA

Recipient country or institution	Project	Date of approval	Amount ($m)
(A) Project-Aid			
1 Senegal	Dakar Port extension	19.02.1993	3.934
2 Botswana	Line of credit to Botswana Development Corporation (BDC)	19.02.1993	4.000
3 Chad	Integrated rural development in Salamat region	19.02.1993	4.350
4 Guinea	Foracariah rural development	19.02.1993	3.930
5 Mali	Livestock development in eastern coast	19.02.1993	3.500
6 Uganda	Gayaza–Kalagi Road	19.02.1993	4.900
7 Burkina-Faso	Bobo Dioulasso–Orodara–Mali Borders Rd	10.06.1993	8.500
8 Cape Verde	Transport	10.06.1993	8.000
9 Zimbabwe	Development and modernisation of telecommunications	10.06.1993	10.000
10 Madagascar	Rehabilitation of some bridges	10.06.1993	7.000
11 Senegal	Construction of embankments against infiltration of feline water to agricultural areas in Casamance Basin	05.10.1993	3.260
12 Chad	Cotton cultivation development	05.10.1993	7.400
13 Mali	Line of credit	05.10.1993	3.200
Sub-total			71.974
(B) Technical Assistance			
1 Senegal	Feasability study of extension and connection of rural water supply facilities	19.02.1993	0.350
2 Rwanda	Technical studies of Municipal Roads Project in Kigali City	19.02.1993	0.380
3 Namibia	Technical assistance to support the Ministry of Finance (Training)	19.02.1993	0.200
4 Mali	Contracting the services of an economist and financial analyst to the Autonomous Fund for Debt Settlement	19.02.1993	0.190
5 Uganda	Feasibility study of Small Ruminants Development Project	19.02.1993	0.320
6 Botswana	Contracting the services of an economist, specialised in marketing of horticultural products, to support Planning Statistics Division, Ministry of Agriculture	10.06.1993	0.190

Table 4.4 continued

Recipient country or institution	Project	Date of approval	Amount ($m)
7 Chad	Support to National Directorate for Water to purchase equipment and materials	10.06.1993	0.100
8 Rwanda	Contracting the services of an engineer to support Water Department, Ministry of Works	10.06.1993	0.190
9 Zimbabwe	Feasibility study of construction and rehabilitation of 3 Roads project	10.06.1993	0.340
10 Mali	Study of Kidal city water supply	10.06.1993	0.350
11 Burkina Faso	Feasibility study of Banzon Plain Development Project	05.10.1993	0.240
12 Zimbabwe	Contracting the services of an architect to the Ministry of Public Construction	05.10.1993	0.150
Sub-total			3.000
Total			74.974

Source: Arab Bank for Economic Development (BADEA) 1994

the start of the Bank's activities, 37 countries benefited from technical assistance operations, in addition to four regional groupings and 13 organisations on the regional and subregional levels (see Table 4.5).

International and regional meetings are always attended by BADEA officials. They are present at regular Islamic Development Bank and OPEC Fund for International Development meetings and participate in Arab Economic and Social Council summits and Islamic Conference Organisation (ICO) meetings. At the African level BADEA attends the African Conference on Environment and Sustainable Development, meetings of the OAU Council of Ministers, summit conferences of ECOWAS and IBRD/IMF annual meetings. Perhaps the most significant contacts it has with an external agency are the 'regular co-ordination meetings' it holds with the World Bank during which it assists BADEA 'in identifying several development projects in a number of beneficiary countries' (BADEA *Annual Report* 1991 p. 10). These meetings with World

Table 4.5 BADEA Grants for institution Support

Group of African countries	Telecommunications seminar	1976	0.080
OCLALAV	Environmental projection	1978	0.300
OICMA	Environmental projection	1978	0.050
DLCO-EA	Environmental projection	1978	0.050
AFAA	Fifth Conference	1983	0.020
ICIPE	Training	1984	0.165
CAFRAD	Training and upgrading	1984	0.100
Comoros	Support to the Department of National Planning and Development	12.7.1984	0.100
IDEP	Vocational training	12.7.1984	0.095
ARCEDEM	Development of manufacturing industries	12.7.1984	0.150
PANA	Support for activities	15.10.1984	0.150
ICRISAT	Regional centre for Sahel	11.7.1984	0.500
Zimbabwe	Support to the Ministry of Transport	16.10.1985	0.100
Botswana	Support to the Ministry of Works	24.7.1986	0.200
Angola	Support for National Bank of Angola	10.12.1987	0.120
RCSSMRS (Nairobi)	Support for activities	10.12.1987	0.300
Burkina Faso	Support to General Administration for International Co-operation	29.12.1988	0.120
ACSAD	Support for activities	26.10.1986	0.125
OCLALAV	Support for activities	29.12.1988	0.200
DLCO-EA	Environmental projection	1989	0.300
CAFRAD	Consolidation of economic and financial administration in African countries	1990	0.100
Lesotho	Support of the services of water and sewerage	15.6.1991	0.167
Mozambique	Support of the Department of Roads and Bridges	15.6.1991	0.145
Rwanda	Consolidation of the General Administration for Roads and Bridges	6.11.1991	0.125
Equatorial Guinea	Institutional Support to the Ministry of Economy	1992	0.140
São Tomé and Principé	Institutional Support to the General Administration of Industry, Energy and Tourism	1992	0.120
Mauritius	Support of the activities of the Department of Sewerage	1992	0.150

Table 4.5 continued

Namibia	Support to the Ministry of Finance (Training)	1993	0.200
Mali	Contracting services of an expert to the Autonomous Fund for Debt Settlement	1993	0.190
Botswana	Contracting services of an expert to the Ministry of Agriculture	1993	0.190
Chad	Support of the National Directorate for Water	1993	0.100
Rwanda	Contracting services of an expert to the Ministry of Works	1993	0.190
Zimbabwe	Contracting services of an architect to the Ministry of Public Construction	1993	0.150
Sub-total			5.191
Total			17.643

Source: Arab Bank for Economic Development (BADEA) 1994

Bank officials are of 'great help' to BADEA in successfully implementing its lending programmes (ibid.). Certainly, BADEA's lending strategy is affected by similar concerns which condition World Bank and IMF programmes. On 1991 figures, BADEA attributed its decrease in lending to West Africa as being attributable to three major factors:

1 Failure of the countries to complete technical preparation.
2 The suspension of new BADEA operations due to the accumulation of arrears by some countries.
3 Revision by countries of their investment programmes and priorities because of political instability and economic and financial difficulties, over and above the conditions applied by international development finance institutions as part of structural adjustments programmes.

(ibid. p. 14)

West Africa received assistance of $21 million for four operations, representing 29 per cent of 1991 lending compared with eight operations in East Africa, amounting to $50 million, which represented around 70 per cent of total lending (ibid. p. 15).

As Tables 4.6 and 4.7 suggest, BADEA does not lend in isolation from other international and regional institutions.

Table 4.6 BADEA: joint financing in 1991

	Amount ($m)	(%)
Total project costs	178,259	100.0
Financing:		
(a) BADEA	68,488	38.4
(b) Arab Funds, OPEC Fund		
and Islamic Development Bank	5,290	3.0
(c) Non-Arab institutions	73,410	41.2
(d) Beneficiary governments and local		
institutions	31,071	17.4
Total	178,259	100.0

Source: Arab Bank for Economic Development (BADEA) 1994

Table 4.7   BADEA: joint financing in 1993

	Amount ($m.)	(%)
1 Total project costs	215,003	100.0
2 Financing:		
(a) BADEA	64,774	30.1
(b) Arab Funds, OPEC and Islamic		
Development Bank	86,415	40.2
(c) Non-Arab institutions	42,070	19.6
(d) Beneficiary governments and		
local institutions	21,744	10.1
Total	215,003	100.0

Source: Arab Bank for Economic Development (BADEA) 1994

RETHINKING THE CAIRO SUMMIT 1977

Looking back to the 1977 Cairo Summit from the vantage point of the mid-1990s, a number of features have changed. Although there existed a readiness for conciliation and co-operation at that time with representatives of 59 Arab and African countries meeting to discuss the possibility of increasing the aid package from Middle Eastern nations, political concerns were very much part of the debate. Economic aid and political unity were linked in 1977 and solidarity was expressed in public and political terms. Imperialism, colonialism, neo-colonialism, Zionism, racial segregation and any other forms of 'racial and sectarian discrimination particularly in

South Africa, Palestine and the Arab and African occupied territories' were condemned. Full support was given for the struggles of
peoples of Palestine, Zimbabwe, Namibia, southern Africa and
Djibouti to 'recover their legitimate national rights' and achieve self-
determination (*Africa Contemporary Record* 1976/1977 pp. A100, A101,
A107).

Specific political issues no longer dominate discussions between
Africans and Arabs although conferences continue to uphold, in
much the same way as they did earlier, the importance of general
statements: respect for sovereignty and territorial integrity, peaceful
co-existence, the establishment of a just economic order, non-
interference in the internal affairs of other states and the peaceful
settlement of disputes. The African and Arab ties of fraternity, based
on 'firm and lasting foundations' were very much part of a rhetoric
of the past and were always weakened by the clear economic imbal-
ance between the regions. The 1977 Summit declared its approval
of a long-term integrated plan for Arab–African co-operation in
economic and financial fields, the clauses of which demonstrated
the inequity in the relationship. The Summit agreed to:

1 Strengthening the resources of the national and multi-lateral
  establishments involved in development in Africa.
2 Contributing to the boosting of the financial resources of the
  African Development Bank through loans from the Arab money
  markets on the best possible terms.
3 Increasing the resources of BADEA to enable it to play a greater
  role in meeting the requirements of African development.
4 Strengthening trade relations between the Arab and African
  states through reciprocal preferential treatment.
5 Co-ordination of the financial aid provided by the Arab states
  and the collective financial organisations to increase the effect of
  that aid on development in the benefiting African states.
6 Encouragement of Arab investment by promoting Arab–African
  joint projects and by seeking to devise a system for guaranteeing
  investment in African states.
7 Encouragement of Arab capital in the African states in the form
  of direct investment, loans or deposits.
8 Encouragement of technical co-operation between Arab and
  African states.
9 Increasing the bilateral aid given through national funds to the
  African states.

The linkage was quite straightforward: the deleterious effect of increased oil prices would be ameliorated by increasing aid and investment in African states. Through such an arrangement 'the Arab countries could use their newly-found power to influence a reformation of the international economic system to achieve more economic justice for developing countries' (OAPEC Report 1977).

A number of multilateral Arab institutions specialising in aid to Arab and Muslim countries had been established in the 1970s, namely: the Arab Fund for Social and Economic Development (1973), the Islamic Development Bank (1973), the Arab Investment Company (1974) and the Arab Monetary Fund (1976). By 1993 a variety of organisations linked Arab financial institutions with African countries (see Table 4.8)

In the 1980s the relationship between oil prices and the Arab world's aid strategies on low income countries led to a debate about the long-term impact of oil price rises on low-income countries.

IMPACT OF OIL PRICE RISES

Heal and Chichilnisky question the assertion that the cost of oil imports by low income countries from 1973 to 1979 produced 'proportionally more hardship on these economies than on the rest of the world' (Heal and Chichilnisky 1991 pp. 96–97). They agree that the value of imports of developing countries rose as a percentage of Gross Domestic Product between 1973 and 1980, when oil prices were highest, thus confirming the view that higher oil prices were a burden to these countries, but this effect, they stress, was offset by foreign aid transfers from oil-exporting countries to low-income developing countries in Africa. In other words, aid, particularly from

Table 4.8 Organisations linking Arab financial institutions with African countries

Arab Fund for Technical Assistance for African Countries.
Islamic Solidarity Fund
Special Arab Aid Fund for Africa
Saudi Fund for Development
OPEC Fund
Islamic Development Bank
BADEA
Arab Fund for Social and Economic Development

the Arab states, which by 1981 represented $US 7.6 billion per year, exceeded the cost of oil imports:

> In summary the low-income developing countries were not particularly harmed by higher oil prices. The growth rates of the oil import bills as proportions of Gross National Product, are comparable with those of the rest of the world and they received very substantial aid flows from the oil producers in the period of high oil prices. In several cases, the incremental OPEC aid flows exceeded the increased cost of oil imports.
>
> (ibid. pp. 99-103)

This argument runs counter to the received view that the oil price rises of the early 1970s contributed directly to the vastly inflationary cost of imported oil and manufactured goods and, more devastingly in the long term, the spiralling Third World Debt crisis (cf. LeVine and Luke 1979; Ismael 1986; Hallwood and Sinclair 1981). Critics of Heal and Chichilnisky suggest that by grouping countries together, their study masks the fact that between 1973 and 1977, the 20 main recipient states of OPEC aid were, with the exception of India and Thailand, all regarded as Muslim countries. According to a 1994 United Nations Conference on Trade and Development (UNCTAD) report: 'The severity and speed of the debt crisis (in Africa) started in the early 1970s when OPEC's first oil price increase in 1973 created an acute need among oil importing countries to finance their large current account deficits.' However, the high inflation rates and wide fluctuations in commodity prices recorded at the end of the 1970s helped to keep the growth of Africa's real debt and debt service within a manageable proportion, although this varied considerably within individual countries (The Projection of Africa's External Debt by the Year 2000, UNCTAD see Thisen 1994). UNCTAD believe the debt crisis occurred in the early 1980s when a second round of OPEC oil price increases in the 1979–1980 and 1980–1982 world recessions worsened the debt servicing position 'as both the price and volume of developing countries' exports were drastically reduced' (ibid. p. 2).

Certainly, non-oil-producing developing countries continue to feel a sense of unease at any instability in the price of oil. In the months before the Gulf War of 1991, Gambia's Finance Minister stated: 'We have no panacea for a continued rise in oil prices, except perhaps, a deepening dependence on external aid. We would hope those experiencing a windfall see fit to help us' (*West Africa* 12–18

November 1990 p. 2,814). This view was echoed in Ghana by the Secretary for Finance and Economic Planning who stated that Ghana would require an extra $US50-60million to meet the country's oil bill for the remainder of 1990 resulting from the sharp increase in the price of oil brought about by the Gulf crisis (ibid.). The price-rise instability of 1990 was reversed in 1991. According to the BADEA *Annual Report*, the year 1991 witnessed a marked decline in oil prices which averaged $17.77 per barrel compared with $22.05 per barrel in 1990, representing a decline of 24.1 per cent. Average prices reached $30.58 per barrel through the last quarter of 1990 during the peak of the pre-Gulf War crisis (BADEA *Annual Report* 1991). In fact, one of the central assumptions in econometric predictions of the prospects for an improved debt position in the non-oil-producing countries of sub-Saharan Africa is the maintenance of a stable price of oil, 'so as not to perturb drastically the balance-of-payments equilibrium, as was the case in the 1973/74 and 1979/80 oil price shocks' (UNCTAD see Thisen 1994 p. 17).

The Organisation of Arab Petroleum Exporting Countries (OAPEC) readily accept the importance of energy pricing because of the 'direct relationship between prices, economic and social activities and their effect on standards of living and economic costs' (OAPEC General Secretariat Economic Report, Kuwait 1994). To illustrate the impact of domestic energy price changes on economic activities in general and on domestic energy-consumption levels in particular, the OAPEC Secretariat prepared a preliminary study on the relationship between prices and consumption, using a paper prepared by the Energy Planning Institute in Egypt as a basis for drawing conclusions on how prices affect economic activities. The preliminary study was based on a statistical analysis of the relationship between per capita consumption of liquefied petroleum gas, automotive gasoline, kerosene, diesel oil and fuel oil, the prices of these products and the per capita income (ibid.). A direct effect on levels of economic activity was produced when price levels of these commodities changed.

ARABS, AFRICANS AND THE 1991 GULF WAR

The invasion of Kuwait by Iraq in August 1990 placed a profound strain on the relationship between Arab countries and other Third World states, despite the seeming unanimity in support of the United Nations condemnation of the Iraqi leader, Saddam Hussein's, actions and its approval of a recourse to military action. An understandable fear was emerging 'in most developing countries, especially non-oil producers, that the war will have a disastrous effect on development and living standards' (*West Africa* 28 January–3 February 1991 p. 87). Ghana was in a difficult situation given its economic ties with the United States and its political relationship with the Arab world, especially the Palestine Liberation Organisation. Accordingly, Ghana maintained a two-track approach to the Gulf crisis, on the one hand stating that Iraq had to vacate its hold on Kuwait, and on the other insisting that the Palestinian issue be addressed as part of an overall settlement. A government statement announced at the beginning of the war: 'In terms of history, President Saddam Hussein must be seen as a product of frustration over years of marginalisation of Arab interests,' thus further pointing to the existence of a linkage between the Palestinian issue and Iraqi actions in Kuwait. *The Ghanaian Times* conducted a survey on 17 January 1991, the morning after the first Allied bombings. The survey revealed alarm among those interviewed at the possible effects of a war in the Third World and a preference for some form of diplomatic settlement of the dispute (*The Ghanaian Times* 18 January 1991).

Nigeria was allegedly 'tilting towards Iraq' despite its condemnation of the invasion of Kuwait, its support for United Nations resolutions and its embargo on trade with Iraq (*West Africa* 28 January–3 February 1991 p. 86). Nigeria had made clear from the start its belief that peaceful and diplomatic avenues should be explored to end the conflict. It would be difficult to overestimate the importance of oil to Nigeria's economy which, at that time, accounted for 90 per cent of the country's foreign exchange earnings. The over-shooting by $8.10 million of the revenue projected in the 1990 Nigerian budget resulted from improved oil prices actually caused by the Gulf crisis. The initial drop from $23.6 per barrel to $18.80 per barrel just three days' into the war caused considerable concern about Nigeria's economic recovery. According to UNCTAD, oil exports represent over 60 per cent of total African export earnings, with Algeria, Libya, Nigeria and Gabon being the major African oil exporters (UNCTAD see Thisen 1994 p. 17). Nigeria, as an OPEC member state, remained on good terms with Iraq following the Gulf War and condemned the UN embargo on the country's oil production (SWB AL/2148 9 November 1994). Nigeria looked to Iraq to enhance 'wider co-operation in the fields of industry and trade, as well as oil' (ibid.).

Nigeria's position *vis-à-vis* the Arab world during the Gulf War was delicate largely because the country's large Muslim population had 'nothing but sympathy for Saddam Hussein, the Iraqi President' (*West Africa* 28 January–3 February 1991). Nigeria's security agencies stopped demonstrations by Muslims in the northern part of the country after the influential Muslim leader, Abubakar Gumi, declared that Iraq was fighting the Muslim's cause and urged every Muslim to support the country. Leaders of the Christian Association of Nigeria appealed to the nation's citizens not to allow the Gulf crisis to mar or disrupt peace in the country (ibid.). One analyst views the support for Iraq during the Gulf War resulting primarily from 'anti-western sentiments', in that irrespective of the rights or wrongs of the affair, any country or political leader who appeared to be confronting the West gained increasing support (El-Affendi; interview). Certainly, relations between the Muslim and Christian sectors of the Nigerian population became increasingly tense over the role played by the Islamic Conference Organization (ICO).

ISLAMIC CONFERENCE ORGANIZATION

The Islamic Conference Organization was established in May 1971 and its aims were set out in a Charter adopted in 1972:

1 to promote Islamic solidarity among member states;
2 to consolidate co-operation among member states in the economic, social, cultural, scientific and other vital fields, and to arrange consultations among member states belonging to international organisations;
3 to endeavour to eliminate racial segregation and discrimination and to eradicate colonialism in all its forms;
4 to take necessary measures to support international peace and security founded on justice;
5 to co-ordinate all efforts for the safeguard of the Holy Places and support of the struggle of the people of Palestine, and help them to regain their rights and liberate their land;
6 to strengthen the struggle of all Muslim people with a view to safeguarding their dignity, independence and national rights;
7 to create a suitable atmosphere for the promotion of co-operation and understanding among member states and other countries.

(Moinuddin 1987 pp. 74-78)

112

At the ICO's first summit conference of Islamic leaders it was decided that governments should 'consult together with a view to promoting close co-operation and mutual assistance in the economic, scientific, cultural and spiritual fields, inspired by the immortal teachings of Islam' (ibid. p. 65). It is an expression of interregional co-operation among Islamic states. In order to give impetus to economic co-operation, the ICO has worked out a set of multilateral treaties such as the 'General Agreement for Economic, Technical and Commercial Co-operation among Member States' and the 'Agreement for Promotion, Protection and Guarantee of Investments among Member States' (ibid. p. 5). (See Table 4.9.)

By 1993, the ICO declared that although it had made commendable efforts towards the fulfilment of its goals 'much more needed to be done to promote cooperation and understanding among Muslim countries', and called for the organisation to 'strive to reinforce the common ties that bind Muslim peoples together' (SWB

Table 4.9 Member States of the Islamic Conference Organization (ICO)

Afghanistan	Malaysia
Albania	Maldives
Algeria	Mali
Azerbaijan	Mauritania
Bahrain	Morocco
Bangladesh	Mozambique
Benin	Niger
Brunei	Nigeria
Burkina Faso	Oman
Cameroon	Pakistan
Chad	Palestine
Comoros	Qatar
Egypt	Saudi Arabia
Gabon	Senegal
Gambia	Sierra Leone
Guinea	Somalia
Guinea-Bissau	Sudan
Indonesia	Syria
Iran	Tajikistan
Jibuti	Tunisia
Jordan	Turkey
Kyrgyzstan	Uganda
Kuwait	the United Arab Emirates
Lebanon	Yemen
Libya	Zanzibar (Tanzania)

FE/1673 27 April 1993). However, the ambivalent principles of the ICO outlined in the Articles of its Charter raise difficulties of interpretation. Article 11 (a) 6 refers to support of the struggle of Muslim peoples which should be undertaken in order 'to safeguard their dignity, independence and national rights' (Moinuddin 1987 p. 82). There are Muslim minorities in non-member states of Asia, Africa and Europe and it is unclear whether 'Muslim peoples' should be construed as Moinuddin suggests: Muslim peoples living under colonial rule or military occupation, or Muslim minorities permanently resident in non-Muslim states (ibid. p. 83). Any interference in another sovereign territory would contravene the principles of self-determination and non-intervention contained in sub-paragraph 2 of Article 11 (b) which upholds 'respect of the right of self-determination and non-interference in the domestic affairs of Member states'. It would also undermine the principle of sovereignty outlined in Article 11 (b) 3 which calls for 'respect of the sovereignty, independence and territorial integrity of each member state' (ibid. pp. 87–92). Equally, the preamble of the ICO Charter reaffirms the commitment of its members states 'to the United Nations Charter and fundamental human rights, the purposes and principles of which provide the basis for fruitful cooperation amongst all people' (ibid. p. 74).

Yet, the ICO does operate on a political level. From its inception it called for Arab territories to be restored by Israel, the rights of Palestinians and of the Palestine Liberation Organisation to be recognised and Jerusalem to be returned to Arab rule. In fact, the 1981 Summit conference called for a *jihad* (holy war) for the liberation of Jerusalem and the occupied territories (*Middle East and North Africa* 1990 p. 108). The ICO was particularly active in the early 1980s following the Islamic revolution in Iran and was quick to affirm the importance of the Iranian Islamic Republic's sovereignty, territorial integrity and political independence, opposing any foreign pressures which might be exerted against Iran. By 1989 it declared that as Muslims in Africa shared a common colonial heritage, there was a need for unity between all Muslims (Brenner 1993). Its proselytising function was clearly outlined in July 1991, when the ICO's Secretary General proclaimed his intention to visit a number of states 'in order to promote the organisation of the Islamic movement in the world' (SWB ME1139 1 August 1991). Continual ICO meetings refer to the fact that over 300 million Muslims live in non-Muslim countries and their rights should be safeguarded (ibid.; SWB

FE/1673 27 April 1993). It is maintained that the potential of the Islamic world will only materialise when there is solidarity between Muslims. President Rafsanjani of Iran referred to the 'enormous powers and resources' the Islamic world possessed, which could be employed in the pursuit of its goals (SWB ME/1253 12 December 1991). Yet it is still unclear precisely what those goals are. King Hussein of Jordan speaks of the Muslim community's (*umma*) 'distinctive cultural identity' and its need to 'draw up comprehensive plans to spread its message in the world, to achieve solidarity, and to protect its rights' but no-one has any doubt about the 'long list of problems, the burden of debts and difficult cirumstances which the African states are enduring' (SWB ME/1253 12 December 1991; Hamid Algabid, ICO Secretary-General. in SWB ME/1252 11 December 1991). ICO member states have been exhorted to unite and join ranks in order to manage 'Africa's' problems and to 'prepare them for a better future' (Hamid Algabid, ibid.).

President Dawda Jawara of Gambia addressed the 1991 ICO Summit on the critical issues confronting Africa: 'Many countries, some of them ICO member states, are affected by increasing poverty, destabilisation, troubles and violence.' The Gambian President urged the Islamic world to draw up the bases for its new global order:

> Islam is not merely a creed but a way of life. God has blessed us with human and material resources so that we do not have to rely on others. The Islamic community must become a recognised power in the international community.
> (SWB ME/1252 11 December 1991)

Links between the OAU and the ICO have been steadily increasing because the majority of ICO members are from the the African continent and are, therefore, members of both organisations. Inevitably, similar problems are debated in both organisations. In fact, some view the two organisations as comparable given their dual emphasis on brotherhood and solidarity 'in a larger unity transcending ethnic and national differences' (Brownlie 1983; Moinuddin 1987 p. 74). Yet there are differences. Whereas the OAU Charter refers to a compact geographical area, the Charter of the ICO refers to the eligibility of every 'Muslim state', regardless of geographical location, to join the ICO. Eligibility exists when a state, anywhere in the world, expresses its desire and preparedness to adopt the ICO Charter (ibid.). According to the Secretary-General

of the OAU, Salim Ahmed Salim, the closeness between the two
organisations was initially the result of their 'joint struggle for the
freedom of peoples in South Africa and Palestine' (Salim Ahmed
Salim 1995; meeting) More recently, the OAU realises the ICO has
dealt with a number of problems and adopts stands supporting
African peoples in economic, political, social and security fields:
'Middle Eastern states within the ICO extend help to many African
states in their struggle for economic development' (ibid.).

However, conditions were always laid down by the Arab world
in their dealings with Africa. African countries were recommended
not to establish relations with Israel and financially punished if they
disobeyed. In the case of Zaïre in 1982, aid was cut off by BADEA
because of the country's resumption of diplomatic relations with
Israel (Ismael 1986 pp. 245–247). In the early 1990s although the
ICO reaffirmed its condemnation of Israel a number of African
states, Liberia, Nigeria, Zaïre, Ivory Coast, Cameroon and Togo all
restored diplomatic links with Israel. Nigeria had for some time
received Israeli investment through the Jewish-owned company,
Goan, which operated a number of construction companies in the
country, and operated security arrangements (Connolly; interview).
In fact, in 1995 it was reported that the Commander of the Israel
Defence Forces' anti-terror academy was in Nigeria 'establishing
an armed presidential guard'. According to the Israeli media a
'group of 50 officers and soldiers were training the presidential
guard' in an arrangement privately financed by the Nigerian
government (SWB AL/2196 9 January 1995). Yet, if the ICO is
less stringent the Arab League continues to threaten to withdraw
economic aid to countries recognising the state of Israel. The
decision of the Republic of Comoros to renege on its promise to
establish diplomatic relations with Israel was attributed to threats
of repercussions from the Arab League and accusations of 'rash-
ness' from Egypt (Al-Hayat 17 November 1995; SWB AL/2156
18 November 1995).

Clearly, then, African states, whether members of the ICO or
not, are affected by political imperatives defined by Middle Eastern
states and these constraints have inevitably led to a reaction.
Nigerian government officials believe the country can no longer
afford to allow itself to be marginalised in world politics: 'No nation
can be said to be politically safe if it is under economic bondage'
(SWB ME/1154 19 August 1991). Decisions to resume diplomatic
relations with Israel were defended in Ghana:

Events in the last few years demand that Africa balances its diplomacy in the Middle East with some realism. We can no longer go in with a blindfold over our eyes. There have been many instances in the past where some influential Africans have tried to belittle Israel's agricultural co-operation with Africa before the 1973 break but if our Arab 'friends' had followed Israel's example, Africa's agriculture would not be in such a sorry state.

(*Africa Contemporary Record* 1988–1989 p. A111)

The President of Senegal, Abdou Diouf, asserted that Arabs should take blacks more into consideration: 'black Africans respect Arabs more than they respect us' (*Africa Bulletin* No. 24 1992). Despite the very strong cultural links 'ill-educated Arabs disparage black Africans', although this tendency is deemed to be changing (El-Affendi; interview).

Certainly the ICO is criticised for devoting too much time to Arab issues and ignoring other areas (SWB ME/1254 13 December 1991). The 1991 ICO Summit, the first of its kind to be held in sub-Saharan Africa, was deeply affected by Iraq's invasion of Kuwait and the subsequent Gulf War. Only six of twenty-one Arab heads of state attended with many leaders, particularly Saudi Arabia's King Fahd and Egyptian President Husni Mubarak, staying away in order to avoid sharing a platform with PLO leader, Yassir Arafat, who had supported Iraq during the conflict. African leaders condemned the Arabs as 'immature' and predicted a worsening of Arab–African relations as a result of the conference (ibid.). Political events in the Middle East and the obvious lack of unity within the Arab world undermined statements concerning the great Muslim community '*umma*'. It was quite apparent that the Arab world was as divided and riven with conflict and animosities as were parts of sub-Saharan Africa.

However, with a Muslim population in Africa having increased by an estimated 50 per cent in the past decade to 149 million, which according to one interpretation now results in Africa having more Muslims than the Middle East, the potential for a closer relationship exists (*Africa Bulletin* No. 24 1992). Yet the ICO has been judged to have failed to unite Muslim states. Hassan Al-Turabi, head of the National Islamic Front of the Sudan, states: 'Perhaps the highest disenchantment is that the ICO, a professedly Islamic association, has turned out to be politically impotent and totally unrepresentative of the true spirit of the community that animates Muslim people' (*Islamica* April 1993). Regional organisations have, he argues, been 'inspired by the concurrence of security or economic national interests, with no Islamic perspective' (ibid.). The ICO admits that one of its roles is to 'promote the collective security of the Muslim community' (SWB FE/1673 27 April 1993). An alternative view, however, sees the ICO has having considerable radical potential. Moinuddin maintains that a change of attitude towards the principles enshrined in the ICO Charter could be accelerated and supported by a steady radicalisation of Islamic orders at a national level. This would give an opportunity for radical elements in the Islamic world to pursue a militant course and, 'perhaps even translate it collectively, that is, through ICO action' (Moinuddin 1987 p. 110). The time is now right for such a move, according to Turabi, on the grounds that the present growth of Islamic revivalism implies a 'deeper experience of the same culture and a stronger urge for united action, nationally and internationally' (*Islamica* April 1993).

MUSLIM CLASHES

One of the recurring features of African politics in the 1990s is the tension between Islamic groups. In numerous countries, including member states of the ICO, clashes have occurred. In Guinea, the government launched an 'offensive against Islamic fundamentalism' by sentencing Islamists for 'violence and inflammatory speeches'. The leader of the group, a young man from Mali, was allegedly trained in Algeria and returned to Guinea, from where he had been banned, with the intention of starting a *jihad* (holy war). Women who did not wear a veil were abused and threatened and anti-contraceptive speeches have been made from mosques. Imams (religious leaders), some of whom come from Pakistan, assert the need for a return to Muslim values: 'The wearing of the Islamic headscarf for women, a toughening up of the Friday prayer sermon and above all the appointment of young imams trained in Iran and Iraq.' These views have alarmed the Secretary-General of the Islamic League who claimed: 'Fundamentalism is dangerous; we shall fight it by all possible means.' Ninety per cent of Guineans are Muslims and the Islamic League fears that 'fundamentalist concepts may strike a chord with thousands of young people with time on their hands' (SWB AL/2178 14 December 1994; SWB

AL/2164 28 November 1994; SWB AL/2193 5 January 1995). The government in Senegal deported two officials of non-governmental organisations (NGOs) from Sudan and Chad for alleged fundamentalist activities and later went on to close the local offices of five foreign Muslim charitable organisations on the grounds that they were acting as a cover for radical groups aiming 'to destabilise the country' (SWB AL/2188 29 December 1994; SWB AL/2166 30 November 1994). Demonstrations and confrontations between supporters of the Islamic Party of Kenya and the Kenyan paramilitary police, (the General Service Unit) have taken place around the Sakina Mosque in Mombasa, a predominantly Muslim area and an IPK stronghold (SWB AL/2104 19 September 1994; SWB AL/2175 10 December 1994; SWB AL/2146 7 November 1994).

Demonstrators in Ethiopia called on the government to give full authority to *sharia* courts and to ban the existing Supreme Council of Islamic Affairs. According to Ethiopian news reports the demonstrators included women, students and religious leaders who asserted that to be governed by religious rules was not fundamentalism. The wearing of the *hijab* (veil) was the religious duty of women and therefore should be respected. Equally, the country's Central High Court should not overrule the rulings of a *sharia* court because it would undermine religious teaching. The government responded by referring the demands to a Constituent Assembly (SWB AL/2166 30 November 1994; SWB AL/2167 1 December 1994). The President of the Central African Republic, Ange-Felix Patasse accused the Muslim community of engaging in acts of violence asserting that 'insecurity in the country was largely caused by the Islamic community'. The Azaouad Arab Islamic Front claimed responsibility for violent outbursts and the killings of civilians in Mali, and Islamic groups in Chad distributed leaflets calling on non-Muslim communities to 'convert to Islam without delay' or to leave the country. Muslim student associations in Liberia warned the Muslim community 'to be mindful of people who may have a hidden agenda under the banner of Islam' (SWB AL/2218 3 February 1995).

The President of Somalia, Ali Mahdi Muhammad, officially inaugurated an Islamic court to operate in accordance with 'pure Islamic shariah', claiming that 'it was regrettable that the Somali people, who were historically of Islamic faith had never been given the opportunity to rule themselves according the Qu'ran'. The following day it handed down death sentences on two accused of murder basing its judgment on a chapter in the Qu'ran (Surat

119

al-Ma'idah) (SWB AL/2147 8 November 1994; SWB AL/2146 7 November 1994; SWB AL/2074 15 August 1994). Ayatollah Khamenei of Iran asserted in 1993 that Muslims living in other regions should pay attention: 'The Islamic struggle is like a traditional military battle. It is confrontation. You sit, think, show initiative and counter any move of the enemy.' He regarded Iran as the main centre for advancing the Islamic revolution (SWB ME/1608 9 February 1993). Accusations were made in Zambia in 1993 that the country's opposition party, the United National Independence Party, had formulated a destabilisation plan, funded by Iran. Iran 'strongly rejected' the allegations (SWB ME/1633 8 March 1993). However, the Interior Minister of the Islamic Republic of Mauritania overtly stated that Islamic groups, especially the Islamic Movement in Mauritania (Hasam) were strongly linked with Islamic organisations overseas. The countries alleged to be involved were Algeria, Sudan, Kuwait and Saudi Arabia. The President of Niger warned the population of the 'danger of Islamic fundamentalism' in the country adding that all efforts had to be made to avoid the events occuring in neighbouring states (SWB AL/2021 14 June 1994). According to reports a popular fundamentalist current was making a comeback in northern Nigeria due to economic problems and largely financed by Iran (SWB AL/2113 29 September 1994).

The Interior Minister of the Islamic Republic of Mauritania accused various Islamic organisations and cultural centres of attempting to 'undermine Mauritainian security by threatening to kill innocent Muslims and creating a climate of fear among believers' (SWB AL/2116 3 October 1994). Sixty Islamic leaders, including a former Religious Affairs Minister, three Egyptians, two Sudanese and a Saudi national were arrested on the grounds that they were part of organisations, linked with foreign groups. Non-governmental organisations (NGOs) were accused of receiving finance from Kuwait and Saudi Arabia and were in regular contact with Hasan al-Turabi of Sudan, the Algerian Islamic Salvation Front and Tunisian Islamic leaders. The secret organisation, Hasam, co-ordinated activities with other groups, the Call to Islam, the Cultural and Islamic Association of Mauritania, the Ben Masaoud Institute, Mis'ab Bin Umayr and the Higher Institute for Islamic Philosophy with the intention of paralysing the government and destabilising the population. The infiltration of the NGOs was especially condemned: 'They exploit the relief organisations residing in our country in order to obtain the necessary revenues to implement their plans, ignoring the rights of the poor and needy who are more entitled to such assistance.' NGOs would be used as channels through which to funnel monies from overseas (SWB AL/2111 27 September 1994). Mauritania, a Muslim country, was deliberately being violated by extremist behaviour which 'contravenes the teachings of true Islamic religion and is a challege to the feelings of the believers' (ibid.).

According to a Mauritanian radio report the plans and policies of the radical Islamic Movement in Mauritania (Hasam), which began in 1978 were clearly delineated into four areas: planning principles, strategic planning, assessment principles and ways of communication. The aim was mobilisation and training in 'jihad guerrilla warfare inside cities and towns with the objective of overthrowing the authorities by every means'. Through a process of infiltration of the official media, NGOs, educational and cultural organisations and a programme of training in military technique, Hasam intended to mobilise the organisation's members and supporters (SWB AL/2125 13 October 1994). Whilst the Kuwaiti Foreign Ministry denied that Kuwait was involved in covert activities in Mauritania and the opposition party, the Union of Democratic Forces, accused the government of engaging in 'repression against Islamic militants' simply in order to please 'certain foreign circles, especially France', the government claimed to have discovered a training contingent of 34 members on the outskirts of the capital city (SWB AL/2119 16 October 1994; SWB AL/2118 5 October 1994; SWB AL/2111 27 September 1994).

Whatever the exact truth of the incident, Mauritania was not the only country affected. By December 1994, a security source in Dakar confirmed that co-operation existed between Senegal and Mauritania to 'curb religious extremism and uncover organisations that operate under the cloak of religion'. Organisations and associations were dissolved, people expelled and deported. Again claims were made that some international NGOs use 'the cloak of religion and humanitarian activities to propagate their ideas' (SWB AL/2182 19 December 1994). Charity NGOs in Mauritania, which number over 200, carry out major social programmes aimed at the underprivileged living in shanty towns around the capital where large numbers of unemployed young people 'are left to their own devices' and, consequently, have enormous potential to influence people's views (SWB AL/2148 9 November 1994). Recognising this potential the Mauritanian government issued radio broadcasts specifically directed at young people warning them against the teachings of extreme Islamic groups (SWB AL/2130 19 October 1994). However, Syrian bureaucrats reluctantly admit that nationalist, socialist politics tend to be resisted by young people increasingly looking to Islam for political direction and identity (Hammade 1993; interview). By 1995, Senegal, Mali and Mauritania held meetings to discuss matters of 'security and religious fundamentalism' on a regional basis in order to more effectively combat threats of stability to all countries (SWB AL/2203 17 January 1995; SWB AL/2204 18 January 1995).

Clearly, tensions exist between Islamic groups within Muslim countries who are members of the ICO. These activities sit uneasily with claims made at ICO summit meetings that only in 'non-Muslim countries' are the 'basic human rights of Muslims violated' and their places of worship undermined (SWB FE/1673 27 April 1993). Splits between Islamists deeply affect the lives of Muslims. Interestingly, the whole of the northern belt countries below North Africa are regarded as 'borderline states' by Sudan because of their close association with the Arab world and the possibility of their integration into the wider Muslim *'umma'*. The increase in Arab education and the Arabic language further promotes the possibility of integration and the formal establishment of Islamic statehood (El-Affendi 1995; interview) Divisions between Islamist groups are largely a result of the Sunni/Shi'a split which was exacerbated by the Iran/Iraq war throughout the 1980s. Propaganda is now played out in the 'borderline states' and Sudan stands accused of pursuing a policy of destabilisation in several countries in the Horn of Africa. Hasan Turabi's Sudanese, National Islamic Front is condemned for encouraging the creation of a group known as the Eritrean Islamic Jihad with the intention of undermining the Eritrean government (SWB AL/2225 11 February 1995, *Observer* 25 June 1995). The National Islamic Front makes no secret of the fact that it would like to see Islam propagated throughout the whole of Africa but Turabi insists that nobody should be forced to convert to Islam (*Light and Hope for Sudan* 1995).

ISLAMIC DEVELOPMENT BANK

One organisation, set up by the ICO, to 'further augment the financial aspects of co-operation between countries' is the Islamic

Development Bank (IDB) which has been judged to be 'a proven and effective instrument of mutual cooperation' (El-Affendi; 1995; Moinuddin 1987 p. 5). The Islamic Development Bank (IDB) based in Jeddah, Saudi Arabia, was formally established by a Conference of Finance Ministers of Islamic Countries under the auspices of the ICO, in 1973. The administrative structure of the Bank is outlined in Figure 4.1. Its aim is to encourage economic development and social progress of member countries and of Muslim communities in non-member states. The Bank adheres to the Islamic principle forbidding usury and does not grant loans or credits for interest. Instead, its methods of financing are: provision of interest-free loans (with a service fee) mainly for infrastructural projects which are expected to have a marked impact on long-term socio-economic development; provision of technical assistance, e.g. for feasibility studies, equity participation in industrial and agricultural projects; and leasing operations. Funds not immediately needed for projects are used for foreign trade financing, particularly for importing commodities to be used in development, such as raw materials and intermediate industrial goods, rather than consumer goods; priority is given to the importation of goods from other member countries. In addition, the Special Assistance Account provides emergency aid and other assistance, with particular emphasis on education in Islamic communities in non-member countries (Islamic Develop-ment Bank *Annual Report* 1991–1992).

At the annual meeting of the IDB in Iran in 1992, President Rafsanjani called for a strengthening of the Bank in Islamic and African countries 'in order to fight against the plundering of their national resources by the West' (SWB ME/WO257 17 November 1992). Islamic countries often needed urgent loans and in obtaining them from the West they were 'ready to give political concessions', a fact which was 'very detrimental to the Islamic world and highly beneficial to the colonial powers' (ibid.). Rafsanjani warned the IDB not to be manipulated by Western policies. Yet the Bank has forged much closer ties with both multilateral financing institutions and other international institutions including UNCTAD, UNESCO and UNICEF and it continues to hold regular consultation/coordination meetings with the World Bank (IDB *Annual Report* 1991–1992 p. 57). When the World Bank announced in 1993 that it had suspended disbursements to Sudan due to the country's arrears of $1.14 billion, the IDB immediately agreed to finance an $8 million road-building project in the country (*Africa Research Bulletin*

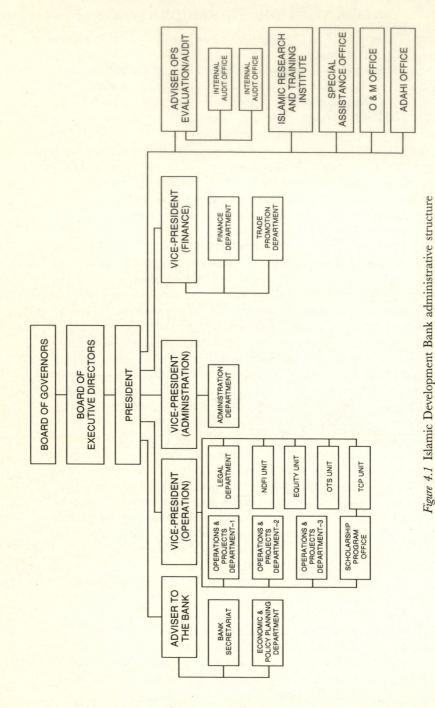

Figure 4.1 Islamic Development Bank administrative structure

Source: Islamic Development Bank Report 1991–92

16 April–15 May 1993). Both the World Bank and the IDB are fully aware of political factors when dealing with Sudan (Van Eeghen 1994; interview; El-Affendi 1995; interview) Tables 4.10 and 4.11 outline the Official Development Assistance (ODA) commitments and net disbursements to member countries of the Islamic Development Bank.

THE WORLD BANK AND INTERNATIONAL AGENCIES

Although the activities of the World Bank will be discussed in detail in the subsequent chapter, it is necessary at this point to outline its objectives and administrative structure. The International Bank for Reconstruction and Development, referred to as the World Bank, was conceived in July 1944 at the United Nations Monetary and Financial Conference in Bretton Woods, New Hampshire, US. The World Bank, based in Washington, opened for business on 25 June 1946 (see Figure 4.2 for administrative structure since 1987). The principle on which the bank was founded was the recognition that many countries would be short of foreign exchange for reconstruction and development and would be insufficiently creditworthy to meet all their needs by borrowing commercially. As an official multilateral institution whose share capital was owned by countries in proportion to their economic size, the Bank would be able to intermediate by borrowing on world markets and lending more cheaply than commercial banks. It would also be able to exercise sound judgement about which projects to help finance.

The goal of the World Bank (1993) as stated in its literature is: 'To promote economic development that benefits poor people in developing countries' (*The World Bank Group* A.01.4.93). Although the first World Bank loans helped finance the reconstruction of post-war Europe, it now lends to developing countries, including those in sub-Saharan Africa, North Africa and certain states in the Middle East. Loans are provided for various uses including investments such as roads, power plants, schools, irrigation networks, agricultural services and health and welfare programmes. Loans also finance changes in the structure of countries' economies to help them to become more efficient and market oriented. Technical assistance is also provided. The Bank operates under the authority of a Board of Governors, and each of its 174 member countries is represented

125

Table 4.10 Official Development Assistance (ODA): commitments to
member countries

Country	1984	1985	1986	1987	1988	1989	1990
Afghanistan	13.8	19.4	17.7	63.6	116.4	187.2	165.9
Algeria	213.4	153.8	122.0	180.5	348.1	540.3	427.5
Bahrain	148.4	59.2	103.3	12.6	29.3	9.7	19.9
Bangladesh	1,655.8	1,530.4	1,539.3	1,930.9	1,723.4	2,200.2	2,178.7
Benin	165.1	95.5	127.0	204.1	290.8	301.6	278.0
Burkina Faso	246.2	249.5	263.1	331.0	366.8	453.3	351.3
Cameroon	304.3	167.3	270.5	336.1	472.8	455.6	503.2
Chad	144.5	210.0	254.8	331.3	309.7	397.5	324.4
Comoros	50.5	26.3	34.6	61.0	54.5	57.4	45.9
Djibouti	111.0	76.1	152.8	117.1	109.2	124.9	88.8
Egypt	1,840.4	1,949.3	1,746.0	1,595.7	2,216.7	2,050.9	16,301.1
Gabon	92.1	67.0	68.0	104.2	150.9	139.4	53.4
Gambia	82.1	33.2	113.6	89.0	137.0	120.1	109.3
Guinea	237.2	176.7	209.2	372.5	466.7	390.0	463.5
Guinea-Bissau	76.1	62.1	62.8	188.5	90.8	193.8	104.8
Indonesia	1,060.9	1,249.3	681.7	2,204.9	2,740.8	2,696.5	2,925.5
Jordan	690.5	617.8	784.9	672.7	485.7	492.9	1,043.7
Lebanon	86.3	93.7	77.1	119.6	149.2	114.4	211.7
Malaysia	361.1	210.5	330.0	115.0	755.2	138.2	675.2
Maldives	18.9	9.7	13.5	35.0	37.8	35.1	22.1
Mali	411.4	438.1	361.5	356.7	568.3	642.1	517.1
Mauritania	191.5	250.2	200.9	260.3	261.0	288.4	257.7
Morocco	539.6	860.1	703.8	527.5	674.8	766.8	1,193.0
Niger	346.0	261.0	457.3	446.4	471.2	270.7	293.0
Oman	73.9	84.6	77.1	119.6	149.2	114.4	211.7
Pakistan	1,403.0	1,393.7	1,303.2	2,099.8	1,916.6	2,044.3	1,708.9
Senegal	445.8	312.9	637.8	935.2	643.0	624.1	741.3
Sierra Leone	84.9	110.9	90.7	130.3	80.0	183.5	111.8
Somalia	417.2	389.5	786.0	700.5	502.0	505.7	447.3
Sudan	720.4	1,301.9	1,303.4	1,017.6	1,024.8	756.9	518.2
Syria	700.7	708.6	898.0	842.4	200.5	74.3	679.1
Tunisia	290.2	296.1	640.2	352.0	659.7	517.9	564.3
Turkey	567.9	364.2	419.0	840.5	458.8	772.8	2,087.7
Uganda	308.8	150.3	216.0	440.2	458.5	484.4	844.2
Yemen Republic	633.7	507.8	475.4	487.9	644.9	322.8	381.8
Total	14,733.6	14,486.7	15,542.2	18,622.2	19,765.1	19,468.1	36,851.0

Source: Islamic Development Bank (Report) 1991–92

Table 4.11 Official Development Assistance (ODA): net disbursements to member countries

Country	1984	1985	1986	1987	1988	1989	1990
Afghanistan	6.7	16.8	2.3	45.0	72.4	167.0	143.1
Algeria	121.8	173.0	165.1	214.4	171.4	152.4	226.8
Bahrain	199.3	72.4	99.6	0.3	−2.6	−2.7	101.0
Bangladesh	1,189.8	1,130.8	1,455.7	1,635.7	1,591.7	1,800.8	2,103.1
Benin	76.5	94.7	138.1	137.7	161.6	262.8	261.5
Burkina Faso	187.4	195.3	283.9	280.5	297.6	271.6	314.4
Cameroon	183.5	153.0	224.8	212.5	284.5	458.3	483.1
Chad	114.1	180.6	165.0	198.2	264.4	241.5	315.0
Comoros	41.0	47.6	46.3	54.3	51.9	44.7	42.4
Djibouti	102.1	81.5	115.1	105.5	93.0	75.2	122.8
Egypt	1,775.3	1,759.9	1,716.0	1,773.6	1,537.3	1,567.7	5,604.2
Gabon	75.5	61.1	78.9	82.5	106.1	132.7	139.9
Gambia	53.0	49.6	101.0	100.1	82.1	92.4	95.1
Guinea	121.2	115.2	174.9	213.4	261.9	346.3	292.0
Guinea-Bissau	55.2	57.7	71.0	110.9	98.8	101.7	122.3
Indonesia	672.7	603.2	710.9	1,245.9	1,631.8	1,839.2	1,724.4
Jordan	687.0	537.7	563.6	577.3	416.7	273.0	891.3
Lebanon	77.4	83.2	62.2	101.1	140.7	119.1	134.3
Malaysia	326.6	229.2	192.0	363.4	103.7	140.2	469.6
Maldives	5.6	9.3	16.3	18.6	27.5	28.2	22.1
Mali	319.0	376.2	372.0	366.0	427.4	453.9	473.8
Mauritania	173.7	206.7	224.7	184.6	184.4	242.1	210.6
Morocco	341.3	766.1	402.7	447.2	480.7	450.3	969.9
Niger	159.9	303.4	307.1	353.1	371.2	296.4	358.1
Oman	66.7	78.0	84.0	16.0	0.6	18.2	68.8
Pakistan	729.4	769.6	970.3	879.4	1,408.1	1,129.5	1,152.3
Senegal	365.1	288.7	566.9	641.6	568.6	649.6	788.4
Sierra Leone	58.7	64.9	87.1	68.4	102.4	100.3	70.1
Somalia	350.1	353.3	511.4	580.1	433.2	426.9	427.6
Sudan	618.7	1,128.6	944.9	898.1	936.9	771.7	792.1
Syria	640.9	609.8	728.4	683.8	191.1	127.2	649.9
Tunisia	178.2	162.7	222.4	274.4	316.3	233.8	315.6
Turkey	241.7	180.9	340.2	378.8	268.9	141.9	1,264.7
Uganda	162.6	180.1	197.5	280.2	363.3	402.6	557.5
Yemen Republic	425.8	391.6	328.6	422.1	303.1	358.1	392.0
Total	10,903.5	11,512.4	12,671.1	13,944.7	13,748.7	13,914.6	22,099.8

Source: Islamic Development Bank (Report) 1991–92

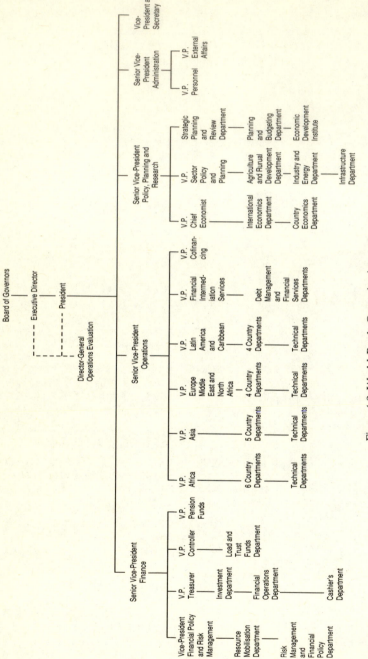

Figure 4.2 World Bank Organisation structure

Source: World Development Report, World Bank 1993

by one governor, who is usually a ministerial-level government official. As Figure 4.2 illustrates, the Board of Governors delegates its authority to a smaller group of representatives, the Board of Executive Directors, which is based in Washington. It is the Board of Executive Directors which is responsible for decisions on policies affecting the Bank's operations and for the approval of all loans. Loan decisions, according to the Bank, are based on 'economic rather than political criteria' (ibid.). The World Bank has three affiliated institutions: the International Development Association (IDA); the International Finance Corporation (IFC) and the Multilateral Investment Guarantee Agency (MIGA), all of which are based in Washington.

Although they were conceived at the same time the World Bank and International Monetary Fund (IMF) are separate institutions with separate goals. Before a country can apply for membership of the World Bank it must first be a member of the IMF. Both richer and poorer countries are entitled to join the World Bank but only poorer countries qualify for assistance from the institution. While the World Bank lends only to poor countries, the IMF can lend to any of its member countries that lack sufficient amounts of foreign currency to cover short-term financial obligations to creditors in other countries. Although both organisations are seen as 'partners in promoting global economic prosperity', their structure, size and country focus are not identical (World Bank (1993) *The World Bank and the IMF* A.02.4.93). The main goals of the IMF are to oversee the international monetary system and to help member countries overcome short-term financial problems. Since international trade and investment cross borders, nearly every country finds itself buying and selling foreign currencies to finance imports and exports. The IMF monitors such transactions and consults with its members on ways they can contribute to a fluid and stable global monetary system. The IMF also offers technical assistance in macro-economic management and extends financial assistance to countries in return for a commitment to economic policy changes. As of June 1992 the Bank disbursed over $200 billion in loans for projects and policy changes since it began operations. The Fund has provided over $140 billion in permanent liquidity and short- and medium-term loans to its members, traditionally to help them overcome balance of payment difficulties. The World Bank is a much larger institution with a staff of over 6,800, while the Fund has a staff of 2,000 (ibid.). The relationship between the World Bank and the IMF, particularly in relation to the structural adjustment programmes, which link economic policy conditions with lending strategies and were introduced in the 1980s, will be discussed in the following chapter.

The International Development Association (IDA), an affiliate of the World Bank, was established in 1960 'to promote economic development in the world's poorest countries' (World Bank (1993) *The International Development Association* A.01.4.93) The IDA provides a supplementary source of development capital but as the World Bank states: 'It is in many respects indistinguishable from the World Bank' (ibid.). Like the World Bank, the IDA helps to finance development projects which have been carefully selected and prepared and both organisations have the same staff. The President of the World Bank is the President of the IDA. The organisation, which accounts for one-fourth of all bank lending, provides developing countries with interest-free loans. Because of these terms the IDA cannot raise funds in capital markets as the World Bank does. Instead, donor nations replenish IDA resources every three years. The IDA has 150 member countries, 70 of which are eligible to borrow. The Association has extended more than $71 billion in credits to 90 countries and states who were once borrowers, including Turkey, are now donor members. Saudi Arabia is one of the donor nations.

IDA credits are directed to the poorest and least creditworthy countries; that is those states with a 1991 per capita income of less than $765. The IDA's funds, then, are allocated broadly in relation to a country's size, per capita income and economic policy performance. As Mosley, Harrigan and Toye point out 'economic performance entered as a determinant of aid flows as early as the 1960s and 1970s', long before the Structural Adjustment Programmes of the 1980s (Mosley *et al.* 1991 p. 31). They argue that with the IDA's highly concessional form of aid 'performance criterion had a quantitatively powerful influence on overall allocations' (ibid.).

As a country's per capita income increases, it becomes ineligible for IDA credits and is then deemed creditworthy for World Bank or commercial bank loans. The IDA helps countries meet the foreign exchange costs of imports of goods such as industrial machinery, spare parts, fertilizers and pesticides which are essential for economic development, e.g. it financed a municipal water supply system in Amman, Jordan. Donor contributions to the IDA replenishments are determined through negotiations taking into account a number of economic criteria, including donors' Gross National Product (GNP), Gross Domestic Product (GDP) and trade-related indicators. Since it was established the IDA has completed 10 'replenishments'. Negotiations for the Tenth Replenishment were completed in December 1992 when 34 donor countries agreed to provide the IDA with $18 billion to fund its aid operations for the three years 1 July 1993 to 1 July 1996. Those funds, together with another $4 billion expected from repayments of earlier IDA credits to it borrowers, made possible total aid from IDA of $22 billion between 1993 and 1996. The donors agreed that the IDA should build on its emphases of poverty reduction, economic reform, sound management and environmentally sustainable development.

The IDA's approach to poverty reduction is twofold: first, it supports a pattern of economic growth which attempts to provide efficient employment and income opportunities for the poor, avoiding subsidies for capital-intensive industry or damaging exploitation of natural resources. Second, it supports investment in people in the areas of primary health, education and nutrition. Investments in family planning and increasing women's access to education are especially important and the share of lending to social sectors for projects specifically targeted to reach poor people rose from 29 per cent in 1988 to nearly 40 per cent in 1993 (World Bank (1993) *IDA and the Tenth Replenishment* B.02.4.93). A Special Programme of Assistance (SPA) is providing for countries under-taking structural adjustment programmes especially those in sub-Saharan Africa. In the fiscal years 1991 to 1992, IDA adjustment lending was $2.6 billion or 27 per cent of all IDA credits. In the fiscal year 1992, new adjustment programmes were launched in Sierra Leone, Zimbabwe, Guinea and Ethiopia (World Bank (1993) *IDA and Economic Reform* B.06.4.93). Clearly, countries who are members of the Islamic Conference Organisation also benefit from World Bank sponsored funding. According to one analyst, sub-Saharan African countries can 'strike better deals with the World Bank' than with the Islamic Development Bank or BADEA because the West has more resources: 'the IMF/World Bank pays much more than the IDB or BADEA'. Also the aid is more focused on development projects and comes as a package. Membership of the World Bank can also facilitate loans from other sources (El-Affendi 1995; interview). Certainly, according to the IDA there is a growing demand for assistance from the organisation. (World Bank (1993) *IDA and Development* B.03.4.93). Of the IDA's commitments for the

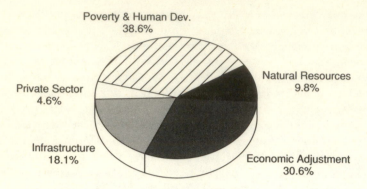

Figure 4.3 International Development Associations commitments 1991–93
Source: World Bank 1994, *IDA and the Tenth Replenishment*

period 1991 to 1993, the highest proportion of resources was devoted to poverty alleviation and human development, with economic adjustment coming second (see Figure 4.3). However, according to one study 'poverty-alleviation was demoted to priority zero' in the 1980s in order that structural adjustment of the developing economies could take place. The IDA decided itself in January 1993 that the organisation should include 'specific poverty-reduction measures in the design of adjustment programmes, whenever feasible' (Mosley *et al.* 1991 p. 22; World Bank (1993) *IDA's Contribution to Poverty Reduction.* B.04.4-93). Poverty-focused conditions supported by IDA in the period 1992 included:

1 Supporting a reorientation of public expenditures towards infrastructure and social services for the poor.
2 Focusing specifically on eliminating distortions that especially disadvantage the poor.
3 Supporting safety nets, such as nutrition programmes, labour-intensive public works and targeted food subsidies.
4 Supporting the gathering of poverty data and monitoring the impact of adjustment on the poor
5 Developing a national poverty reduction strategy and improving policy formulation and coordination for reducing poverty (ibid.).

Satisfactorily implementing poverty-focused conditions is necessary for obtaining the next tranche of the loan in a number of adjustment loans. In order to identify investment projects whose primary purpose is the reduction of poverty of identifiable groups, as distinct from those projects that contribute to poverty reduction in a more general way, the World Bank introduced in 1991, the 'Programme of Targeted Interventions' (PTI). The definition of a PTI project is that it either includes a specific mechanism for identifying and reaching the poor or, where no such mechanism is used, the participation of the poor in the project significantly exceeds the country-wide incidence of poverty. Examples of PTI projects are cited as those: designed to increase the productivity of groups such as small and marginal farmers, landless labourers and slum dwellers; provision of primary education, basic health care, nutrition services, water supply and sanitation to those, especially women and children, who lack access to these basic services; projects confined to regions of concentrated poverty, compensatory programmes introduced as part of adjustment operations; and projects concerned with safety nets for the poor (ibid.).

Similarities exist between the BADEA, the IDB, the IMF and the World Bank in a number of ways: all assist developing countries in sub-Saharan Africa and the Middle East with similar patterns of lending, e.g. technical assistance, projects, education, infrastructure, etc. The IDB and the World Bank have similar administrative structures and both have political agendas in that they impose conditions about political issues on their lendee nations, that is, conditionality arrangements, democratisation and transparency or furthering and upholding the interests of Muslims within the solidarity of Islam. Both organisations are concerned with development issues and attempt to introduce economic practices, either liberalisation or Islamic economics, to their donee states. Finally, all organisations meet and negotiate with each other.

So where does this place the borrowing nation? Caught between international organisations and attempting to get the best deal. Disbursement agreements may be agreed in Washington but it is at state level that conflict emerges over power and resources (Connolly 1994; interview) When countries receive aid from Western development agencies and from Islamic quarters, there can be conflicting demands and animosities over access to economic benefits. One aspect is clear, however, the relationship between sub-Saharan Africa and the Middle East is evolving. It is in the sphere of Islamic revivalism and economic strategy that a future relationship will be played out.

5

ECONOMIC PRESSURES

Major statements on African development were made in the early 1990s by United Nations Secretary General, Boutros Boutros-Ghali. Progress in Africa was identified as being dependent on co-operation and investment in human resources. The solution to Africa's problems would be found in debt reduction, regional integration and the diversification of economies. These main objectives could be achieved as part of patterns of co-ordination and regionalisation with national and international agencies, including the UN agencies themselves co-ordinating their activities. At national level there should be a strong and unified presence which facilitates inter-agency efficiency. Regional aid is preferable to bilateral aid in many areas because it follows practical requirements and need not stop at political boundaries. Water, electrification, air transport, communication, hospitals and health delivery systems all called for region-wide answers and other countries could provide training. Egypt serves as an African Training centre for nurses and police officers. Regional development banks should channel aid and donor governments could increase the capital of these banks to allow them to make more loans at concessional or non-repayable terms. Foreign aid and technical assistance should promote efforts to make African markets more attractive to domestic and foreign investment and where possible donors should mandate programmes such as regional professional training. Basic mechanisms such as customs, banking, insurance and a legal framework could not remain vague. The UN New Agenda believes that economic progress requires both access to information and an informed population (United Nations Focus on the New Agenda for Africa 1993).

The United Nations and World Bank are not the only organisations setting an economic agenda for the developing world. The application of Islamic economic principles to countries of the Third World as a means of promoting and developing their economies is also recommended as a development strategy by countries of the Middle East. Islamic economics is conceived as a self-contained ethical–economic system, which can play three distinct roles that may be expressed in terms of neo-classical economics (Choudhury 1989 p. xxvii). First, it can adopt an 'inspirational' role, urging people to work better, harder, longer and be reliable and honest in their co-operation with others. In neo-classical economics, labour productivity would be increased and resources would be maximised. The second role is called 'reallocational' in that the Islamic injunction against personal consumption and its prohibition of alcohol reallocates resources in favour of capital formation rather in the model of Calvinist teachings. However, Islam's commitment to redistributive justice marks a separation from Calvinism and potentially a break on capital accumulation. Redistribution inevitably increases overall consumption and may undermine a work ethic. The third role is referred to as an 'institutional restriction' and emphasises the Islamic prohibition of '*Riba*': the payment of interest (ibid. p. xxviii). Whereas the fundamental concept of neo-classical economics rests on the individual operating within economic rationalism, the Islamic approach considers wider issues including 'social, ethical, and religious circumstances, inclinations and beliefs' of people. Consequently, the notion of 'ethico-economics' or 'humanomics' cannot be viewed in the sense of economic maximisation (ibid.). A reformulation of development criteria on the basis of ethico-economic goals is necessary in the Third World claims Masudul Choudhury: 'The principle of sharing resources in the context both of national economies and of the world economy as a cornerstone for development co-operation can be seen to be well-shaped in the crucible of ethics and values' (ibid. p. xxxi). So, in our examination of economic factors in countries of Africa and the Middle East, consideration will be given to different development agendas.

DEVELOPMENT AGENDAS

The Islamic Development Bank (IDB) and the World Bank link economic progress to the wider issue of development. Interestingly, both institutions identify the same priorities for assistance: food security, trade among member countries, infrastructure, human resource development and technological advancement. As the World

Table 5.1 Africa: Social and economic data

	GNP per capita ($US)		Life expectancy (yrs)			Adult literacy (% of pop)		Access to safe water (% of pop)	Under-five mortality (per 1,000 live births)		Daily calorie supply (% of requirements)	
	1976	1992	1960	1975	1990	1970	1990	1988–90	1960	1990	1964–66	1988–90
Angola	330	*	33	39	46	12	42	38	345	292	81	80
Benin	130	410	35	41	47	16	23	50	310	147	88	104
Botswana	–	2,790	46	52	60	41	74	56	174	85	88	97
Burkina	110	290	36	42	48	8	18	67	363	228	91	94
Burundi	120	210	42	45	49	20	50	38	260	192	103	88
Cameroon	290	820	40	46	54	33	54	34	275	148	89	95
Cape Verde	–	850	52	–	67	–	–	74	164	56	–	125
CAR	230	410	37	42	50	16	38	12	308	169	91	82
Chad	120	220	35	40	47	11	30	–	325	216	99	73
Comoros	–	510	–	–	55	–	–	–	279	151	–	90
Congo	520	1,030	38	44	54	35	57	20	241	110	101	103
Côte d'Ivoire	610	670	39	47	53	18	54	83	264	136	102	111
Djibouti	–	*	–	–	48	–	–	43	–	–	–	–
Equatorial Guinea	–	330	–	–	47	–	50	–	316	206	–	–
Eritrea	–	**	–	–	–	–	–	–	–	–	–	–
Ethiopia	100	110	36	42	46	–	–	18	294	220	77	73
Gabon	–	4,450	41	46	53	33	61	72	288	164	81	104
The Gambia	–	390	–	–	44	–	27	77	375	238	–	103
Ghana	580	450	45	51	55	31	60	56	224	140	87	93
Guinea	150	510	33	37	44	14	24	33	336	237	81	97
Guinea-Bissau	–	210	–	–	43	–	37	25	336	246	–	97
Kenya	240	330	45	52	60	32	69	28	208	108	98	89

Country												
Lesotho	170	590	42	50	57	62	–	46	208	129	89	93
Liberia	450	**	41	49	54	18	40	50	310	205	94	98
Madagascar	200	230	41	48	55	50	80	–	364	176	108	95
Malawi	140	210	38	42	48	30	–	53	366	253	91	88
Mali	100	300	35	39	45	8	32	49	369	284	83	96
Mauritania	340	530	35	41	47	–	34	66	321	214	88	106
Mauritius	–	2,700	59	64	70	68	83	100	104	28	103	128
Mozambique	170	60	37	43	48	22	33	22	331	297	86	77
Namibia	–	1,610	42	50	58	–	–	–	262	167	–	–
Niger	160	300	35	40	46	4	28	59	321	221	85	95
Nigeria	–	320	40	46	52	25	51	46	316	167	95	93
Rwanda	110	250	42	45	50	32	50	64	248	198	73	82
São Tomé and Príncipe	–	370	–	–	66	12	–	–	–	–	–	103
Senegal	390	780	37	41	48	12	38	53	299	185	104	98
Seychelles	–	5,480	–	–	70	–	–	99	–	–	–	100
Sierra Leone	240	170	32	36	42	13	21	43	385	257	79	83
Somalia	110	**	36	42	46	3	24	56	294	215	92	81
South Africa	1,340	2,670	49	55	62	–	–	–	192	88	107	128
Sudan	290	**	39	44	51	17	27	–	292	172	79	87
Swaziland	–	1,080	–	–	57	–	–	30	226	167	–	105
Tanzania	180	110	41	48	54	33	–	52	249	170	85	95
Togo	260	400	39	47	54	17	43	71	305	147	101	99
Uganda	240	170	43	48	52	41	48	15	223	164	96	93
Zaïre	140	**	42	47	53	42	72	34	251	130	98	96
Zambia	440	290	42	48	54	52	73	59	228	122	91	87
Zimbabwe	550	570	45	53	60	55	67	–	181	87	87	94

Source: GNP per capita 1992: *World Bank Atlas 1994*; all other figures: UNDP *Human Development Report* 1991, 1992, 1993. Adapted from *Keesing Record of World Events* (1994)

** GNP per capita estimated to be less than $675; * GNP per capita estimated to be in the range $676–2,695

Table 5.2 Africa: Social and economic data

| | Breakdown of labour force (%) | | | | | | Urban pop. (%) |
| | Agriculture | | Industry | | Services | | |
	1965	1989–91	1965	1989–91	1965	1989–91	1991
Angola	79	74	8	10	13	17	28
Benin	83	70	5	7	12	23	38
Botswana	89	43	4	5	8	52	28
Burkina Faso	89	87	3	4	7	9	9
Burundi	94	93	2	2	4	6	6
Cameroon	86	74	4	5	9	22	41
Cape Verde	–	52	–	23	–	25	29
CAR	88	84	3	3	9	14	47
Chad	92	83	3	5	5	12	30
Comoros	–	83	–	6	–	11	28
Congo	66	62	11	12	23	26	41
Côte d'Ivoire	81	65	5	8	15	27	40
Djibouti	–	–	–	–	–	–	81
Ethiopia	86	80	5	8	9	12	13
Equatorial Guinea	–	66	–	11	–	23	29
Gabon	–	76	–	11	–	14	46
Gambia	–	84	–	7	–	9	23
Ghana	61	59	15	11	24	30	33
Guinea	87	78	6	1	7	21	24
Guinea-Bissau	92	82	3	4	5	14	20
Kenya	86	81	5	7	9	12	24
Lesotho	92	23	3	33	6	44	20
Liberia	79	74	10	9	11	16	46
Madagascar	85	81	4	6	11	13	24
Malawi	92	82	3	3	5	15	12
Mali	90	86	1	2	8	13	19
Mauritania	89	69	3	9	8	22	47
Mauritius	37	19	25	31	38	50	41
Mozambique	87	85	6	7	7	8	27
Namibia	–	44	–	22	–	35	28
Niger	95	85	1	3	12	12	20
Nigeria	72	45	10	4	18	51	35
Rwanda	94	93	2	3	4	4	8
São Tomé and Príncipe	–	–	–	–	–	–	33
Senegal	83	81	6	6	11	13	38
Seychelles	–	–	–	–	–	–	–
Sierra Leone	78	70	11	14	11	16	32
Somalia	81	76	6	8	13	16	36
South Africa	32	14	30	24	39	62	60
Sudan	82	64	5	4	14	32	22
Swaziland	–	74	–	9	–	17	33

Table 5.2 continued

| | Breakdown of labour force (%) | | | | | | Urban pop. (%) |
| | Agriculture | | Industry | | Services | | |
	1965	1989–91	1965	1989–91	1965	1989–91	1991
Tanzania	92	86	3	5	6	10	33
Togo	78	64	9	6	13	29	26
Uganda	91	86	3	4	6	10	10
Zaïre	82	72	9	13	9	16	40
Zambia	79	38	8	8	13	55	50
Zimbabwe	79	65	8	6	13	30	28

Source: UNDP *Human Development Report* 1991, 1992, 1993. Adapted from *Keesing's Record of World Events* (1994)

Bank and the International Development Association emphasise their continuing commitment to health and education projects, IDB Reports stress their financial support of social sector projects such as education and health (see Tables 5.1, 5.2 and 5.3). Equally, as food security and poverty reduction are highlighted in World Bank literature, the IDB declares its full participation in the 'achievement of the goals and objectives of the Decade of Food Security for the Islamic Countries' declared at the ICO summit in 1991. With regard to infrastructure, the IDA believe good roads, ports, water supply and irrigation to be the 'lifelines of a nation' underpinning production and 'creating the channels vital to bringing goods to domestic and foreign markets', whilst the IDB pronounce the development of infrastructure to be vital 'in order to stimulate the flow of investments, especially from the private sector, and to make these investments more productive' (World Bank (1993) IDA and Infrastructure; Islamic Development Bank *Annual Report* 1991–1992 p. 33). In essence, parts of a development agenda for poor nations, advanced by organisations which are essentially the aid agencies of the West and Islamic worlds, are virtually identical. Yet, according to Choudhury the emphasis is different: the Islamic formula looks to 'an integrated co-operative socio-economic model of development as opposed to a neo-classical competitive equilibrium model' (Choudhury 1989 p. 88). Islamic economics, however, upholds the market and assumes that forces of supply and demand will give rise to a just price (Hardie and Rabooy 1991 p. 53). Equally, whilst monopolies are condemned 'Muslim societies impose little tax upon

139

Table 5.3 Middle East/Arab World: social and economic data

capita $US	GNP per capita $US 1976	GNP per capita $US 1992	GDP ($US bn) 1989	GNP ($US bn) 1992	Life expectancy (yrs) 1960	1975	1990	Adult literacy (% of pop) 1970	1990	Population with access to safe water (%) 1988–90	Under-five mortality rate (per 1000 live births) 1960	1990	Daily calorie supply (as % of requirements) 1965	1988–90
Algeria	990	1,830	—	48.3	47	55	65	25	57	69	270	98	72	123
Bahrain	—	—	—	3.7	—	—	71	—	—	100	17	17	—	—
Egypt	280	630	39.8	34.5	46	54	60	35	48	86	300	85	97	132
Iran	1,930	2,190	—	130.9	50	57	66	29	54	89	254	59	87	125
Iraq	1,390	*	31.6	—	48	59	65	34	60	93	222	86	89	128
Israel	3,920	13,230	150.3	67.7	69	72	76	88	—	—	40	—	109	—
Jordan	610	1,120	—	4.4	47	59	67	47	80	99	218	52	93	110
Kuwait	15,480	***	46	—	60	68	73	54	73	100	128	19	—	130
Lebanon	—	*	3.9	—	60	65	66	69	80	98	92	56	125	127
Libya	6,310	**	23.5	—	47	54	62	37	64	95	268	112	83	140
Morocco	540	1,040	23.0	27.2	47	54	62	22	50	73	265	112	92	119
Oman	—	6,490	22.4	10.7	40	48	66	—	—	57	378	49	—	—
Qatar	—	16,240	7.7	8.5	—	—	69	—	—	91	36	36	—	—
Saudi Arabia	4,480	7,940	80.9	126.4	44	56	65	9	62	97	292	91	79	121
Syria	780	—	—	—	50	59	66	40	65	79	218	59	89	126
Tunisia	840	1,740	11.5	14.6	48	58	67	31	65	65	255	62	94	131
UAE	—	22,220	—	14.6	53	65	71	16	—	100	239	30	—	151
Yemen	—	—	8.9	—	—	—	52	8	39	—	—	—	81	—

Table 5.3 continued

| | Public expenditure as % of GNP | | | | Military | | Debt service (% exports) | Annual inflation | | Urban pop (%) | Breakdown of labour force (%) | | | | | |
| | Health | | Education | | | | | | | | Agriculture | | Industry | | Services | |
	1960	1987–90	1960	1989–90	1960	1990	1990	1980–89	1991	1991	1965	1989–91	1965	1989–91	1965	1989–91
Algeria	1.2	6.0	5.6	9.1	2.1	1.5	59.4	5.2	50.0	52	57	14	17	11	26	75
Bahrain	–	6.0	–	5.4	–	5.0	–	-1.3	–	83	–	3	–	35	–	62
Egypt	0.6	5.0	4.8	6.0	5.5	4.6	25.7	11.0	22.3	47	55	34	15	22	30	44
Iran	0.8	3.2	2.4	4.1	4.5	–	3.5	13.5	14.3	57	49	25	26	28	25	47
Iraq	1.0	–	5.8	5.1	8.7	20.0	–	–	–	71	50	13	20	8	30	79
Israel	1.0	2.1	8.0	–	2.9	8.4	–	117.1	–	92	12	3	35	24	53	73
Jordan	0.6	6.0	3.0	4.4	16.7	10.9	23.0	–	6.6	68	37	10	26	26	37	64
Kuwait	–	–	–	5.0	–	6.5	–	-2.7	–	96	2	–	34	–	64	–
Lebanon	–	–	–	–	–	–	–	–	–	84	29	14	24	27	47	59
Libya	1.3	9.6	2.8	7.4	1.2	8.6	–	0.2	–	70	41	18	21	29	38	53
Morocco	1.0	3.2	3.1	3.7	2.0	4.5	23.4	7.4	5.7	48	61	46	15	25	24	29
Oman	–	2.1	–	3.4	–	15.8	13.0	-6.6	–	11	62	49	15	22	23	29
Qatar	–	3.1	–	–	–	–	–	–	–	89	–	3	–	28	–	69
Saudi Arabia	0.6	2.1	3.2	5.8	5.7	17.7	–	-4.4	–	77	68	48	11	14	21	37
Syria	0.4	–	2.0	4.4	7.9	13.0	26.9	15.0	–	50	52	22	20	36	28	42
Tunisia	1.6	2.4	3.3	6.0	2.2	3.2	25.8	7.5	6.5	54	49	22	21	16	29	62
UAE	–	9.0	–	1.9	–	4.7	–	1.1	–	78	21	5	32	38	47	57
Yemen	–	–	–	–	–	–	5.4	–	29.0	29	73	63	8	11	19	26

Source: UNDP Human Development Report 1991, 1992, 1993; World Bank Atlas 1994. Adapted from Keesing's Record of World Events (1994)

profits' which might, at first sight, appear to undermine redistributive policies. However, Islamic banks have social welfare duties, such as the payment of *zaka* on their deposits. The payment of *zaka* is a religious obligation for Muslims and the money is used to assist the poor and for other designated purposes (ibid. p. 62)

The Islamic Development agenda does not detach the countries of the south from the industrialised world but it demands that 'international multilateral resource flows', i.e. aid, concessional lending, grants, must be 'untied' from conditionality arrangements (Choudhury 1989 p. 62). These unconditional resources, together with indigenous resources, could be mobilised on the basis of shared interests and co-operation. This approach is allegedly different from IMF and World Bank strategies because it overrides the emphasis on the needs and requirements of the nation state in favour of a 'collective self-reliant integrated development of the South' as a whole (ibid.). OAPEC countries would be expected to contribute more to the poorer areas of Africa. The difficulties with this model is not its economic imprecision nor its predominantly theoretical basis but rather its unwillingness to acknowledge that resources which flow from the Middle East to Africa are also conditional or 'tied' to an Islamic political agenda.

Nevertheless, from both Western and Islamic perspectives infrastructural consolidation is considered essential in building modern economies and connecting urban and rural areas, promoting higher agricultural output, providing electricity and helping integrate diverse economic activities. Infrastructure, then, is an umbrella term for many activities referred to as 'social overhead capital'.[1] The term refers to technical features such as economies of scale, and economic features, such as spillovers from users to non-users. Over the past two decades developing countries have rapidly expanded their infrastructure systems. By the 1990s the generating capacity for electric power in poorer nations was over four times that of twenty years earlier. Between 1989–1990 an additional 1.3 billion people gained access to fresh water (World Bank (1993) *IDA and Infrastructure*). IDA credits assisting the expansion and lending for infrastructure since 1961 totals almost $23.5 billion, which includes over $4 billion for power, $3.2 billion for water supply and sanitation, over $8 billion for irrigation and drainage systems and more than $8.3 billion for transportation (ibid.).

Between 1975 and 1991, the Islamic Development Bank allocated 21.6 per cent of its budget to transport and communication works,

Table 5.4 Islamic Development Bank Sectorial Distribution of Ordinary
Operations

Sector	1990 1410H		1991 1411H		1992 1412H		1976–1992 1396–1412H	
	Amount	(%)	Amount	(%)	Amount	(%)	Amount	(%)
Agriculture and Agro-Industry	30.25	18.3	58.19	33.0	39.66	18.3	374.22	16.6
Industry and Mining	48.20	29.2	53.85	30.6	43.28	19.9	682.95	30.3
Transport and Communication	26.98	16.3	20.36	11.6	59.04	27.2	487.98	21.6
Utilities	18.39	11.1	27.47	15.6	30.97	14.3	387.83	17.2
Social Sector	34.96	21.2	12.88	7.3	44.26	20.4	286.13	12.7
Others**	6.24	3.8	3.38	1.9			36.29	1.6
Total	165.02	100.0	176.13	100.0	217.21	100.0	2255.40	100.0

Source: Islamic Development Bank (*Report*) (1991–92)
Note: * Including only project financing and technical assistance. Cancelled
projects are excluded from all figures. ** Includes mainly approved amounts for
Islamic banks. Please note that ID means Islamic dinar, which is equivalent to
one Special Drawing Right of International Monetary Fund

and in 1991, it accounted for the highest level of expenditure. Figure
5.1 and Table 5.4 show that the share of resources devoted to transport and utilities expenditure has been increasing over the period.
Monies were allocated to the building of roads to link
the economies of West African countries such as Senegal, Niger,
Mali, Guinea and Burkina Faso (IDB Report 1991–1992 pp. 67/68).
Yet many IDA countries found that better management of existing
systems became a higher priority than building new capacity (World
Bank (1993) *IDA and Infrastructure*). By the end of the 1980s, over
half of IDA's lending for roads was for maintenance or rehabilitation
and such programmes were implemented in 19 African countries.
The payoff for these programmes is high. Every dollar spent on
maintenance and rehabilitation of roads can save one dollar no
longer needed for road reconstruction, and reduced wear and tear
on road users' vehicles saves another dollar (ibid.).

For the IDA 'improving the financial and institutional capability
of organisations that manage and deliver infrastructure systems has
become critical' (ibid.). Rehabilitation has often taken precedence
over new construction. These considerations have prompted a refo-
cusing of the IDA's infrastructure operations in many developing
countries as projects have increasingly addressed weaknesses in

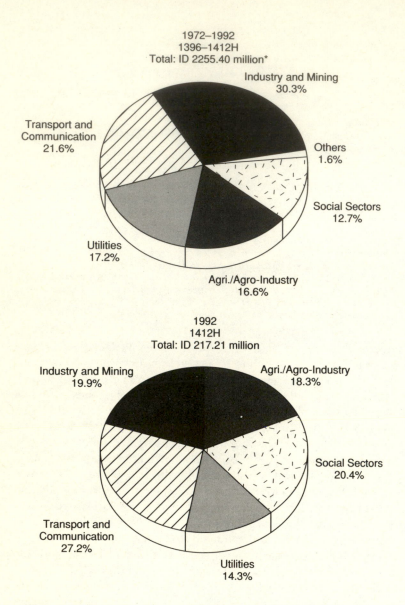

1972–1992
1396–1412H
Total: ID 2255.40 million*

Industry and Mining
30.3%

Transport and
Communication
21.6%

Others
1.6%

Social Sectors
12.7%

Utilities
17.2%

Agri./Agro-Industry
16.6%

1992
1412H
Total: ID 217.21 million

Industry and Mining
19.9%

Agri./Agro-Industry
18.3%

Social Sectors
20.4%

Transport and
Communication
27.2%

Utilities
14.3%

Figure 5.1 Islamic Development Bank, sectoral distribution – ordinary
operations, years, 1976–92

Source: Islamic Development Bank Report 1993
Note: Please note that ID means Islamic dinar, which is equivalent to one Special
Drawing Right of International Monetary Fund

144

service institutions. Consequently, some of the changes the IDA has urged include: fostering greater autonomy of local organisations, insulating them from political interference, incorporating incentives for efficiency and improving technical capability. This broader approach requires changes in economic policy and management techniques largely because of requirements to move away from state-controlled industry towards a market economy.

Power projects are undertaken by both the IDB and IDA. Cairo and Mali both received aid from the IDB for the construction of a gas distribution project and a thermal power plant. However, assistance from the IDA takes into account wider issues and maintains that power utilities have often been hampered by 'inadequate legal frameworks, excessive regulation and unrealistic pricing of services to consumers' (ibid.). To combat these features, the IDA encourages countries to set up independent, open regulatory processes, consider alternative institutional structures for utilities, and perhaps, more importantly, to use the private sector for some functions. Again countries which are members of both the ICO and IDA have received assistance: a revamped management structure for Guinea's power utility; an autonomous electricity corporation in Guinea-Bissau; and help for the use of the private sector for the management of electricity utility companies in Cote D'Ivoire and Guinea (ibid.).

In water and irrigation projects the IDA has also emphasised improving 'service quality' and efficiency. In Cote d'Ivoire and Guinea-Bissau, the World Bank and the IDA have supported management agreements with the private sector for services such as design, billing and accounting. With irrigation and drainage projects the need to improve efficiency has been stressed. More emphasis has been placed on ensuring that services pay their way and become more effective operations. Two approaches have shown promise according to the IDA: increased involvement by farmers to encourage better allocation of water resources and provide incentives for meeting operating costs and moves to privatise certain aspects of the service. However, while functions can be contracted out to the private sector in some cases, in most IDA-recipient countries, the public sector is likely to retain the primary responsibility for providing infrastructure services. Nevertheless, the IDA urges that greater attention be paid to institutional strengthening, of which the prices charged for electricity, water and other public services are a vital part. The IDA argues that even the poor are prepared to pay for basic services that improve their wellbeing if the quality is good enough. Tariff increases must, therefore, be linked to better services.

STRUCTURAL ADJUSTMENT LOANS

A study of World Bank and policy-based lending maintains that the 'step which initiated Structural Adjustment Loans (SALs)' came in early 1980 (Mosley *et al.* 1991 p. 34). The then President of the Bank, Robert McNamara, raised the issue at an UNCTAD meeting: long-term non-project assistance would be made available to countries prepared to 'embrace economic policies which the Bank regarded as necessary for development' (ibid.). This decision was made at management level within the Bank and presented to the Executive Board who initially felt uneasy that loans would be made to 'buy policy change or to persuade reluctant developing countries to undertake reforms' (ibid. p. 35) Yet, that was entirely the case, as Mosley *et al.* point out:

> Policy conditionality attached to loans does not make sense if both the Bank and the borrower are truly like-minded about the need for reform and the right methods to go about it. Only when real differences exist in objectives or perceptions about how best to achieve those objectives does the device of policy conditionality become relevant.

(ibid. p. 36)

Also, if World Bank loans were to carry a prescribed set of economic objectives which potentially could overlap with IMF economic stabil- isation programmes, how would these two organisations co-operate? Not surprisingly, perhaps, tensions between the IMF and the World Bank appeared. In the early 1980s, the Bank decided that SALs would be awarded to countries already in receipt of an IMF stabili- sation programme. Yet, the introduction of structural adjustment lending raised what Mosley *et al.* refer to as a 'moral hazard'. How far could borrowing countries be pushed into accepting conditional lending and how much leverage would the Bank use? Certainly, SALs could be used to place pressure on countries to 'follow orthodox liberal economic prescriptions of price reform and privati- sation'. But equally, it was possible for 'some hard-pressed devel- oping countries to take a short-sighted view of their national interest and accept a SAL without having any serious intention of fulfilling the policy conditions' (ibid. p. 38). In short, how much pressure was the Bank willing to exert on a borrowing nation and how much evasion could a poor country employ in avoiding the introduction of 'politically dangerous and administratively complex tasks' (ibid. p. 39). As President Chiluba of Zambia announced at a trade union conference; 'as much as I dislike the adjustment programme there is no alternative but to implement it if the country is to come out of its economic doldrums' (Economic Report, Lusaka, SWB ALW/0349 6 September 1994). Although World Bank officials recognise in the 1990s that 'structural adjustment programmes were, perhaps not the right way, particularly in Africa', there existed uncertainties about their efficacy in the mid 1980s (Van Eeghen 1994; interview).

However, in 1983 SALs were 'defended as a means of persuading more governments to change their economic policies'. Poor development performance was attributed to internal rather than external factors (Mosley *et al.* 1991 p. 40). This policy led to a process of bargaining with the consequence that weaker countries were more likely to accept conditional loans simply because they had little choice. But, ironically, those countries were just as likely not to meet the conditions. In fact, early SALs have been seen as 'extravagant and naive in their conditionality with conditions spread across a broad range of policy areas including trade policy, public finance, price reform in agriculture/energy and institutional change in the civil service, parastatals and public corporations' (ibid. p. 43). Table 5.5 illustrates the variety of measures. According to the African Development Bank, structural adjustment programmes were designed and implemented without much consideration for the interaction between national, regional or subregional consequences (African Development Report 1993). Developing countries were simply overloaded with a set of conditions which often placed too great a strain on local administrative capacity. In fact, one of the reasons cited as being partly responsible for the problems of SALs in sub-Sahara Africa was the absence of agencies and more generally, civil society which could cope with the demands of the World Bank (Van-Eeghen 1994; interview). The varied nature of the conditions made their implementation more difficult to monitor and the rapid timescale by which reforms were introduced are two weaknesses pinpointed as reasons for the difficulties of SALs in the 1980s, especially in deeply impoverished states (ibid.). By the second half of the 1980s changes in the design of SALs were attempting to come to terms with these problems. The sectoral adjustment loan

Table 5.5 Types of policy measure requested in return for SAL finance, 1980–86

Measure	Percentage of SALs subject to conditions in this area
Trade policy:	
Remove import quotas	57
Cut tariffs	24
Improve export incentives, etc.	76
Resource mobilisation:	
Reform budget or taxes	70
Reform interest rate policy	49
Strengthen management of external borrowing	49
Improve financial performance of public enterprise	73
Efficient use of resources:	
Revise priorities investment programme	59
Revise agricultural prices	73
Dissolve or reduce powers of state marketing boards	14
Reduce or eliminate some agricultural import subsidies	27
Revise energy prices	49
Introduce energy-conservation measures	35
Develop indigenous energy sources	24
Revise industry incentive system	68
Institutional reform:	
Strenthen capacity to formulate and implement public investment programme	86
Increase efficiency of public enterprises	57
Improve support for agriculture (marketing, etc.)	57
Improve support for industry and subsectors (including price controls)	49

Source: Mosley *et al.* (1991)

(SECAL) was introduced, as was the increased use of 'tranching', that is, 'the slicing of a given loan up into smaller and smaller elements, the release of each tranch being made dependent on the performance of certain conditions' (Mosley *et al.* 1991 p. 45). These moves responded to the worries expressed in 1986 by the Joint Audit Committee's Sub-Committee on Project Performance Audit Results (ibid.).

But why should there be economic reform at all in developing countries? According to the World Bank 'economic liberalisation and privatisation should not be seen as a goal itself but as a means of enhancing economic and social welfare in poorer nations' (Van Eeghen; interview) Three central factors are important. First, ownership of companies does matter, second privatisation and economic reform provides an encouraging signal to the private sector and third, the public sector is released to concentrate on other areas (ibid.). Because the private sector has an incentive to make profits, there is greater efficiency. If private businesses fail, the enterprise goes out of business and resources are transferred to other areas, therefore, an efficient allocation of resources is achieved. Also the private sector raises expectations and affects public sector behaviour by creating 'almost a transfer of efficiency' in that the public sector cannot be entirely immune to the private sector (ibid.). The public sector, then, can concentrate on what it does best, that is, provide a legal and enabling environment for the private sector (ibid.).

These views are not only those of the World Bank. The Gesellschaft für Technische Zusammenarbeit (GTZ), the German Development Agency, supports privatisation and economic reform for a number of reasons: greater efficiency, an increase in the range of products, the introduction of modern technologies, the diversification of ownership and an increase in income for the state. Many state-owned enterprises are considered unproductive and inefficient, whilst the private sector is geared to the market, efficient and adaptable (Klenk 1994; interview) Equally, the British Overseas Development Administration asserts its support for economic liberalisation. Baroness Chalker, Minister for Overseas Development, urges developing countries to move away from controlled economies and 'develop and encourage private sector activity' (Chalker 1994; meeting).

PRIVATISATION

In order to move towards a market economy, certain 'rules' are laid down in World Bank guidelines. While recognising that each country is different, some features are considered common to all: price and trade reform are necessary to enhance competition and promote foreign investment; tax reform and a system of unemployment insurance must follow quickly, in part to offset social and political pressures; measures to encourage small private businesses and small-scale privatisation help in a variety of ways such as encouraging a new distribution system, strengthening domestic competition, and absorbing some of the impact of diminished employment in larger state firms (*World Bank* (1993) *Toward a Market Economy*). Competition is seen as 'absolutely vital for the success of the private sector' (Van Eeghan 1994; interview) The German organisation, GTZ, maintains that privatisation needs basic macro-economic reforms. In creating a competitive economy, monopolies must be broken up and customs duties should encourage trade. Efficient money and credit systems must be in place in order for deregulation to take place. There should be no state restructuring before privatisation except perhaps in management because new owners will be responsible for introducing changes. Foreign investment must not be excluded and it is necessary for privatisation and social security services to be intact to protect against the realities of unemployment. (Klenk 1994; interview).

Looking at privatisation from the perspective of a developing nation, the situation is not so clear cut. If countries were to respond to the privatisation demands of the World Bank, there had to be a 'national consensus, from the president of the republic, through parliament, the government, to civil society as a whole.' No-one could escape the impact of economic reform (Zaïre Prime Minister, SWB AL/2156 18 November 1994). From the vantage point of Zaïre, where inflation escalates by the hour, prospects of economic growth seem remote (ibid.). However, African countries have approved a series of privatisation plans: various agricultural companies in Zambia are preparing for privatisation; the Congolese National Assembly approved the privatisation of enterprises involving Water Distribution, National Electricity, Post and Telecommunications; and the Botswana Development Corporation decided to privatise its brewery assets (Economic reports, SWB ALW/0338 21 June 1994; SWB ALW/0363 13 December 1994). Yet in the Congo privatisation 'jeopardised the social pact between the government and trade unions'; and in Kenya the privatisation of some government parastatals have been condemned as 'flawed' with mismanagement and corruption (ibid.).

GTZ has considerable experience in African states. In responding to the question: 'Why privatisation?', the organisation's spokesperson attempted to understand the initial reasons behind state intervention: 'In many parts of the world there has in past decades been a hope that state control of the economy might make good the imperfections of the market and that governments might function as a driving force for their country's development' (Klenk 1994; interview). State activities in the economic sector were to be used to establish and promote strategic enterprises, regulate existing monopolies, offset the power of foreign enterprises and promote social objectives such as job creation or better distribution of income. Attitudes to private enterprise were distant because capitalism was equated with poverty, social disequilibrium and exploitation by the former colonial powers (ibid.). In many African countries there was also a predominance of economic models, especially the quasi-Soviet model, where rapid industrialisation was to be brought about by planned state action.

In spite of all the reasons given for the establishment of state-owned enterprises, there have been difficulties with the state-centred economic model – noticeably an absence both of economic success by individual state enterprises and of macroeconomic development. In many cases, state-owned enterprises have become permanent recipients of subsidies. An example cited by GTZ shows that in Ghana, state grants to 14 public enterprises from 1985 to 1989 amounted to 2 per cent of the country's GNP, although it is important to remember that the country was undergoing structural adjustment programmes at the time and had resident World Bank officials constantly monitoring the economy (ibid.; Mosley *et al.* 1991 p. 159). Arguments against central planning, of course, fit in with the generally held criticism of the command economy following the breakup of the Soviet Union. Once the USSR changed political and economic direction it was inevitable that state-run economies in other countries would come under critical scrutiny. But what is the relevance of privatisation to impoverished sub-Saharan African countries when even the World Bank admits that successful privatisation requires 'a well-developed economic structure and a much wider economic strategy?' (Van Eeghen 1994; interview). The World Bank has increased its attention on countries of the Middle East but GTZ continues to be especially involved in Africa and has adopted a 'specific approach to poorer nations' (Klenk 1994; interview).

GTZ's approach to Africa is to engage a partnership with the particular country not necessarily in an adversarial bargaining role as played out in the 'conditionality game with the World Bank' but through a process of discussion (ibid.; Mosely *et al.* 1991 pp. 67–69). Initially, the German organisation enters into talks with the partner country in an attempt to define the problem identified by the state/government. Co-operation is the standard policy and a flexible response is necessary. In any case, according to GTZ, it must be a partner-led process and the state has to define the framework for economic policy and entrepreneurial promotion. In countries where the private sector is not very well developed, some form of consensus is sought. GTZ's view is that even in poorer developing nations there exists some kind of market activity and efficiency which operates outside the realm of the state.

However, GTZ does not view privatisation as a strategy for the complete withdrawal of the state. What is needed, the organisation argues, is a reduced, specialised and effective public sector, first to push ahead with privatisation on a targeted basis, and second, to guarantee the basic preconditions for continuing economic development and the emergence of new enterprises. Basic questions should, however, be asked when the privatisation debate is introduced: which state enterprises should be privatised, which should merely be restructured or reorganised and which should remain in the public sector? (Klenk 1994; interview). GTZ pinpoints one useful classification system for this procedure and that is to group enterprises in the categories 'strategic' and 'nonstrategic', 'efficient' and 'inefficient'. Depending on the initial situation in a given country, these terms may be defined in different ways. This yields a clear overview of those enterprises which are to be privatised and those which are not, and results in the following enterprise types and reform recommendations:

Stategic + efficient enterprises   = remain in state ownership
Strategic + inefficient enterprises   = restructuring/
                                            reorganisation
Non-strategic + efficient enterprises   = privatisation
Non-strategic + inefficient enterprises = privatisation/liquidation
                                            (Klenk 1994)

In many reform programmes, as in SECAL arrangements with the World Bank, the intention is to privatise only specific sectors of an economy. In such cases, the choice of sectors to be privatised can also be based on the answers to the questions: in which sectors does privatisation have a particularly positive impact on the economic and social objectives of a country and which sectors are most likely to be competitive or become competitive? According to GTZ, if privatisation programmes are for individual companies only, the basic principle should be to privatise as quickly as possible, as the period between the decision to privatise and the formal transfer of ownership is the most difficult time for the enterprise. Before privatisation, the enterprise has to operate in an economic vacuum, management and employees have unclear targets for the achievement of specific corporate objectives and problems with maintaining old purchasing and selling practices. All members of staff become 'unmotivated because of no threat of redundancy' (Klenk 1994).

Yet, privatisation may result in a sale to private individuals, a public sale of shares or management or employee buyouts but these last two possibilities are more appropriate to advanced economic systems such as those of the East European kind. GTZ maintain that foreign investors should not be excluded from privatisation programmes from the start, because they can bring 'new capital, new markets, new management strategies and new technologies into the country'. But they acknowledge that redundancies can occur and social security systems should exist in order to assist 'the population's initial ability to put up with hardship' (Klenk 1994, *GTZ Experiences in the Design*). In the course of its projects GTZ endeavours to implement a comprehensive privatisation approach that is capable of flexible application. In this sense, GTZ describes its approach as 'a modernisation strategy' that aims to promote the 'economic participation of broad sections of society and a large measure of social consensus' (ibid. p. 10). Looked at from that perspective GTZ's policies could contribute to a new interpretation of the old 'modernisation theory' presented over 30 years ago: privatisation will now lead to the establishment of capitalist, competitive economic structures, which will differentiate the labour market and create social change.

GTZ call their approach a 'system-policy consultancy' in that it seeks to promote 'suitable stability-orientated framework conditions at the macroeconomic level' whilst simultaneously attempting to establish and strengthen supporting institutions at the 'meso' or middle level (ibid.). Consultancy at the macroeconomic level is important, because large-scale privatisation projects that take place without changes in the macroeconomic framework conditions and without the creation of effective competition involve the risk that state monopolies may be replaced by private ones. This results in no benefits being achieved either at macroeconomic level or for the consumer through more cost-effective or better-quality production of goods. GTZ regards intermediary organisations and enterprises such as: chambers of commerce, trade associations, agencies, export institutions, finance institutions, etc. to be a vital part of the privatisation process as they act as a bridge between government and the private sector. In short, a functioning civil society plays a central part in the practical implementation of privatisation programmes and in the subsequent support and follow-up process. They form the control and communication centre of privatisation activities because they have a great deal of vertical influence both upwards, at government level, and downwards, at enterprise level.

GTZ advocate 'close to the people' ventures, that is private enterprise production, perhaps in the agricultural sector, which increases the availability of goods and services to consumers. Initially, this type of privatisation sequence does not involve social hardship, brings about social support for the privatisation process and permits the introduction of market-economy practices on a small scale from the bottom up (ibid.). Without the existence of market relations based on long-term considerations and without the presence of the necessary institutions, the privatisation of larger enterprises is doomed to failure, argue GTZ. Unquestionably, privatisation and economic liberalisation both raise political and sociological responses.

In December 1991, the World Bank established a new Regional Office covering the countries of the Middle East and North Africa region, stretching from Morocco in the east to Iran in the west. Despite their strong individual identities and unique historical backgrounds, the countries of the region were deemed to have much in common, economically, socially and culturally. The region shared economic and sociopolitical development aspirations and challenges including the need to restore economic growth, to address problems of poverty and inequality of opportunity and to increase the physical wellbeing of all its citizens. In an important series of speeches delivered both in the United States and in the Middle East, the World Bank set out its priorities for the region. In 1992 a speech on 'Economic Reform and Regional Co-operation' was given in Washington, an address on 'Coping with Population Growth' was presented at the Arab Population Conference in Jordan in 1993. Later that year a speech on 'Meeting the Challenges of Environmental Degradation' was delivered in Casablanca.

ECONOMIC REFORM AND CO-OPERATION IN THE MIDDLE EAST AND NORTH AFRICA

In the post-Cold War and post-Gulf War world, a rethinking is taking place within the region both on the issues of economic development and peace. These processes provide a unique opportunity, the World Bank believes, that the countries of the Middle East and North Africa may pursue economic and social progress and be able to forge a lasting peace (see Appendix pp. 257–60 for text of World Bank speech). In the eyes of the region's people, political and economic aspirations have not been realised; nationalism, socialism, capitalism and the new wealth have all been unable to resolve political problems and achieve better living standards. These failures have fuelled protest, created tensions and divisiveness, and driven populations in the region to support radical movements that are generating political unrest. Of course, many analysts have judged economic impoverishment and disappointment to be powerful reasons why young people have found radical Islam so attractive (Goytisolo 1994; Ghiles 1993; Hammade 1993; interview; Dembri 1995; meeting). Algerians, for example, have complained of their disposable incomes falling sharply as a result of harsh austerity measures imposed by the government and having 'to put up with shortages and spiralling food prices' (Ghiles). In fact, Algeria's Foreign Minister recognised that 'fragility of the economy' together with the immediate effects of economic restructuring' contributed, in part, to the dislocation and polarisation of Algeria's political system in the early 1990s (Dembri).

Clearly, beyond the important issues of Islam and the Palestinian/Israeli dispute in the Middle East rests the whole issue of economic stagnation within the region as a whole. The World Bank points to the fact that in 1960 South Korea and Egypt had approximately the same income per capita. By 1992 Korea's was almost 10 times as high as that of Egypt. Yet, more positively, basic elements for economic and social progress are present:

1 The region is and will continue to be relatively rich in resources. Almost two-thirds of the world's total known oil and gas reserves are located within its boundaries.
2 The location of the region, close to Europe and at the doorstep of Africa and the fast-growing East, is strategic.
3 The region has been a major exporter of capital to OECD countries, with Gulf Co-operation Council holdings in the hundreds of billions of dollars.
4 The region has a large pool of skilled and relatively inexpensive manpower and a dynamic entrepreneurial and trading class.

Two key questions remain, stated the World Bank. Will the interplay between stagnating living standards, political instability and the quality of economic management perpetuate the vicious cycle in which the region has found itself in the recent past or is there any cause for optimism that the cycle could be reversed and the success of some other regions of the world, such as East Asia, be reproduced in the Middle East? The World Bank believes that this could be possible (see Appendix, pp. 257–60). A report was prepared at the request of the Multilateral Working Group on Regional Economic Development which included an overview of economic development and regional co-operation in the Middle East and North Africa, a review of financial flows to the region, and an analysis of the Occupied Territories (World Bank (1993) *Economic Development and Co-operation in the Middle East and North Africa*). The region, as defined by the report included: Algeria, Morocco, Tunisia; (the Maghreb) Egypt, Jordan, Lebanon, the Occupied Territories, Syria, (the Mashreq) Yemen and Israel.

It is interesting that subsequent consideration of the Palestinian/Israeli peace process both by economists in the region and by political practitioners all maintain that economic progress provides the key to sustainable peace. The Israeli diplomat Uriel Savir spoke of the need for the region to be seen as 'successful and prosperous' in order to attract private investment and other experts argue that economic regeneration and co-operation in Jordan, Israel and the Palestinian entities is essential (Savir 1994; meeting; Fischer *et al.* 1994). Economic liberalisation in the Middle East, then, is not simply about reforming the efficiency of the region's economies but about very real political and security concerns at the very heart of the peace process.

Looking at past regional performances the *Economic Development Report* (World Bank 1993) stated that since the beginning of the 1980s economic growth has been unable to create sufficient job opportunities for rapidly expanding labour forces and displaced persons. In 1993 more than 10 million people were unemployed. Also, although the swing in performance from boom in the 1970s to bust in the 1980s can be related to many factors, two are particularly important: capital inflows and domestic policies. The boom and bust periods were closely linked to changes in inflows of capital, although with the exception of the Occupied Territories. The changes in capital inflows were of major proportions, often amounting to swings of about 10 per cent points of Gross National Product. In the Mashreq the swings mirrored the rise and fall in the price of oil. Elsewhere changes in OECD assistance were more important, and in the case of Algeria, commercial borrowing was a major factor. However, the report pointed out that regardless of the source and the fluctuations, 'net inflows of capital between 1970 and 1990 averaged 16 per cent of GNP in the Mashreq, 14 per cent in Israel and 3.5 per cent in the Maghreb, unusually high flows by international standards' (Fischer *et al.* 1994 p. ii).

During the first half of the 1970s the region enjoyed high and, at least in the case of the Maghreb and Mashreq (east and west) regions, accelerating rates of economic growth. But by the second half of the 1980s, growth had collapsed. In both parts of the region economic growth was barely keeping pace with population growth and in Israel the economic stagnation of the early 1980s moderated slightly but growth remained modest. However, the link between capital inflows and economic performance rests in investment: in both the upswing and the downswing periods domestic investment increased and declined with changes in capital inflows. The report found that changes in economic performance did not always match the increase in investment in the upswing, and the subsequent collapse in performance was much greater than could easily be explained by declining levels of investment during the downswing. This trend suggested a decline in the productivity of investment (ibid.; Van Eeghen 1994; interview). The declining productivity of capital could be attributed to domestic policies. Of almost $55 billion that flowed into the region on a net basis in the 1970s, more than 90 per cent accrued to the public sector (*Economic and Development Report*, World Bank 1993). This inflow, the report maintained, helped finance a rapid expansion of the region's public sectors, an expansion that was associated with a policy framework inhibiting the growth of private entrepreneurship, shunning the use of markets and protecting public production from foreign competition – all policies, of course, which were compatible with the quasi-socialist political programmes of many of the countries' leaders. Numerous public sector jobs were created and practically every organisation was dependent on the state (Van Eeghen 1994; interview). When the flow of external capital began to shrink, the rationing of increasingly scarce resources led to inflation and capital flight which reached an estimated average annual outflow in the 1980s of $1.6 billion in the Maghreb and $4.5 billion in the Mashreq (*Economic Development Report*, World Bank 1993). Region-wide population growth was running at 2.8 per cent per year in 1994 and standard measures of education attainment and health status fell short of those in other countries.

The Economic Development Report (ibid.) suggested the need for a strategy that combined three elements: increased regional co-operation, reform of domestic economic policy and a new approach to external financing. The key points relating to each component and their role in the overall strategy are as follows:

1 Regional co-operation in the areas of trade, labour, capital and especially multi-country projects should contribute to regionwide prosperity and help solidify interaction in political and social spheres. But by itself, regional co-operation will not solve the development problems confronting the region.
2 Domestic reform is central to both a resurgence in private investment and a redirection of public investment towards human resources, infrastructure and protection of the environment. An additional $10 to 15 billion a year in investment will be required regionwide.
3 External financing from official sources will not be as plentiful as in the past. Attracting the back part of the savings held abroad – estimated to be $180 billion – is important. This will require a credible domestic economic programme and careful management of the existing debt overhang of $140 billion.

Regional co-operation is a potentially important mechanism for improving regionwide economic performance. Co-operation in the area of trade, for example, enlarges the market and allows for gains from economies of scale. But at present intra-regional trade accounts for only 6 per cent of total trade, so that even a doubling is unlikely to generate an adequate number of new jobs. A similar point applies to labour migration. Even a return to the pre-Gulf War levels of migration would make only a small dent in the existing unemployment problem. Capital flows from the Gulf can, however, be significant and the OECD may be attracted to the labour-surplus countries of the region, that is, non-Gulf states, if conditions became sufficiently appealing.

The implementation of high-return regional projects in the fields of communication, water, energy and environmental management is possibly the most beneficial form of regional co-operation. However, unless the productivity of investment in all uses increases, expansion and improvements in one area, that is regional projects, cannot solve the problems of low growth and high unemployment. Domestic reform, with an emphasis on increasing private investment and an incentive structure conducive to the development of private entrepreneurship and an open trading environment is vital. There have to be improvements in public sector management including: a redefinition of the role of the state towards enabling and supporting, rather than substituting for, private economic activity; civil service reforms; provision of physical infrastructure and the reallocation of some military expenditures to the social sectors. Of course, macro-economic stabilisation, liberalisation and public sector management are the familiar ingredients of economic management that have generally been advanced for some years. But achieving long-term economic sustainability also depends on human resource development and natural resource management.

The Economic Development Report emphasised developing human resources as not only an important social goal in its own right but also a necessary ingredient for long-run growth. Without complementary progress in human development and without efforts to reduce population growth, policy and institutional reforms to improve economic efficiency could not yield sustainable results (*Economic Development Report*, World Bank 1993 p. iv). The priority programmes for the Middle East, as with the sub-Saharan African states, stressed: special attention to the education, training, health and employment of women; increasing the role of the private sector and voluntary organisations in the delivery of services; and effective policies for employment and social assistance including well-targeted social safety nets (see Appendix 5). Yet as one World Bank economic analyst asserted: 'Social safety nets are not completely satisfactory nor are training programmes, the only thing that will protect people and provide a solution to poverty is economic growth' (Van-Eeghen 1994; interview).

THE LABOUR MARKET AND ECONOMIC LIBERALISATION

The first calls for the Egyptian government to shed its parastatal enterprises was heard in 1974. More recently privatisation and public sector reform has become 'the mantra of both developing and industrialised economies suffering from chronic fiscal and external deficits and/or declining industrial efficiency' (Posusney 1994). As Posusney argues, although joint ventures in Egypt have been initiated in manufacturing, and foreign leasing is becoming commonplace in the tourist sector, only two small factories have actually been transferred from public to private ownership. Public support for privatisation has not been forthcoming and as late as 1988, responding to popular concerns, Egyptian President Husni Mubarak pledged 'las masas wala bi' al-quita' al-'amm' (no diminution or sale of the public sector) (ibid.). Although, since the mid-1980s the Egyptian economy had been in severe crisis with declining growth, rising inflation and declining real earnings, significant opposition to privatisation still existed, particularly from organised labour (ibid.; Assaad 1994)

In a sense, this reaction was not surprising. To understand fully the priorities of the Egyptian Trade Union Federation (ETUF) (al-Ittihad al-'am li-niqabat), it is neccesary to consider briefly some aspects of recent Egyptian labour history. In the period from the end of the Second World War to the revolution on 23 July 1952, job security became the key demand of Egyptian workers reacting to former widespread dismissals. Protection from dismissal without cause or as a result of production cutbacks or other market considerations was one of the first demands granted to Egyptian workers by the new revolutionary government under Nasser (Bianchi 1986 pp. 429–444; Goldberg 1992 pp. 147–162). Bianchi argues that the main feature of Egyptian labour relations since 1952 has been the gradual corporatisation of the trade union movement, in that labour has been co-opted into the decision-making process through a process of worker representation in management, seats in legislative bodies at national level and contributions to advisory economic planning councils (ibid.; Posusney 1994 p. 2). The system that has emerged over the years is one in which the 'state secures the loyalty and self-restraint of union leaders in exchange for job security and other long-standing demands' (Assaad 1994 p. 23). Workers, then, traded a level of autonomy and the right to strike for security in the labour market. In Posusney's views 'workers in post-colonial Egypt came to believe in a type of moral economy – a sense of entitlement from the government so long as they fulfil their obligation to meet production goals' (Posusney). It is not surprising, then, that workers oppose reforms which threaten these entitlements and that is exactly what the policy of economic liberalisation and privatisation implies. However, it is not simply a question of rates of pay; high school graduates are guaranteed a government job for life and are prepared to wait, sometimes for nine years or more, to obtain that position often foregoing higher-paid work in the private sector. Equally, since most union membership is in the public sector a reduction or erosion of that sector would inevitably reduce their membership base. With the private sector flouting the protective labour laws, privatisation becomes even less attractive to workers (ibid.).

Egypt, of course, is not the only country affected by economic liberalisation. In Algeria firms are allowed to lay off workers for economic reasons after negotiation with the relevant labour union and dismissed workers are entitled to a severance pay equal to one month's salary for each year of service up to a maximum of 15 months (World Bank (1992) *Algeria: Labour Market Overview Study*). In Sudan laid-off workers are compensated with six month's pay plus one month paid notice. In Zimbabwe severance pay is limited to one month's pay but permission has to be obtained from the government before layoffs can occur. One consequence of the introduction of government permission provision is that employers are increasingly reluctant to hire workers (Assaad 1994 p. 27).

There is no doubt that notwithstanding the economic deficiency and stifling of incentive attributed to the public sector, privatisation brings with it hardship to many social groups in terms of: increases in unemployment, elimination of subsidies, inflation, business collapse, and increasing social inequalities. The negative features associated with a competitive market economy are unlikely to escape the polities of the Third World. As Algerian economist Abed Bendjelid states, attempts at privatisation in Algeria would be difficult for any government simply on account of the 'population's deep attachment to the public sector' (Bendjelid 1994). He argues that the 'opening up to a liberal economy is a difficult road for the country', with the obvious political implications of increasing popularity of Islamic groups. In Algeria, Bendjelid states, privatisation is seen as a 'compulsory move', forced on the country by IMF and World Bank imperatives which further contribute to the general antipathy towards the policy. Yet in other countries, Tunisia, for example, the government's decision to structurally reform the economy and to sell all but strategic enterprises goes back to before the introduction of the SALs by the World Bank. Also, in the case of Egypt there were indigenous incentives to liberalise the economy (Harik 1994; Abdel Monem Said Aly 1992). The oil era, in its rise and fall, led to an extensive change in the Arab world in that it contributed vast resources to the Arab countries of North Africa and the Middle East. 'The well-known phenomenon of labour migration to the Arab oil-producing countries has provided extensive employment opportunity as well as capital to Egyptian individuals' (Abdel Monem Said Aly). According to conservative estimates for 1974 to 1984, 3.3 million Egyptians migrated to work in the Gulf states and transferred to Egypt $33 billion in cash transfers, bank deposits, goods and commodities (ibid. p. 48). Abdel Monem Said Aly asserts that the results of a survey show that 35 per cent of the proprietors of manufacturing enterprises who were former labour emigrants used their remittances as a principal source of capital to establish new workshops of their own (ibid. p. 49). Consequently, one result of this flow of capital to Egypt has been the consolidation of the Egyptian private sector

Although privatisation and public sector reform is popular in the West it can dislocate economies in financial terms and in social and political areas (Posusney 1994). Labour is, of course, exceptionally important in privatisation programmes and workers are likely to lose their advantages. Yet it would be wrong to think problems arise only in developing nations. Israel's attempts at economic liberalisation met with opposition from the Israeli Trade Union organisation, the Histadrut (Murphy 1994). There tends to be opposition to privatisation from those members of society who have little or nothing to gain from the policy. In a sense what is being played out in some states of Africa and the Middle East is the classic divide between the interests of capital and labour which the old corporatist or neo-corporatist economic structures with their attempts to unite government, business and labour in some form of concordat, tried either to destroy or manipulate. Strong authoritarian states may manipulate corporatism and emasculate the labour movement, whilst others bludgeon the economy by ensuring that no economic change can ever take place. Weak states, however, find themselves almost unable to institute change on their own and seek regional assistance.

REGIONAL TRADE

In response to the continuing economic crisis in Africa, the African Development Bank (ADB) has attempted to put in place a series of strategies in order to 'improve the efficiency of resource allocation and utilisation' (African Development Report 1993). One strategy is to bring together 'small and pristine' African economies so they can reap economies of scale both in production and consumption. Through a co-ordinated approach to development, the ADB hopes that economic integration may contribute to the growth of African economies. To a large extent the moves towards structural adjust-

ment and regional co-operation have been pursued independently
of each other. Structural adjustment programmes tend to be national
in character and 'designed and implemented without much consideration for their regional or subregional consequences' (ibid.).
Economic integration, meanwhile, is pursued among groups of
contiguous countries, again often without reference to the conduct
of national macroeconomic policies.

The ADB in seeking to identify interactions between these two
strategies concludes that it might be possible to adopt an approach
to reinforce the two strands in the future. If structural adjustment
is to interact with economic integration so that both can jointly
influence economic development, the ADB considers the design and
implementation of structural adjustment programmes could be one
area of reform. For instance, if it were possible to design a subregional structural programme, its implementation could assist the
countries involved in their mutual trade liberalisation schemes. By
liberalising their trade regimes and granting regional tariff preferences, subregional structural adjustment programmes would be
facilitating intra-regional trade and economic integration. The
ECOWAS (Economic Community of West African States) Economic
Recovery Progamme (ERP) is one such sub-regional programme
which although suffering from resource constraints is, asserts the
Bank, 'a unique experience in the history of economic integration
in Africa' (ibid.). In future, the Bank would encourage and promote
such initiatives through its lending programmes. The leaders of
ECOWAS, who signed a protocol establishing an ECOWAS parliament in 1994, see regional integration as their objective and have
called upon their 16 member states to implement progressive
economic programmes (SWB AL/2069 9 August 1994). Some
moves have been made towards uniting policies: a motor insurance
scheme established a common system for the settlement of claims
and provides the same guarantees in all ECOWAS countries
(Economic Report. SWB ALW/0356 25 October 1994). However,
the ECOWAS Summit meeting in August 1994 highlighted other
concerns, particularly anxiety at the deepening debt crisis facing
their member states. By far the greatest threat to the 19-year-old
organisation is the volume of unpaid contributions, estimated at $20
million. ECOWAS could cease to function it this situation continues
(SWB AL/2069 9 August 1994).

The seven-member, Francophone economic grouping within
ECOWAS, the West African Economic and Monetary Union

163

(EUMOA) was set up in 1994 in an attempt to reverse the adverse effects of the devaluation of its common currency, the CFA franc. The CFA franc, which is pegged to the French franc at a fixed parity of 100:1 was devalued in January 1994. The organisation was formed because countries could not afford individual national currencies and seek a convergence of monetary policies (ibid.). In 1995 the EUMOA commission, established in Burkina Faso, announced its task was to define major policies and programmes for implementation with the objective of economic integration (SWB ALW/0370 7 February 1995). The organisation saw itself as a 'catalyst within ECOWAS' rather than a threat to it (SWB AL/2069 9 August 1994).

A number of organisations supporting the aim of regional co-operation exist. A summit of the Common Market for Eastern and Southern African states (COMESA), an organisation which replaced the old Preferential Trade Area (PTA) was held in December 1994. A number of countries ratified its treaty: Angola, Somalia, Jibuti, Eritrea, Ethiopia, Kenya, Burundi, the Comoros, Malawi, Mauritius, Rwanda, Sudan, Tanzania, Uganda and Zambia. Again the objective is the expansion of their economies through regional integration. COMESA hopes to attract domestic and external investors to set up industries to process raw material into finished products (SWB AL/2175 10 December 1994). COMESA could provide the institutional framework for market integration and development and provide a link with the Southern Africa Development Community (SADC). This organisation, whose members include Malawi, Zambia, Lesotho, Swaziland, Mozambique, Tanzania, Zimbabwe, Namibia, Botswana, Angola and since August 1994, South Africa, is looking for 'sustainable economic interaction to be based on more equitable flows of capital goods and services' (SWB AL/2088 31 August 1994). Yet, perhaps, reflecting the importance of the addition of South Africa to its membership it also hopes to change the 'existing post-colonial relationship' between itself and the European Union. The EU is, in fact, the main trading partner of South Africa, buying 40 per cent of its exports. SADC member states intend to take advantage of 'the emerging belief in Europe that Southern Africa holds the best chance of political and economic success on the African continent', by attempting to broaden their access to European markets and 'secure stable commodity prices under the Lome Convention, and a trade and aid pact with the European Union (SWB AL/2087 30 August 1995). Meetings between SADC and the EU took place in September 1994 to ensure the region was treated as a whole. The trade volume of the EU with the former SADC (without South Africa) had run at DM 10 billion in 1992. It was agreed in a joint statement that both the EU and SADC would 'promote greater co-operation between the two regions' (Economic Report SWB ALW/0350 13 September 1994).

A well-articulated subregional structural adjustment programme could contain measures for harmonising national macroeconomic policies. Unrecorded trade among African countries is traceable in part, the African Development Bank believes, to 'policy disharmony among groups of countries'. One possible outcome of structural adjustment is the convertibility of national currencies. According to the ADB, the inconvertibility of currencies is one of the factors limiting the growth of intra-African trade. If countries could permit current and capital account convertibility, this could usher in the possibility of cross-border investment, including mergers, acquisitions and takeovers. The co-ordinated approach to investment decisions which this would entail would gradually assure increasing complementarity of the economies involved in such an exercise (ibid. p.188).

At the Organisation of African Unity's (OAU) summit in 1994, reference was made to the creation of an African Economic Community which would create mechanisms to encourage subregional economic communities paying special attention to communications, telecommunications, energy, health, education, and the management of water resources (SWB AL/2024 17 June 1994) In a sense, these statements and this level of activity seems very encouraging but warning voices are coming from Africa and the United Nations. President Museveni of Uganda spoke on the question of economic modernisation at an East Africa Summit meeting of Uganda, Kenya and Tanzania: 'When it comes to our countries – are they adequate? No, they are not adequate. The reasons they are not are very clear: underdevelopment in productive forces, that is science,technology, managerial capacity, and skilled labour.' Co-operation must not simply be fanciful; it was necessary as a means of survival. There had to be a 'more pragmatic model of co-operation' which provided tangible results (SWB AL/2164 28 November 1994). Equally, the United Nations Secretary-General, Boutros Boutros-Ghali, cautioned against Africa imagining grandiose schemes and artificially raising aspirations which bring 'bitterness and deeper despair' when they fail to be achieved (UN

Focus on the New Agenda for Africa 1993). It must be remembered, of course, that the Organisation of African Unity (OAU) is in 'desperate' financial circumstances given the failure of most its member states to pay up contribution arrears. Member states now owe the OAU $77.5 million in unpaid contributions. Out of a total approved budget of $29.5 million for the 1994–1995 financial year, the organisation received only $3.2 million. According to Adullahi Sa'id Uthman, the OAU Assistant Secretary-General, the cash flow problem led to the suspension of most of the activity programmes approved for that financial year. Only six countries, Botswana, Lesotho, Mauritius, Namibia, South Africa and Swaziland, have fully paid up their contributions (Economic Report, SWB ALW/0360 22 November 1994). Although the OAU has decided against sanctioning those states who do not pay it is nevertheless a serious situation (Salim Ahmed Salim 1995; meeting; SWB AL/2214 30 January 1995).

Despite the African Development Bank's wish to see closer economic integration, it recognises the difficulties of such a policy. Despite the existence of numerous regional organisations, real economic integration is 'minimal' (African Development Report 1993 p. 189). One major problem is that attempts at integration can create conflict. One specific area of conflict arises when problems of unemployment force a country to repudiate existing protocols concerning the free movements of persons and the employment of non-nationals. Such decisions, which are invariably responses to national problems, do not advance the cause of economic integration. Similarly, fiscal pressures may also force a country to disregard tariff reduction measures previously agreed with other members of an integrated market. Economic integration cannot be viable unless member states perceive themselves as beneficiaries (ibid. p. 190). Religious and ethnic animosities, together with the propensity for dispute within the continent, have not produced a sufficiently stable political and social environment to sustain economic integration. Even at regional ECOWAS meetings accusations have been made against member states' involvement in neighbouring conflicts. However, having raised a note of pessimism, the ADB believes that just because integration is slow and at times problematic it would be wrong to assume it it may never take place, or that 'the scope for integration cannot exist or be engineered in the future' (ibid. p. 189).

Some attempts are being made to overcome difficulties. Three railway corporations in Kenya, Uganda and Tanzania introduced a common fares and documentation policy in 1995 with the intention of implementing joint maintenance and marketing of Lake Victoria transportation; a new road linking Zambia and Zimbabwe began construction in 1994; Zimbabwe's Grain Marketing Board exports grain to Malawi and Mozambique; a Conference of Southern African Maize Producers was formed in 1994 to establish closer agricultural ties and a Pan-African Telecommunications Union Conference resolved to work towards improving all forms of communications within the continent (Economic Reports/ SWB ALW/0364 20 December 1994; ALW/0367 17 January 1995; ALW/0359 15 November 1994). Of course, there is much to improve and Table 5.6 demonstrates the disappointingly low levels of trade between member countries of the Islamic Development Bank. Tables 5.7 and 5.8 highlight the indicators and values of merchandise trade.

Questions of greater economic integration have relevance in Middle Eastern states. 'Islamic Sudan always looked to the Arab world but now is becoming more aware of its African neighbours' (El-Affendi 1995; interview). Poor communications, however, inhibit trade between African states and between African and Arab worlds. Also general levels of development in marketing, packaging and production contribute to the poor levels of intra-country trade (ibid.). Although international economic integration programmes usually start with measures for trade liberalisation, given the structures of production in Islamic countries the effects of far reaching programmes can only be very limited (Choudhury 1989 p. 359). For Islamic countries, as indeed for other poor nations, the main problem lies not in stimulating mutual trade by removing trade barriers but in 'facilitating trade by the creation of industries which produce those commodities which are needed by other Islamic countries and have been imported in the past from countries outside the Muslim world' (ibid.). An Islamic development agenda may promote the establishment of intermediate goods industries.

ISLAMIC ECONOMICS

The Islamic Development Bank promotes intra-Islamic trade because it is 'convinced of the role that intra-trade plays in consolidating economic co-operation and integration' (Islamic Development Bank 1991–1992 p. 47). The Bank's financing schemes have assumed greater proportions and expansion with respect to the

Table 5.6 Country-wise periodic change in the ratio of intra-trade of IDB member countries

Country	Exports 1980–1985	1986–1990	Change	Imports 1980–1985	1986–1990	Change
Afghanistan	12.0	2.2	–	3.5	2.5	–
Algeria	0.6	2.4	+	2.1	4.8	+
Bahrain	33.4	23.4	–	56.9	46.4	–
Bangladesh	19.6	10.0	–	17.2	11.7	–
Benin	4.0	9.0	+	7.8	3.7	–
Brunei	0.5	0.1	–	4.7	6.1	+
Burkina Faso	3.6	4.4	+	1.9	2.6	+
Cameroon	2.8	4.2	+	6.5	6.1	=
Chad	9.2	11.2	+	11.8	13.3	+
Comoros	..	..	..	..	..	..
Djibouti	75.7[a]	80.5[b]	+	13.4[a]	23.4[b]	+
Egypt	5.0	6.3	+	2.7	5.1	+
Gabon	2.3	2.3	=	3.4	5.7	+
Gambia	11.4	5.2	–	5.9	3.3	–
Guinea	7.3	8.6	+	4.1	4.8	=
Guinea-Bissau	6.0	3.6	–	4.7	5.5	+
Indonesia	1.6	3.8	+	7.1	7.0	=
Iran	..	9.6[f]	..	..	10.6[f]	..
Iraq	15.1	17.6	+	13.2	20.5	+
Jordan	47.6	38.1	–	20.6	25.9	+
Kuwait	16.9	15.8	=	6.6	12.5	+
Lebanon	55.1	45.8	–	15.2	16.4	+
Libya	5.2	4.0	–	4.0	6.7	+
Malaysia	4.4	5.1	+	6.7	3.7	–
Maldives	4.8[d]	1.5[b]	–	1.8	1.6[b]	=
Mali	4.8	21.5	+	9.3	6.5	–
Mauritania	1.1	4.4	+	11.5	12.6	=
Morocco	10.4	9.4	–	21.7	10.8	–
Niger	4.4	1.5	–	5.4	2.9	–
Oman	0.6	1.1	=	20.7	25.8[b]	+
Pakistan	27.4	16.5	–	33.6	22.4	–
Qatar	4.9	8.7	+	7.1	11.6	+
Saudi Arabia	10.9	11.1	=	5.3	7.3	+
Senegal	9.1	10.9	+	8.8	5.3	–
Sierra Leone	1.5[c]	0.3	–	4.3	1.3	–
Somalia	75.8	62.5	–	22.1	16.0	–
Sudan	31.6	30.8	=	23.1	25.3	+
Syria	13.3	15.2	+	18.3	13.9	–
Tunisia	6.7	11.8	+	7.9	8.6	=
Turkey	30.8	27.0	–	27.1	16.1	–
Uganda	5.1	4.3	–	3.3	7.0	+
U.A. Emirates	6.3	9.0	+	12.7	12.1	=
Yemen Republic	..	10.2[c]	..	..	23.1[c]	..

amount of financing, the number of beneficiary member countries and the range of tradeable commodities. The Foreign (Import) Trade Financing Operations of the Bank (ITFO), launched in 1977, contributes to meeting the short-term financing needs of member countries for the importation of basic commodities. The Longer-Term Trade Financing Scheme (LTTFS), developed under the auspices of the COMCEC (ICO Standing Committee for Economic and Commercial Co-operation) and the Islamic Banks' Portfolio (IBP) were established in 1987. The LTTFS encourages exports of commodities among member states. Managed by the Bank and having a membership of 24 Islamic banks and financial institutions, the IBP is oriented towards private sector exporters and importers in ICO member countries and its financing is carried out on the basis of the Islamic '*murabaha*'. The *murabaha* is a contract of sale between a buyer and a seller at a higher price than the original price at which the seller originally bought the goods. As a financing technique, it involves the purchase by the seller (financier) of certain goods needed by the buyer and their re-sale to the buyer on a cost-plus basis. Both the profit and the time of repayment (usually in instalments) are specified in the initial contract. In a sense, it is very close to the usual contract of sale used in Western societies.

The accruing of interest, usury, is prohibited by Islam but different forms of trading agreements are utilised. Loans are a mode of financing used by the IDB to finance infrastructure projects in member countries, particularly the least developed. They are interest-free but they carry a service fee intended to cover the actual costs of administering them. Normally, the repayment period ranges from 15 to 25 years, including a grace period of 3 to 5 years. The '*Mudarabah*' is a form of partnership where one party provides the funds while the other provides the expertise and management. The latter is referred to as the '*Mudarib*'. Any profits accrued are shared between the two parties on a pre-agreed basis, while capital loss is borne by the partner providing the capital. Another Islamic

---

Table 5.6 continued

Source: Figures are based on the data provided in the previous issues of the IDB's Annual Report. Adapted from Islamic Development Bank Report 1991–92
Note: .. not available; (a) data for 1982–85; (b) 1986–89; (c) 1981–85; (d) 1983–85; (e) 1988–89; (f) 1988–90; – sign indicates decline; + sign denotes increase; whereas = sign presents no significant change.

Table 5.7 Some indicators of merchandise trade of IDB member states

Country	Exports ($US mil.) 1991	Imports ($US mil.) 1991	Trade Balance ($US mil.) 1991	Average annual growth rates (%) 1980–90	
				Exports	Imports
Afghanistan	933	1,670	−737	..	..
Algeria	12,314	9,104	3,210	5.3	−4.6
Bahrain	3,161	3,993	−832	..	..
Bangladesh	1,688	3,381	−1,693	7.6	8.0
Benin	121	637	−516	..	..
Brunei	2,597	1,781	816	..	..
Burkina Faso	197	552	−355	10.1	1.0
Cameroon	1,910	1,345	565	−1.3	−3.3
Chad	90	158	−68	..	..
Comoros	28	120	−92	..	..
Djibouti	55	376	−321	..	..
Egypt	3,838	8,227	−4,389	2.1	−1.7
Gabon	2,573	962	1,611	1.4	−1.8
Gambia	166	287	−121	..	..
Guinea	638	605	33	..	..
Guinea-Bissau	20	134	−114	..	..
Indonesia	29,142	25,869	3,273	2.8	1.4
Iran	15,916	21,688	−5,772	21.1	8.0
Iraq	297	284	13	..	..
Jordan	879	2,512	−1,633	10.3	−0.5
Kuwait	422	3,882	−3,460	−11.1	−5.7
Lebanon	490	3,748	−3,258	..	..
Libya	10,775	6,001	4,774	1.8	−10.4
Malaysia	34,405	36,749	−2,344	10.3	5.6
Maldives	54	161	−107	..	..
Mali	294	570	−276	9.9	6.7
Mauritania	515	472	43	3.8	−5.1
Morocco	5,149	7,458	−2,309	6.1	2.9
Niger	241	407	−166	4.3	−8.8
Oman	7,236	3,310	3,926	..	..
Pakistan	6,494	8,432	−1,938	9.0	4.0
Qatar	3,198	1,862	1,336	..	..
Saudi Arabia	51,719	34,587	17,132	−9.7	−10.0
Senegal	737	1,359	−622	5.6	4.6
Sierra Leone	145	246	−101	−1.4	−2.3
Somalia	106	197	−91	−3.3	−4.3
Sudan	358	1,419	−1,061	−0.9	−8.3
Syria	3,700	2,857	843	8.7	−8.3
Tunisia	3,827	5,445	−1,618	4.8	1.1
Turkey	13,335	22,576	−9,241	9.1	7.0
Uganda	171	464	−293	−1.9	3.2
U.A. Emirates	24,261	16,049	8,212	..	..
Yemen Republic	1,205	2,555	−1,350	..	..

financing technique, the '*musharakah*', adopts 'equity sharing' as a means of financing projects. Thus, it embraces different types of profit-and-loss sharing partnerships. The partners (entrepreneurs, bankers, etc.) share both capital and management of a project so that profits will be distributed among them according to determined ratios of their equity participation.

Up to the end of 1992, total trade financing commitments under ITFO, LTTFS and IBP (including both import and export financing) have reached around $US8 billion (ibid.). Yet some academics maintain that Islamic economic processes have a tendency to stifle trade, in that prices fail to reflect real costs (Wilson 1994). Although the IDB does 'good work' it is also recognised that it 'has not achieved its economic goals' (El-Affendi; interview). In a sense, the Bank is constricted by the economies of the Arab world which fail to generate high levels of resources over and above oil production. The agricultural sector has traditionally been weak in the Arab world with poor levels of irrigation, low degrees of mechanisation and use of fertilisers and pesticides. Equally, industrialisation and technological development has been restricted. According to some economists economic co-operation and integration among Islamic countries has now become urgent largely because of the deficiencies in the economies of individual nation states (Adnan and Saleh pp. 155–157 cited in Choudhury 1989).

Attention is now focusing on the role of 'Islamic Investment Companies' (IICs) or 'Islamic Finance Houses' (the translation from Arabic of Sharikat Tawzif Al-Amwal is 'Capital Employment Companies,) which are thought to number around 104 in Egypt with an estimated deposit value of $US 2.3 billion (Abdel Monem Said Aly 1992 p. 58; Zubaida 1990). They are, in fact, closed companies which attract savers either to deposit their savings in exchange for returns (without participation in the decision making) or to own shares and stocks in the company. The companies utilise 'Islamic' forms of investment such as those outlined above: *mudarabah*: capital–labour participation; *musharaka*: venture-capital participation and *murabaha*: cost-plus operations (ibid.).

Table 5.7 continued

Source: IMF Direction of Trade Statistics *Yearbook* (1992) and World Bank, *World Development Report* (1992). Adapted from Islamic Development Bank (*Report*) 1991–92

171

Table 5.8 Values of merchandise trade

Country	Exports					Imports				
	1987	1988	1989	1990	1991	1987	1988	1989	1990	1991
Afghanistan	620	694	727	803	933	1,297	1,295	1,355	1,551	1,670
Algeria	8,606	8,207	9,293	12,653	12,314	7,042	8,148	8,931	10,424	9,104
Bahrain	2,387	2,357	2,716	2,847	3,161	2,659	2,667	2,944	3,835	3,993
Bangladesh	1,077	1,291	1,305	1,671	1,688	2,730	3,034	3,618	3,656	3,381
Benin	114	83	110	110	121	349	567	424	549	637
Brunei	1,901	1,707	1,921	2,270	2,597	641	744	1,498	1,723	1,781
Burkina Faso	155	141	146	181	197	375	448	455	523	552
Cameroon	808	1,582	1,768	2,026	1,910	1,718	1,281	1,348	1,555	1,345
Chad	52	58	72	93	90	127	140	165	141	158
Comoros	19	27	26	23	28	71	66	76	91	120
Djibouti	29	45	42	49	55	205	201	197	215	376
Egypt	2,037	2,120	2,648	2,569	3,838	7,595	8,657	7,448	9,170	8,227
Gabon	1,291	1,209	1,522	2,461	2,573	792	927	830	851	962
Gambia	63	96	138	171	166	182	211	182	215	287
Guinea	500	477	585	624	638	412	434	453	539	605
Guinea-Bissau	6	10	7	20	20	85	96	122	120	134
Indonesia	17,170	19,376	21,936	25,675	29,142	12,850	13,489	16,467	22,005	25,869
Iran	11,036	8,154	11,360	15,329	15,916	9,369	8,171	12,807	15,716	21,688
Iraq	9,705	9,688	12,246	10,401	297	7,342	9,332	9,769	6,545	284
Jordan	919	1,020	1,098	923	879	2,708	2,802	2,136	2,607	2,512
Kuwait	10,300	8,359	11,044	8,149	422	5,608	6,265	6,394	4,050	3,882
Lebanon	497	629	484	496	490	1,832	2,408	2,263	2,578	3,748
Libya	8,047	6,908	8,617	10,759	10,775	4,339	4,275	4,393	5,557	6,001
Malaysia	17,934	21,096	25,049	29,420	34,405	12,701	16,567	22,589	29,170	36,749
Maldives	31	40	45	52	54	98	113	143	148	161
Mali	146	166	196	283	294	467	484	499	578	570
Mauritania	428	508	451	469	515	382	447	351	388	472
Morocco	2,946	3,464	3,312	4,130	5,149	4,244	4,703	5,489	6,546	7,458
Niger	402	359	304	274	241	357	404	390	410	407
Oman	3,223	4,031	4,363	4,584	7,236	1,959	2,202	2,258	2,726	3,310
Pakistan	4,168	4,509	4,660	5,587	6,494	5,819	6,588	7,107	7,383	8,432
Qatar	1,995	2,078	2,490	3,292	3,198	1,134	1,267	1,326	1,695	1,862
Saudi Arabia	22,602	23,737	27,741	44,416	51,719	20,110	21,784	21,153	24,069	34,587
Senegal	755	591	670	722	737	1,176	1,080	1,235	1,434	1,359
Sierra Leone	130	106	138	138	145	137	156	183	216	246
Somalia	141	126	120	150	106	456	312	403	403	197
Sudan	492	490	587	516	358	1,058	1,094	1,299	1,185	1,419
Syria	1,353	1,345	3,006	4,218	3,700	2,487	2,231	2,084	2,401	2,857
Tunisia	2,135	2,425	3,035	3,954	3,827	2,837	3,696	4,434	5,944	5,445
Turkey	10,238	11,753	11,823	12,959	13,335	14,655	14,695	17,051	22,302	22,576
Uganda	303	319	273	184	171	513	473	458	463	464

Table 5.8 continued

Country	Exports					Imports				
	1987	*1988*	*1989*	*1990*	*1991*	*1987*	*1988*	*1989*	*1990*	*1991*
U.A.										
Emirates	14,178	13,935	17,951	23,539	24,261	6,901	8,526	9,559	11,472	16,049
Yemen										
Republic	110	828	1,205	1,582	1,205	1,541	2,086	2,015	2,420	2,555
Total:	161,049	166,144	196,870	240,772	245,400	149,360	164,566	184,301	215,569	244,491

Source: Islamic Development Bank (*Report*) 1991–92

These organisations, apart from syphoning money away from other institutions, can convey political overtones:

> The IICs are the economic symbol of rising Islamic tendences in Egypt. The shift in the ideological makeup of Egyptians toward Islam has made them ready to deposit their money in the IICs. They use nonusurous concepts of economics and Islamic symbols. They open their speeches and their advertisements with Qu'ranic verses.
>
> (Abdel Monem Said Aly 1992 p. 53)

Some IICs are linked to the Muslim Brotherhood but generally religious leaders and personalities are recruited as consultants. Islamic groups 'propagate the idea of an independent Islamic economy' and these companies play an important role (ibid.). From the perspective of Egypt and other countries with strong Islamic communities, the position is complex; whilst the IMF/World Bank hand down strictures on privatisation and economic liberalisation, Islamic companies are organising alternative forms of economic exchange. When the Egyptian government passed Law 146 in 1988 legalising and regulating Islamic companies, Hasan Al-Gamal,a Muslim Brotherhood member of the People's Assembly condemned the law as representing a 'conspiracy against the Islamic solution and the Islamic movement.' (ibid. p. 54). At this point it is, perhaps, appropriate not to lose sight of the fact that petro-dollars were invested in Western banks suggesting that the adoption of 'Islamic economics' has not always been entirely obligatory under Shariah. Equally, a number of the Islamic investment companies have been criticised for resorting to 'Islamic rhetoric to legitimise their activity' (Zubaida 1990).

173

From its inception the IDB has been keen to develop a close working relationship with national development finance institutions (NDFIs) in order to reach various sectors of the economies of member countries and to contribute to the financing of small-and medium-scale industries. NDFIs submit requests for development project funding to the Board of Executive Directors of the IDB for approval. Lines of financing can be established between the IDB and approved NDFIs in which case the institutions themselves approve finance for projects up to a certain amount. Close links are also established between the IDB and various Islamic banks, the Islamic Centre for Development and Trade, the Islamic Chamber of Commerce and Industry and Commodity Exchange in attempts to increase the role and influence of the private sector in member states. The bank set up the Islamic Research and Training Institute and also allocates monies for the opaquely named 'Assistance for Islamic causes' (Islamic Development Bank 1991 p. 159). Its relationship with the Saudi Arabian Monetary Agency is that of a depository and trustee and the Agency manages certain funds in consultation with the Bank. Interestingly, the Bank has deposits with commercial banks which are used in the purchase and sale of commodities. Trading is conducted by commercial banks on behalf of the IDB. The discretion of the commercial banks over buying and selling is limited by the terms of the agreement between IDB and the commercial banks. However, it is the commercial banks who guarantee the liability of third parties in respect of all trans-actions, thereby acting as a form of underwriter. Transactions take place between 'Western' banks and 'Islamic' banks to the obvious benefit of both sectors. The IDB itself, however, is cautious about the economic environment and admits that 'a shadow over the economic prospects of IDB members and other developing countries persists' (ibid. p. 33). Economists maintain, however, that notwithstanding the efforts of the IDB, Islamic banks in general have invested very little in industry. The reason for this omission is largely because finance for industry has to be long term whereas the banks can only offer finance on a short-term basis (Hardie and Rabooy 1991 p. 66).

The UN Economic Commission for Africa (UNECA) set up the first Arab–African Trade Fair in Ethiopia in 1993. UNECA believes that the Trade Fair could 'rekindle links between Africa and the Arab world which have existed for centuries' (UNECA, *African Trade* 1993). The main elements in the Fair were: investment, trade promotion, cultural linkages and tourism. UNECA listed the challenges facing Africa:

1 How to restore the African people's sense of self-pride in order to reactivate the spirit of self-determination and self-reliance.
2 How to make the development process human centred and thereby ensure that development is an effort of, by and for people.
3 How to internalise the development process in Africa by increasing the domestic contribution to that process and reducing the heavy dependency of the continent on technical assistance.
4 How to improve Africa's adaptive capabilities to respond to international developments.

(ibid.)

The challenges are, of course, enormous but some trade linkages have been established between certain countries of the Middle East and Africa. Since 1993 trade co-operation agreements have been signed between Sudan and Iraq, Zambia and Iran, Nigeria, Egypt and Israel, Comoros and Egypt, Eritrea and Yemen and Kenya and Israel. South Africa and Iran have agreed to co-operate in the banking sector and have established a joint economic commission. African and Arab member states of the ICO do not lack the necessary resource base for a better future. They command, as a group, 'a rich endowment of natural resources and minerals, a big market of around one billion consumers and a relatively important number of scientists and experts in various disciplines scattered all over the world' (Zeinelabdin 1993). Their relative underdevelopment results from technological backwardness and dependence: most of the ICO countries lack the basic technologies essential for the realisation of their industrial revolution' (ibid.). The phenomenon of modern and traditional economic sectors in many countries stems from an alienation of science and technology from production systems with the result that the modern sector enjoys the benefits of imported technology, whilst the traditional sector is left technologically backward. These factors, combined with misguided government policies and a lack of labour skills create a situation in which firms operate within 'highly unfavourable structures and institutional set-ups from the very beginning' (ibid.). Zeinelabdin looks to the newly industrialising countries, such as South Korea, with their export promotion policies and adaptability, to provide lessons for the countries of Africa and the Middle East. Also, the linking of the ICO and the UN in a co-operation programme could ensure a flow of information and a more structured dialogue about technology–environment–economic policy.

Certainly, the increasing 'technology gap' between the developed and developing world is of growing signficance. However, another issue defined by international organisations as important is the need to integrate environmental considerations into development and economic policymaking.

ENVIRONMENT

The United Nations Conference on Environment and Development, often referred to as the 'Earth Summit', held in June 1992 maintained that accelerated, sustainable economic and human development could be consistent with improving environmental conditions if major changes of policy took place. The World Bank Report on the Environment and Development believes a two-fold strategy is required: first, the positive links between income growth and the environment need to be 'aggressively exploited.' For example, this calls for the removal of distortionary policies, such as subsidies for energy, chemical inputs, water and logging, that encourage the overuse of national resources. It also calls for expanded emphasis on population programmes, female education, agricultural extension and research, sanitation and clean water and for more local participation in the design and implementation of development programmes. Second, strong policies and institutions need to be put into place which cause decision-makers – corporations, households, farmers and governments, to adopt less-damanging forms of behaviour (World Bank (1993) *Environment and Development*).

The Islamic Development Bank (IDB) recognises that growing international concern with environmental problems presents challenges to its member countries, but it fears the 'international preoccupation with environmental protection might be one-sided and to the detriment of developing countries' (IDB 1991–1992 p. 32). Ghayth Armanazi of the League of Arab States admits that 'the environment is not a burning issue in the Middle East today' (Armanazi 1995; conference). In the name of environmental protection, obstacles may be raised which impede developing countries from exploiting some of their natural resources, such as forest reserves or fossil fuel, or from vigorously pursuing their industrial development objectives (ibid.). Environmental concerns may cause new conditions to be imposed on developing countries which add to the costs and burdens of economic development. It is, therefore, essential, the IDB asserts, that while pursuing environmentally sound policies and practices, IDB members continue to stress the importance of economic development and the need for the developed countries to shoulder their fair share of environmental protection costs (IDB 1991–1992 p. 32–33). According to the IDB the environment remains a subject of controversy between the developed and developing countries and the 'Earth Summit' contributed to a feeling of disappointment in the developing world mainly because of the failure of the developed world to make 'significant financial commitments towards the implementation of Agenda 21'. Agenda 21 is a blueprint for environmental and global development for the twenty-first century which addresses most of the world's environmental and development problems with urgent corrective action. Yet out of a prospective financial requirement of $US 70 billion, pledges of barely $US2.5 billion were made by the industrialised countries.

The countries of the Middle East have, however, co-operated with the United Nations Envrionment Programme over resolutions concerning industrial pollution control, diversification and improving environmental information. A Council of Arab Ministers Responsible for Environment (CAMRE) has been established to draw up a clearly defined Arab Plan for Action for international co-operation. Nevertheless, as far as actual policies are concerned, few have been introduced. A Global Environment Facility set up in 1990, initially on a three-year demonstration project, acknowledged that developing countries are 'financially hard-pressed' and find it difficult to 'grapple with their domestic environmental difficulties' (World Bank (1993) *Global Environment Facility*). The GEF linked three agencies – the World Bank, the United Nations Environment Programme and the United Nations Development Programme. Its work falls into four main areas: reducing global warming, protecting international waters, preserving biological diversity and preventing further depletion of the ozone layer. The International Development Association (IDA), who lends to the poorest nations, maintains that poor people are often the most vulnerable to environmental degradation:

The health of hundreds of millions of people is endangered by contaminated drinking water and polluted air. The productivity of natural resources is being lost in many places because of the overuse and pollution of renewable resources such as soils, water, forests and the atmosphere

(World Bank (1993) *IDA and the Environment*)

177

Certainly the wood fuel crisis in sub-Saharan Africa is judged to be 'alarming and needing urgent action', by the UN Environment programmes assistant executive director, Dr Jan Huismans. The most pressing problem relates to the unsustainable and inefficient use of wood, charcoal and dung which particularly affect women and children through inhallation of smoke fumes (Economic Report SWB/0356 25 October 1994).

The Heritage 2000 World Conservation Union and Commission on National Parks and Protected Areas conference held in South Africa in 1994 was attended by 123 delegates from over 30 African countries. Because protected areas are being eroded by wars, civil disorder, the collapse of administrative structures and an expanding human population, a declaration was issued calling on all governments in Africa:

1 To protect areas with sufficient resources to enable them to yield benefits to all people;
2 To negotiate additional resources from international sources;
3 To work in partnership with each other.

Good environmental practices are seen not only to improve the quality of people's lives but also to have high economic returns particularly if valuable natural resources are managed well and produce permanent benefits (World Bank (1993) *IDA and the Environment*). However, it may not be that straightforward. One study points to the low world prices for primary product exports of sub-Saharan African states which means they have to export more in order to earn foreign income. In the process, unsustainable exploitation of natural resources is involved which leads to environmental degradation (Kainyah 1995). Viewed from this perspective a more equitable international trade system is called for. Clearly then, environmental factors, important though they are, are only part of the economic difficulties facing poorer nations. One other major concern is that of debt.

DEBT

The debt crisis in the developing world has become a predominant issue. The obligation to repay debt has become a heavy burden for developing countries with other pressing needs that also require financing. The debt crisis, which began in the 1980s, was marked by three major turning points: the suspension of loan payments to commercial banks by Mexico in 1982; the 1985 Baker Plan of new lending to indebted countries; and the Brady Initiative for debt reduction devised in 1989 (see Appendix 2). The World Bank accept that in the 1990s 'debt will continue to be a burden for some developing countries', and that further debt reduction, rescheduling and cancellations are needed so highly indebted, developing countries can devote a greater portion of their resources to productive investments (World Bank (1993) *The Debt Crisis* – See Appendix 2 for details of debt measures and a glossary of debt terms). In recognising the severity of the debt situation, the IDB points to the fact that the total external debt of all its member countries, including the oil exporting states, the non-oil exporting states and the least developed states, increased in 1990 and 1991 (Islamic Development Bank 1991–1992 p. 30).

Table 5.9 contrasts Africa's debt picture between North Africa and sub-Saharan Africa by country. With the exception of Libya, which normally has a credit position and whose obligations to the outside world are fairly small, Egypt, Morocco, Tunisia and Algeria, in spite of the disproportionate structure of their debts, have regularly honoured their commitments. Net transfers relating to debt can be improved by an influx of direct investment. The volume of the North African region's commitments declined by 6.3 per cent from $123.4 billion in 1991 to $115.6 billion in 1992, resulting from the measures taken by creditors to write off and reschedule part of Egypt's debts. However, the commitments of sub-Saharan Africa countries, including Sudan, were estimated to have amounted to $US182.3 billion in 1992, increasing by 3.8 per cent compared to the 1991 level. In spite of the fact that drawing from official lenders in 1992 and the infusion of concessional loans continued at a rate similar to that of 1991 and in spite of an 8.7 per cent growth in the disbursement of medium- and long-term loans, the net-resource flows were appreciably reduced by the transfers made to cover debt servicing.

Jean Thisen, analysing a projection of Africa's external debt by the year 2000, asserts that although in the early 1990s Africa was ranked as the 'least indebted continent' the fragile structure of African economies makes the problem of debt service 'one of the most crippling and constraining factors in their process of economic development'. This situation can only be eased by either a cancellation and/or conversion into grants of around 20 per cent of official debts and the restructuring of the remainder with a lengthening of the debt maturity to possibly 40 years (Thisen 1994 p. 4). Economic factors in Africa and the Middle East are complex. An inspection of social and economic data for both regions reveals differences in most categories: literacy rates, life expectancy and in the breakdown of the labour force. It would appear that in economic terms the regions are moving further apart.

NOTES

1 Development economists Paul Rosenstein-Rodan, Ragnar Nurkse and Albert Hirschman consider this issue in *World Development Report, Infrastructure for Development,* World Bank 1994.

Table 5.9 Trends in African external debt stock, 1971–92 ($US bn)

Region/ Country	1971	1975	1980	1985	1990	1991	1992*	Distribution (%) 1992	Growth rate per annum (%) 1971–91
North Africa:	**4.90**	**13.12**	**58.78**	**91.07**	**116.56**	**123.35**	**115.59**	**41.02**	**17.1**
Algeria	1.26	4.63	19.36	18.40	29.79	28.64	28.50	10.12	16.9
Egypt	1.81	4.35	20.92	42.13	40.10	49.18	40.62	14.41	16.8
Libya	–	–	–	–	–	–	–	–	–
Morocco	0.87	1.73	9.71	16.53	23.62	21.22	21.56	7.65	17.3
Sudan	0.34	1.38	5.26	9.13	15.34	15.91	16.10	5.71	21.2
Tunisia	0.62	1.03	3.53	4.88	7.71	8.30	8.81	3.13	13.9
West Africa	**2.85**	**5.31**	**24.55**	**44.14**	**75.39**	**79.51**	**84.50**	**30.00**	**18.00**
Benin	0.05	0.08	0.42	0.82	1.22	1.34	1.48	0.52	17.7
Burkina Faso	0.02	0.06	0.13	0.33	0.51	1.02	0.96	0.34	20.1
Cape Verde	0.00	0.01	0.02	0.01	0.15	0.16	0.16	0.06	18.9
Côte d'Ivoire	0.37	1.04	5.85	9.74	18.08	18.85	22.23	7.89	21.7
Gambia	0.01	0.01	0.14	0.25	0.35	0.39	0.41	0.15	19.5
Ghana	0.54	0.73	1.41	2.23	3.76	4.21	4.59	1.63	10.8
Guinea	0.43	0.76	1.11	1.45	2.48	2.64	2.70	0.96	9.5
Guinea-Bissau	0.00	0.01	0.13	0.31	0.60	0.65	0.65	0.23	29.8
Liberia	0.16	0.18	0.69	1.24	1.87	1.99	2.01	0.72	13.4
Mali	0.27	0.36	0.73	2.47	2.43	2.62	2.73	0.97	11.8
Mauritania	0.04	0.19	0.85	1.50	2.21	2.29	2.69	0.95	22.4
Niger	0.04	0.11	0.86	1.21	1.83	1.65	1.69	0.60	20.4
Nigeria	0.65	1.14	8.93	19.55	34.55	34.50	35.31	12.53	21.9
Senegal	0.15	0.35	1.47	2.56	3.34	4.66	4.13	1.47	17.1
Sierra-Leone	0.07	0.16	0.76	0.44	0.72	1.18	1.29	0.46	15.2
Togo	0.05	0.12	1.05	0.94	1.29	1.36	1.47	0.52	17.9
Central Africa:	**0.91**	**2.34**	**11.39**	**14.91**	**27.99**	**29.99**	**30.91**	**11.0**	**19.1**
Burundi	0.01	0.02	0.17	0.46	0.91	0.96	1.11	0.39	25.6
Cameroon	0.17	0.42	2.51	2.94	5.99	6.88	6.97	2.47	20.3
Central African Republic	0.03	0.08	0.19	0.35	0.77	0.88	0.92	0.33	18.4
Chad	0.05	0.09	0.23	0.19	0.51	0.61	0.67	0.25	13.3
Congo	0.14	0.35	1.53	3.03	4.82	4.70	4.95	1.76	19.2
Equatorial Guinea	0.01	0.03	0.08	0.13	0.24	0.25	0.27	0.10	17.5
Gabon	0.13	0.77	1.51	1.21	3.64	3.84	4.17	1.17	18.5
Rwanda	0.01	0.02	0.19	0.37	0.74	1.01	1.07	0.38	20.5
São Tomé and Principe	0.00	0.01	0.02	0.06	0.15	0.16	0.18	0.07	18.9
Zaïre	0.36	0.55	4.96	6.17	10.22	10.70	10.63	3.78	18.5

Table 5.9 continued

Region/ Country	1971	1975	1980	1985	1990	1991	1992*	Distri- bution (%) 1992	Growth rate per annum (%) 1971–91
East **Southern** **Africa**	**2.49**	**6.86**	**16.56**	**27.55**	**45.37**	**47.44**	**50.80**	**18.0**	**15.8**
Angola	–	–	–	–	–	–	–	–	–
Botswana	0.03	0.15	0.13	0.33	0.52	0.68	0.74	0.26	15.5
Comoros	0.01	0.02	0.04	0.13	0.18	0.19	0.20	0.07	15.9
Djibouti	0.01	0.02	0.03	0.14	0.20	0.22	0.24	0.08	16.7
Ethiopia	0.20	0.34	0.81	1.88	3.26	3.61	3.82	1.36	15.3
Kenya	0.43	1.11	3.45	4.18	7.01	7.01	7.50	2.66	14.9
Lesotho	0.01	0.02	0.07	0.17	0.39	0.43	0.49	0.17	20.7
Madagascar	0.10	1.84	1.22	2.47	3.63	4.37	4.09	1.45	19.8
Malawi	0.14	0.26	0.82	0.88	1.58	1.61	1.89	0.67	12.9
Mauritius	0.03	0.05	0.47	0.63	0.95	0.99	1.08	0.38	19.1
Mozambique	0.01	0.02	1.41	2.86	4.92	5.35	6.03	2.14	36.9
Seychelles	0.00	0.01	0.01	0.01	0.20	0.20	0.21	0.07	16.2
Somalia	0.08	0.23	0.66	1.64	2.37	2.44	2.77	0.98	18.6
Swaziland	0.09	0.15	0.21	0.22	0.28	0.29	0.30	0.11	18.3
Tanzania	0.26	0.89	2.48	3.75	6.13	6.46	6.85	2.43	17.4
Uganda	0.17	0.21	0.70	1.23	2.64	2.83	2.97	1.05	15.1
Zambia	0.69	1.35	3.26	4.62	7.26	7.28	7.86	2.79	12.5
Zimbabwe	0.23	0.19	0.79	2.41	3.85	3.48	3.76	1.33	14.5
Total developing Africa		15.40	39.50	100.60	174.40	278.80	281.00	281.80	100.00	14.8
Sub-Saharan Africa		10.84	27.76	47.08	92.46	177.58	175.56	182.31	64.70	14.4

Source: UN Conference on Trade and Development, no. 82, Geneva, 1994

Part IV
CONFLICT

6

VIOLENCE, WARS AND
CIVIL DISORDER

INTRODUCTION

Perhaps one of the most distressing and debilitating features of states in the Middle East and Africa in the recent past, and one which has profoundly affected the lives and life-chances of many people, has been the seemingly endless capacity for violent struggle. Wars, racial hatred, civil disorder and spiralling military expenditure have been characteristics of the two regions. In the Middle East, the Arab/Israeli dispute has given rise to conflicts in 1967 and 1973 and both the Islamic Republic of Iran and the Arab Republic of Iraq have contributed to regional beligerency largely because of their assumed roles of respective regional pre-eminence. Iraq's invasion of Kuwait in August 1990 was one demonstration of a deluded step towards leading the 'Arab nation', and the Islamic Revolution in Iran in 1979 set down a challenge to the Arab world.

A feature apparent in both the Middle East and Africa has been the linkage between political organisations and military groups. In Lebanon, a number of parties had their own militias and similar associations can be found in Africa, eg. the Rwandese Patriotic Army (RPA) is the armed wing of the Rwandese Patriotic Front (RPA). Between 1975 and 1990 Lebanon was plunged into a civil war which threatened to split the country and since 1994 Rwanda has suffered an appalling ethnic conflict which at times witnessed the indiscriminate slaughter of thousands of people (*Observer* 10 July 1994). Some wars have lasted almost a generation. In Angola a civil war continued for 19 years between the National Union for the Total Independence of Angola (UNITA) under the leadership of Dr Jonas Savimbi and the Popular Movement for the Liberation of Angola (MPLA) headed by the country's President José Eduardo dos Santos. The war began at the country's independence from Portugese colonial rule. Civil wars have taken place in the early 1990s in Ethiopia, Sudan and Somalia. A high-ranking expert on Somalia has spoken of the conflict and insecurity in Somalia being a function of the country's politics.

Certainly, Islamic influences have been powerful factors in a number of conflicts and so too has been the ease with which weaponry is imported. Writing in the late 1980s of civil/military relations in Uganda, Kokole and Mazrui referred to the 'sheer availability of arms and ammunition' within the country (Kokole and Mazrui 1988 p. 279). Sometimes arms are imported illegally, at other times they are stolen. Richard Dowden claimed that Rwandan militias had stolen weapons from army barracks in the neighbouring country of Uganda (*The Tablet* 18 June 1994). Militias armed with an array of weaponry hunted both ethnic groups, the Hutus and the Tutsis in Rwanda 'with a diabolical frenzy'. According to one refugee everyone was under threat: 'They kill you just for looking at them' (ibid.). However, some African and Arab political leaders have attempted to control the power of militias and armies. After the 1991 Gulf War, militias were disbanded in the Lebanon and encouraged to lay down their arms. The Prime Minister of Zaïre announced to parliament in 1994 that attempts would be made 'to ban all units of the armed forces from roaming about in uniform with weapons, when not on duty'. Zaïre TV reported the sense of relief and support for the policy from parliamentary members who recognised that such activity was contrary to military discipline and a 'dangerous threat to public order' (SWB ALW/0342 19 July 1994). Yet reports emerged in 1995 that Kenyan youths were being trained in guerrilla warfare in Sudan with the purpose of inciting Muslims against Christians (SWB AL/2275 11 April 1995). Although all states need strong, disciplined, well-equipped, well-trained and motivated armies, weak and dilapidated states create a malaise and lack of order within the military and lead to a breakdown of security. If armies become linked with modernity and are seen as providing a service in the process of development they become more than adjuncts of government and can come to regard themselves as actual embodiments of the state.

The fact that separate military groups and ex-guerilla organisations supporting various political factions gained access to powerful positions often reflected the struggle against imperialism and the weak structures of the post-colonial state. But as Kokole and Mazrui proclaimed:

Most African countries have no external foes; in many cases the soldiers are trained to fight external enemies. In reality, they end up fighting domestic political rivals. The soldiers are trained in the arts of killing and fighting but should have been trained in the skills of law enforcement.

(Kokole and Mazrui 1988 p. 285)

Conflicts within states, rather than between states, have inevitably inflicted heavy suffering on innocent populations. This is a central problem which finds echoes in numerous countries. In July 1994, representatives of the government of Burundi together with a number of opposition parties admitted that weapons were being distributed to people and that illegal imports of arms were available in most provinces. Groups of armed activists terrorised people and attacked peaceful citizens (SWB AL/2044 11 July 1994). Concern was expressed about the degree of insecurity which had become widespread throughout the country with growing disorder in several provinces.

In speeches given by Baroness Chalker, the Minister for Overseas Development in 1994/1995 attention focused on the issue of civil/military relations in the developing world. The Overseas Development Administration (ODA) was helping many countries develop civil police capacity in place of military alternatives particularly in Ethiopia, Somalia, Gaza and the West Bank. Efforts were concentrated on making the police more responsive to local communities. More than 30 countries were receiving training by the British police (Chalker July 1994 and March 1995; meeting). However, in attempting to discover reasons for the continuing influence of military groups and the fact that civil–military relations are often tense, it is necessary to consider the role of the military in the recent past.

MILITARY

Lucian Pye wrote in the 1960s that it 'occurred to few students of the underdeveloped regions that the military might become the critical group in shaping the course of nation-building' (Pye 1966 p. 291). Certainly, army-dominated government became a feature of post-independent Third World states and to a degree defined a political process which linked the countries of the developing world. Weak political institutions in transitional polities, the importance of nation building and national integration and the significance of the army in pursuing anti-colonial struggles before independence were contributory factors which prompted a number of academics to conclude that the military could provide a modernising function in underdeveloped countries (Huntington 1967; Finer 1962; Pye 1966). To some analysts, the military came to represent sovereignty and independence and consequently became the 'ultimate coercive force in the state' (Apter 1967 p. 406). David Apter maintained that military oligarchies emerged in different political systems in a number of ways: first, where military rule followed a *coup d'état*; second, where societies were highly structured and discipline was required of everyone, where workers were referred to as 'soldiers of the state', eg. China; third, in a modernising autocracy, such as existed in early post-colonial states, 'a military oligarchy comes to power through the institutionalisation and professionalisation of authority which has come to rely on the military as an organisation' (ibid.).

Military organisations could change in character: workers' militias, people's armies as in Ghana, hierarchical armies as in Nigeria, armies associated very closely with ruling political groups, eg. Ba'th Parties in Iraq and Syria. Yet the nature of the combatant army suggests that conflict is never very far away. Lucien Pye explains that 'armies are created for future contingencies and in many underdeveloped countries these contingencies have never to be faced' (Pye 1966 p. 299). Nevertheless, in some instances the military saw itself as saving a country from corrupt civilian government, but in Nigeria in 1966, Ghana in 1972 and Sierra Leone in 1968 it was democratic systems, however faltering, that were overthrown. According to Apter the military may see themselves as representing modern forces against all forms of traditionalism, 'whether of caste, class or premodern cultural attributes' (Apter 1967 p. 407). Some even see the distinction between civilian and military regimes to be more apparent than real in that often in the developing world there is very little to choose between two invariably authoritarian forms of government (Luckham 1991 p. 367).

Samuel Finer, in his seminal work on the military, *The Man on Horseback*, argued that there is 'a distinct class of countries where governments have been repeatedly subjected to the interference of their armed forces'. Neither liberal democratic nor totalitarian societies, these states fall somewhere on the margins of political efficacy and often have continual military interventions. Finer saw military interference not 'as a mere set of ephemeral, exceptional and isolated adventures' but as a political phenomenon far more profound; one that was 'abiding, deep seated and distinctive' (Finer 1962 p. 4). In part, he saw the prevalence of the military as a reflection of society at a low level of political culture, one that was in a process of transition, where legitimacy and consensus were largely irrelevant and, perhaps more significantly, ones that were 'deeply divided by cultural and ethnic pluralism' (ibid. p. 129). It was not necessarily the case that the peoples of those states had no political ideas or were unable to act from political conviction but rather there was little cohesion within the population. When issues arose they were often decided by force or the threat of it and in countries divided by tribalism or race this could involve whole masses in bitter internecine conflict. Inevitably, under these conditions the military would emerge as a superior organisation with the additional benefit of possessing arms. In a sense, a culture would develop among the population which accepted the power and influence of the military as authoritative and potentially violent. In these circumstances the military did not require the assistance or association of civilian institutions in order to maintain power; it was itself the sole political force (ibid. p. 130). Finer's interpretation carries a resonance in the 1990s and partly explains the ease with which armies and militias operate almost uncontrollably in some countries.

Some analysts, however, have suggested that the military is capable of contributing radical social renewal (Falola and Ihonvbere 1985). More usually armies tend to follow their own interests as the events surrounding Nigeria's attempts at electoral politics indicates. The presidential elections of 1993 were annulled by Nigeria's military government on the alleged grounds of fraud and the presumed winner of the elections, Moshood Abiola, was subsequently imprisoned. The head of state, General Sani Abacha at Army Day celebrations stressed the need for members of the armed forces to remain committed to the protection of the territorial integrity of Nigeria, and expressed confidence in the combat readiness of the Nigerian Army (*Financial Times* 14 July 1994; SWB AL/2043 9 July 1994). According to Lasswell and Kaplan, 'an arena is military when the expectation of violence is high; civic when the expectation is low' (Lasswell and Kaplan 1950 p. 252). Some societies seem to be in permanent political crisis and ultimately military force is used as the last resort.

Although commitments have been made by Nigeria's military government to move towards a system of civil administration, there has been a clear reluctance on their part to carry such a policy through. This tendency supports the view that the military becomes distanced from the needs of society as a whole and as a result rules in its own interests and allocates resources for its own purposes. Shehu Othman maintains that: 'Coups have merely provided a means of creating further opportunities for soldiers' (Othman 1991 p. 144). Since the Second World War, especially in the Middle East and Africa, incidents in which a 'non-governmental body attempts to overthrow and replace an established government has become a common if not normal pattern of political change' (Garnett 1991 p. 81). John Garnett believes that the 'frequency and persistence of military violence provides prima facie evidence that large numbers of people continue to think that military power is useful, perhaps even an indispensable, instrument of policy' (ibid).

The military expenditure of numerous states in Africa and the Middle East often vastly exceeds resources devoted to, say, education or healthcare. Pye asserts that for all their supposed concern with rationality and efficiency the military are relatively immune to real pragmatic tests of their capabilities (p. 298). There are no elections, they are not accountable, there is always the option of a recourse to violence; in short, military governments are under no obligation to meet any requirements of the population as a whole. These facts are often compounded because certain ethnic groups are over-represented in particular armies and under-represented in others. The military wing of the Ba'th Party of Syria is predominantly Alawite in ethnic composition, a group which represents only 10 per cent of the population. Table 6.1 indicates the regional aggregates of military expenditure and resource-use imbalances.

According to the United Nations Development Programme (*Human Development Report*):

> The concept of security must change from an exclusive stress on national security to a much greater stress on people's security, from security through armaments to security through human development, from territorial security to food, employment and environmental security.
>
> (UN Development Programme 1993 p. 2)

These views were echoed at the OAU Summit in Tunis in June 1994 when President Ben Ali of Tunisia in his opening address spoke of the African continent as an arena for a number of conflicts and wars caused by 'various aspects giving rise to the spread of

VIOLENCE, WARS AND CIVIL DISORDER

Table 6.1 Military expenditure and resource-use imbalances

	Sub-Saharan Africa	Arab States
Military expenditure as % of GDP		
1960	0.7	4.9
1990	3.8	–
Military expenditure as % of health/education expenditure		
1977	86	154
1990	108	275

Source: United Nations Development Programme 1993

violence and extremism'. Mutual dialogues should replace mutual killing and co-operation between countries should 'rise above political, racial and national differences'. The president called for the establishment of a 'behaviour charter' which would organise relations between the continent's states on the basis of their unanimous attachment to the principles and aims of the OAU and the UN. The basis of this charter would be a respect for the principles of good-neighbourliness, brotherhood, solidarity, non-interference in the countries' internal affairs, the peaceful settlement of conflicts and the avoidance of all forms of violence and extremism (SWB AL/2023 16 June 1994).

A centre for conflict management, established in Cairo in order to boost efforts to resolve and prevent conflicts in Africa, intends to provide an apparatus which trains African military and civilian groups in the fields of pre-emptive diplomacy and peace keeping. Through such a process an understanding could be consolidated between peoples. Funding for the centre would come from Egypt initially as well as from the United Nations. Egypt's Foreign Minister, Amr Moussa, declared that a process of disarmament must take place within the countries of the continent. Egypt sees itself as a medium-sized power with a responsibility to maintain peace and stability in other areas, especially, Africa. The question of demobilising armies is one which has exercised the political acumen of African leaders. A workshop on post-conflict demobilisation held at the Uganda International Conference Centre in November 1994 was organised by the OAU in conjunction with the international

191

organisation, Global Coalition for Africa. It was co-chaired by the OAU's Assistant Secretary-General, Dr Mapulanga and the former US Assistant Secretary of State, Hermann Cohen, and was attended by more than 70 delegates from Africa and elsewhere. Ugandan President Museveni spoke of the importance of demobilisation for the good of the national economy because of the release of funds and resources for services such as education and health. But he also raised a note of caution when referring to the army as one of the 'pillars of the state', along with the police, the civil service, the judiciary and the legislature. In situations where the institutions of democracy were not secure, he asserted, there must be someone to 'enforce the decisions of democracy' (Radio Uganda, SWB AL/2150 11 November 1994). Demobilisation must not, then, be treated as an end in itself and account must be taken of the political circumstances which gave rise to the strength of the army in the first place. In any case, demobilised soldiers would have to be retrained, equipped with new skills, and prepared for civilian life (ibid). Nevertheless, with assistance from the international community and at the initial cost of $US18 million, 12, 500 Ugandan soldiers were demobilised in 1995 (Radio Uganda, SWB AL/2254 17 March 1995). One of the most positive developments during the period of elections in Mozambique has been the rapid pace of demilitarisation. At the end of the war, Frelimo had 62, 000 troops and Renamo 21,000. Most former combatants have returned to the land but other demobilised soldiers are organised by the Association of Demobilised Soldiers (AMODEG) (Haines and Wood 1995).

Proposals have been made that a Pan-African armed force should be formed in order to resolve conflicts within the continent; Africans would largely be responsible for policing African disputes. However, some African leaders have not supported this notion. President Daniel arap Moi of Kenya opposed the creation of such a force because of suspicions that it would be as likely to kill the people it was intended to protect (SWB AL/2054 22 July 1994). President Moi's fears provide a savage picture of the untrustworthiness and potential volatility and brutality of the armed forces across the continent. Repeated news reports from a number of African states stress the desperate need to curb the power and enhance the discipline of military forces and abolish separate militia groups. In Zaïre, the maintenance of militias or any other private paramilitary organisation is prohibited by law. Any citizen in possession of firearms was requested to hand them over to the Ministry of Defence and Security of Territory by 31 July 1994 (SWB AL/2050 18 July 1994). Regional organisations have attempted to suppress conflicts. Ecomog, the Economic Community of West African States Cease-Fire Monitoring Group, has established itself as a peace-keeping force and draws attention to any illegal arms trading. Ecomog can deploy troops on borders and provide a buffer zone. Equally external countries can call on African states to curb outbursts of violence. Saudi Arabia asked Somalia to 'end the bloodshed' and start rebuilding the country in the interest of the Somali people and Islam (SWB AL/2242 3 March 1995). Yet the impoverished economic environment of many African states impedes their attempts to deal with regional conflicts. The defence ministers from east, central and southern African countries agreed to create a rapid deployment force to cope with disputes and attempt to stop *coups d'état* but they complained they had no resources to pay for such a force which would need to be mobilised at short notice. In co-operation with the South African Development Community, defence ministers called for the support of the international community (SWB AL/2152 14 November 1994). A United Nations mission in Niger considered the problem of the movement of weapons between countries which profoundly increases the incidence of violence. One well-known NGO, Medecin du Monde, working in north-eastern Ghana decided to withdraw from an area because of the increase in violence largely caused by the availability of automatic weapons. Medecin du Monde admitted they had witnessed automatic weapons arriving in the the area by various different ways (SWB AL/2250 13 March 1995; SWB AL/2255 18 March 1995).

However, Adda B. Bozeman believes that incongruities exist between occidental theory and African reality when it comes to conceptualising violence. Western typologies of violent action: war, aggression or defence, fail to adequately accommodate African 'orientations toward the uses of physical force' (Bozeman 1976 p. 27). Adopting a culturally specific approach, she considers magic, rituals and violence as expressions of traditional society, especially, in Yorubaland. Her view is specific:

> No culturally distinct subsystem comes to mind in which resort to violence is as tenuously linked to a validating ideology or master plan, as closely controlled by pre-modern beliefs in magic and as unaffected by the rules of the game as it is in Africa
>
> (ibid. p. 30–31)

Irrational, arbitrary and indiscriminate acts of violence indicate to Bozeman the senselessness of violent attack in Africa and she conjures images of a Hobbesian state of Nature.

Yet in order to situate violence in its political context, it is necessary to consider the nature of the state in Sub-Saharan Africa, its use of power and its general interaction with the larger society. The legacy of colonialism is seen to have contributed to the establishment of weak post-colonial states and distorted political practices. The trajectory of violence, it is argued, must be traced to the colonial period, which itself was an act of violence against indigenous peoples (Crowder 1987). The political inheritance of those years is clear: 'Government rested not on consent but force' (ibid. p. 12) The imprisonment and criminalisation of nationalist leaders who confronted and challenged the colonial power were hardly lessons in representative, accountable and responsible government. But neither was the spectre of a political elite who cared less for the concepts of freedom, human rights and dignity than for the 'fashioning of a network of patronage and brokerage necessary for accession to office and for its retention' (Ade Ajayi 1982). The conceptualisation of the state in sub-Saharan Africa can be problematic if viewed from a Weberian perspective: a system of permanently institutionalised roles; exclusive right to the legitimate use of force; sovereign power over a given territory. According to one line of argument Western 'political technology' does not readily transfer to other developing nations, and therefore, must remain an 'imported artifact' (Badie and Birnbaum 1983 p. 98). But these views suggest an inherent peculiarity about 'developing nations' whilst overlooking the fact that violence was very much a part of the state-building process in the 'developed' world. Equally, if Western patterns of political behaviour are judged to be inappropriate and inadequate, what of the suitability of the political institution of the Islamic *sharia* state? From the perspective of a secular sub-Saharan African state is an Islamic model of government also an 'imported artifact'.

MILITARY MARXISM

Recourse to violence, then, may be a reflection of the political problem of self-styled leaders, accountable to no-one and largely ignoring the welfare of their peoples. It might also have arisen because of the ideological currents running through the region after the colonial period. Chinese socialist ideas of people's armies and the stress on the inequity of capitalism led to an intellectualising about the role and influence of people's militias in the Third World generally. As recently as 1983, writers were imagining the existence of a 'block of revolutionary nation-states in Southern African' which would maximise the possibility of socialist construction within Africa and elsewhere in the world system (Bush 1983). Militias were examined in terms of their relationship to capital and class division. Robin Luckham looked at military rule from a Marxist perspective questioning: 'To what extent do those who control the superstructure rely on repressive rather than ideological mechanisms to establish their hegemony?' (Luckham 1991 p. 366). It was possible for militias to have a revolutionary function; to represent excluded classes and groups in times of crisis and to harness anti-imperialist, anti-capitalist sentiment. Viewed as such, militias almost became desirable features of the developing world's politics. The process of proletarianisation could be combined with the struggle for national liberation (Magubane 1983 and Nzongola-Ntalaja 1983).

In certain countries, Angola, for example, the Soviet Union and China competed with each other in their support of the armed struggle. Initial tensions between militias regarding the direction 'national liberation' should take ultimately led to killings and a drift into civil war. In Angola, socialist rivalries between the Chinese-supported FNLA and the Cuban and Soviet-backed MPLA resulted in a conflict which continued into the 1990s. These wars were more a consequence of international spheres of interest and competition between different manifestations of the socialist world than outcomes of the rigours of international capitalism. Yet societies were pitched against societies on the basis that the black bourgeoisie were 'couriers of imperialism'. The further advancement of the national liberation struggle, therefore, required that 'African people settle matters with their own bourgeoisie', who had become reformist rather than revolutionary (ibid.). Class struggle connected politicised movements with active militancy and contributed to 'a heightened collective revolutionary consciousness' (Immanuel Wallerstein 1983) An intellectual climate existed which both legitimised and defended violence: 'Military action which toppled a civilian regime must be seen in the context of wider societal class contradictions.' Struggles would inevitably take place depending on the 'correlation of class forces, the degree of organisation of the working class and its enemies' (Aidoo 1983).

To an extent, 'scientific socialism' came to be seen in some quarters as the answer to the Third World's political problems. 'Scientific socialism', based on the principles of Marx and Lenin, was an intellectual amalgam. According to Arnold Hughes 'two parallel routes to what was asserted to be a more orthodox Marxism in Africa emerged by the mid-1970s but in their origins they both differed significantly from the classical Marxist path to power' (Hughes 1992 p. 10) These movements were referred to as 'Afro-Marxist', or 'Afro-Communist' (cf. Young 1980; Ottaway and Ottaway 1986). One important feature of these movements was the fact they were invariably led by disaffected soldiers. Country followed country, Somalia, Benin, Ethiopia, Madagascar, Ghana and Burkino Faso in their eagerness to pronounce People's Republics led by radical, revolutionary, Marxist military groups.

Elsewhere anti-colonial guerrilla movements were developing in the old Portuguese colonies of the Cape Verde and São Tomé who also articulated revolutionary sentiments. In fact, by 1977 Frelimo, an anti-colonial movement in predominantly rural Mozambique, formally declared itself a 'Marxist-Leninist party of the Working Class'. By the 1980s, estimates put about one-fifth of the countries of Africa under the Marxist–Leninist umbrella, all with a military component. The disturbing aspect of this development is not necessarily that variations of Marxist

Leninist rhetoric became a chant to be repeated in various underdeveloped states, but that credibility was given to military rulers in the name of 'revolutionary' politics. People's militias were not simply tolerated, they were almost revered by those who defended their strategies. More damagingly in the long term and one reason why militias, arms trading, immediate recourse to military solutions and, at times, indiscriminate killing continue to be features of African states, is that populations became conditioned into accepting the politico/military as one ideological entity. In such political environs opposition was meaningless without access to weaponry. Also, Afro-Marxist jargon could be employed to defend the activities of any military elite.

It is easy now to see Marxism–Leninism as inappropriate to newly independent states just emerging from the yoke of colonial rule but in some instances the methods of rule, the social control, the stress on unity and nation-state building provided an appealing ideology. Markakis maintained:

> In situations of acute material deprivation, political oppression
> and social conflict, its Marxism–Leninism appeal rested on
> the promise of rapid development, social justice and popular
> sovereignty. The radical soldiers shared the illusion that
> socialism could be attained speedily and by decree.
>
> (Markakis 1992 p. 14)

At times, however, the adoption of Marxist terminology was simply
a means of gaining control over the state. As Sam Decalo observes
in cases such as Ethiopia and Madagascar, military leaders often
lacked 'previous ideological convictions' and pursued pragmatic and
parochial political courses (Decalo 1995; interview).

Of course, the adoption of Marxism also provided newly independent countries with a form of anti-colonial imperative which provided them with the means of cutting associations with the West. The
Soviet Union could be the provider of aid, practical assistance and
military hardware. Ethiopia, Somalia and Guinea, three countries
which received assistance from the USSR have subsequently either
become Islamic states or are now looking to the Islamic world for
assistance. Guinea has established close links with Iran in the form
of a joint economic commission and technical assistance with its
bauxite resources together with political links at governmental level.
The Iranian Foreign Minister Ali Velayati regularly visits Guinea and
hailed the 'positive bilateral cooperation between the two countries'
(*Kayhan* 21 July 1994). Again, this may suggest a continuing attempt
by developing countries to distance themselves from their former
colonial rulers or alternatively demonstrates a search for a former
Islamic cultural affinity. Either way these shifts of allegiance are more
important with the disintegration of the Soviet Union and provide a
challenge to the military strategies of a number of states. In the words
of one government adviser: 'Marxism as an ideology has gone but as
a method of struggle it has remained.' The chain reaction of a Marxist
cycle of violence continues in African states and is 'difficult to break
out of' (El-Affendi 1995; interview).

ETHNIC CONFLICT

Recent conflicts in Africa are often expressed as manifestations of
ethnic clashes with rival groups fighting for control of government
and access to resources. One academic believes that in respect of
Africa 'the increasing loss of legitimation on the part of single-party

197

governments, resulting from the lack of development success, leads virtually by default, to the politicisation of ethnicity'. Consequently, for those groups affected by relative deprivation, a recourse to ethnicity may be the most 'cost-effective way of defending their own interests' (Tetzlaff 1992 p. 23). Yet, interestingly, ethnic conflicts are not usually referred to as civil wars between competing nationalities within a specific country. Consequently, the implications of the term 'ethnicity' is that it can only be used in the context of a dislocated state. No-one referred to the past conflict between Israelis and Palestinian Arabs as an 'ethnic' conflict, nor indeed, was the confrontation between Kuwaiti Arabs and Iraqi Arabs decribed as ethnic.

In Africa most conflicts are described as 'ethnic'. Populations are seen to be vulnerable to persuasion largely because patterns of personal rule or patrimonialism have alienated or excluded large sections of society. The reaction of those elements within society to such a political system can be 'voice, exit or loyalty' (Hirschmann 1970). Loyalty can be extracted from inclusive segments of society, exit can usually be demonstrated by an actual withdrawal or disengagement from the state, or the physical expatriation out of the country. Voice, however, can be more exacting and potentially violent especially under an authoritarian setting. A decision to challenge the state may manifest itself through riots, a resort to arms or attacks on groups associated with the primordial circles of the ruling elite.

Patrick Chabal attributes the incidence of violence in Africa to bad government (Chabal 1992). Perhaps, however, it is not only 'bad' government which occasions violence but also it may be 'wrong' government, i.e. secular or Islamic. Radio Burundi news reports referred in 1995 to the 'widespread dissemination of written material, articles published in certain newspapers, pamphlets, messages and instructions' which incite inter-ethnic hatred and violence among the population. (SWB AL/2944 11 July 1994). One example of such activity was the existence of a pirate radio, Rutomorangingo Radio (the radio that tells the truth), which allegedly broadcast inflammatory programmes to the country. In a similar vein, a broadcasting station, Radio-Television Libre Mille Collines (RTLM), transmitted allegedly extremist views of the Hutu ethnic group. RTLM established in July 1993 by Ferdinand Nahimana, a political adviser to the government, regularly called for the murder of opponents and the other ethnic group involved in the conflict, the Tutsis, in the local language, Kiswahili, a derivative of Swahili and in French.

Concern has been expressed in Burundi, Rwanda and other countries of East Africa that 'subversive elements are dangerously threatening the life of nations and their peoples', but the references tend to be oblique and generalised (ibid.). Certain publications are available in a number of states which carry Islamic religious poems and political statements. According to Justo Lacunza Balda, 'the *Sauti ya Umma* is printed in the Islamic Republic of Iran by the government-controlled "Taasisi ya Fikra za Kiislamu" (The Foundation of Islamic Thought) and sent to East Africa and to other countries in Africa where Kiswahili is spoken, i.e. Burundi, Malawi, Rwanda, South Africa, Zambia and Zaïre' (Balda 1993 p. 226). *Sauti ya Umma* has been published since 1985 and has regularly reported on political events in Iran, United States policy in the Middle East, cultural relations between Iran and East Africa and the development of Islam. Balda maintains that 'the knowledge and teaching offered by *Sauti ya Umma* and more particularly the inspiration of Iran's Islamic revolution, have found a welcoming echo among many Muslim leaders and readers in East Africa. Another publication, *Mizani* published by UWAMDI ('Umoja wa Wahubiri wa Kiislamu wa Mlingano wa Dini') (Union of Muslim Preachers of Related Religions), is distributed widely in the region including Burundi and Rwanda. Both publications support the Islamic Revolution of Iran as the example for African Muslims to follow and emulate (ibid.). The Iranian President, Hashemi Rafsanjani in July 1994 stated that the country's 'first priority' in foreign policy was to 'develop further our relations with African and Muslim nations in political and economic spheres' (*Kayhan* 21 July 1994).

Throughout the twentieth century the 'use of Kiswahili has contributed to the popularisation of Islam and to its spread in many parts of Africa outside the geographical limits of East Africa' (Balda 1993 p. 231). African Muslims are taught about Islam in Kiswahili, which according to Balda, has become a 'lingua-franca' in the region (ibid. p. 232). There is, of course, nothing unusual or indeed necessarily reprehensible in publications reflecting a particular creed or promoting a particular political programme. It might even be argued that such publications are an essential part of an emergent civil society. But as previous chapters have demonstrated, there is tension between certain states and Islam within Africa. Balda concludes that 'in the context of Islam in East Africa the issue of

199

Islamic Swahili politics is a contentious and elusive topic' (ibid. p. 237). When the Burundi government and various opposition parties refer to the need for the population to ignore the 'preachings' of certain publications and broadcasts, to defend national sovereignty by 'refusing any foreign political or military interference in national affairs and to defend the state against any attempts to destabilise or overthrow legitimate and democratically elected institutions', it points to the depth and breadth of ethnic division (SWB AL/2044 11 July 1994). Ethnic conflict may take generations to disappear believes one Burundian politician: 'Peace will not be achieved immediately and spontaneously. It depends on a new tradition and the consolidation of a new democratic culture. We shall be the pioneers but it is our children and grandchildren who will see the results' (SWB AL/2243 16 March 1995).

Some agreements between nations can be brokered by other states. Sudan and Uganda agreed in 1995 not to allow their territory to be used for attacks on the other country and not to provide support for opposition movements. The agreement, known as the Tripoli Declaration and brokered by Libya, included a number of principles:

1 Acknowledging and affirming the principle of equality and respect between the two countries in order to protect their stability and security.
2 Respecting either side's policies on local matters which do not prejudice the interest of the other side.
3 Commitment to non-interference in either side's internal affairs, pledging to refrain from providing aid to any opposing gang in either country and barring the use of either side's territory for attacks against the other side.
4 Refraining from the use of force by either side and agreeing to seek recognised peaceful channels for resolving disputes through dialogue and negotiations.
5 Guaranteeing co-operation and consultation between the two countries in economic trade and cultural spheres.
6 Agreeing to convene a tripartite summit meeting between Colonel Qadhafi of Libya, President Museveni of Uganda, and Lt General Hasan Ahmad al-Bashir, President of Sudan.

(SWB AL/2272 7 April 1995)

These agreements may be guided by the principles of the OAU and its recent calls for good neighbourliness but they enhance the significance of Islamic states in the region. In fact, Salim Ahmed Salim, Secretary-General of the OAU spoke of Colonel Qadhafi's radical proposal to create separate Tutsi and Hutu states as one way of resolving ethnic tensions. Salim believed, however, that this suggestion would be problematic given the large population movements required and the fear that in creating different states a form of state-expansionism might develop (Salim Ahmed Salim, 1995; meeting)

CONFLICT AND DEVELOPMENT

War and conflict inevitably push development policies into the background. In the Nigerian Civil War of 1967–1970, the government attempted to finance the war without triggering high inflation or deterioration in the balance of payments. It restricted bank credit to the private sector in hopes of restraining the growth of internal demand; it raised taxes, cut capital investment and sharply decreased non-defence expenditures, including those for general administration, social and community welfare and economic services. Emeka Nwokedi considers the significance of violence within a state's political process lies in its 'costs as measured by the opportunity cost of the resources it consumes, the material damage it inflicts on its victims and on society at large, as well as by the number of lives lost' (Nwokedi 1994). Table 6.2 displays the deaths during wars between 1900 and 1989. According to the World Bank the opportunity costs of some conflicts are greater than the number of casualties might suggest. The Iran–Iraq War illustrates how high these costs can become in a regional war. Each side successfully struck at the other's economic jugular, their oil fields. One study has put the total cost to the countries in military expenditures, oil loss and lost output during only the first five years of fighting at $416.2 billion. This exceeds total oil revenue, some $364 billion, that Iraq and Iran previously received throughout this century. Some 450, 000 lives were lost during the nine-year war (World Bank (1993) *War and Development*).

Economic disruption is similarly severe in civil wars. The conflict in northern Ethiopia's Eritrea territory decreased the labour force and bombing and mining caused farmers to avoid certain land, which effectively took it out of production. According to one account, 40 per cent of land was left idle in 1987 because of the impact of war. It also helps explain between one-third and one-half

201

Table 6.2 Deaths during wars, 1900–89

Period	Civil	International	Death during international wars (thousands)			Death during civil wars (thousands)			Total deaths as percentage of world population
			Civilian	Military	Total[a]	Civilian	Military	Total[a]	
1900–09	10	6	230	12	243	25	139	166	0.02
1910–19	15	9	7,045	13,470	20,556	1,140	139	1,327	1.13
1920–29	11	8	21	42	109	39	111	371	0.02
1930–39	11	8	933	838	1,770	646	1,109	1,796	0.17
1940–49	13	7	20,176	19,110	39,285	1,007	5	2,182	1.70
1950–59	20	5	1,073	1,926	3,031	1,571	253	1,879	0.17
1960–69	12	9	622	605	1,256	1,827	1,222	3,301	0.13
1970–79	18	7	639	606	1,246	3,543	1,236	4,957	0.16
1980–89	29	6	702	931	1,733	1,899	179	2,081	0.08
Total	141	63	31,440	37,539	69,229	11,697	4,393	18,059	–

Source: World Bank (1993) *War and Development.*
Note: All but 11,000 of the war deaths following 1949 took place in developing countries. All numbers are estimates and are subject to significant error. Domestic conflicts are not always clearly definable as civil wars, and thus coverage of these statistics varies among studies. A variety of civil disruptions are excluded. For example, estimated deaths during purges and collectivisation in the Soviet Union during the 1930s, which range from 5 to 20 million people, are not included. Figures for deaths resulting from other such events after World War II are also excluded because of poor data. Rough estimates for these range up to 15 million. Also, some wars are counted as civil even when foreign intervention occurred. Deaths during the Korean War, deaths during the Vietnam War for the 1965–75 period, and the war in Afghanistan for the 1978–89 period are included under international wars.
[a] Totals include total estimated deaths. When breakdowns are unavailable, deaths are omitted from civilian and military subcategories. Totals may also differ as a result of rounding. Deaths were prorated when reporting periods spanned more than one decade.

of the food shortages in the region (ibid.). Despite increases in international trade, constantly improving worldwide communications networks and other constructive global interactions, international and civil wars have remained a constant threat to development. Some commentators have attempted to establish a link between political violence in developing countries and their external economic dependency. Dependence upon international assistance leads to conflict by exacerbating the cycle of deprivation which is already entrenched in those societies. (Oberschall 1969). Foreign investment in such states operates within an enclave economy

Table 6.3 Power Longevity of selected sub-Saharan and Middle East leaders

F. Houphouet-Boigny	1960–93	Ivory Coast
J. Nyerere	1961–86	Tanzania
M. Traore	1968–91	Mali
A. Ahidjo	1960–82	Cameroon
L. Senghor	1960–80	Senegal
M. Kerekou	1972–91	Benin
D. arap Moi	1978	Kenya
R. Mugabe	1980	Zimbabwe
S. Hussein	1979	Iraq
H. al-Assad	1970	Syria

Source: ITN Factbook (1990) M. O'Mara, London

dominated by elite groups from which most people are excluded. Certainly, Table 6.3 reveals the extent to which political leadership in Africa and the Middle East is often considered as a personal and, indeed, a life long occupation. Until the onset of democratisation in the 1980s/1990s, the only obstacles to longevity in office were *coups d'état* and death in office.

Yet, paradoxically, the transitional period between moving from one form of political structure to a pluralist, multi-party system can dislocate a country. Algeria's Foreign Minister, Mohamed Salah Dembri, who set up the National Institute for Global Strategic Studies, maintains that the collapse of the one-party system and the country's move towards pluralism led to a crisis and a rupture in the process (Dembri 1995; meeting). The absence of an ordered transition was caused by the increase in adversarial debate, the raised expectations of the electorate, the desire for economic improvement and the extent of corruption in a political class which became obsolete because of its involvement in the former political order (ibid.). Dembri sees Algeria as only one example of countries in Africa many of whom are in 'deep political crisis'. He sees the absence of a national consensus about political change, a political elite whose main preoccupation was to retain power and the flagrant violation of laws guaranteeing certain freedoms as the main reasons which the country fell into a 'state of political anarchy, violence, terrorism and Islamic extremism' (ibid.). Some 35,000 people are reported to have been killed, the majority of them since the beginning of 1994 (Roberts 1995 p. 247). Some analysts maintain that it is now time for the army 'to come to terms with the principle of the sovereignty of the people . . . and to resume its proper role as the guarantor of Algeria's territorial integrity and national unity' (ibid.). The Foreign Minister asserts that the security forces are active in a programme of 'sustained security' which is resulting in the decline of and increasing abandonment of violence by a number of Islamic groups (Dembri 1995; meeting).

PALESTINE/ISRAEL

The Palestine/Israeli issue has been the source of conflict in the Middle East for nearly half a century. The United Nations Resolution 181 passed on the 29 November 1947 recommended the partition of Palestine into Arab and Jewish states. Palestine had been governed by Britain under a League of Nations Mandate since 1922 and upon British withdrawal in May 1948, the Jewish state of Israel was declared. Israel was not recognised by the Arab community who saw the state as an act of imperialist intervention with land taken from the Palestinian Arabs without agreement. The Arab/Israeli War of of 1967 resulted in the Israeli occupation of lands including the West Bank and Gaza and the subjugation of Palestinians. The degree of population mobility and displacement created a volatile political environment in neighbouring Arab states: 60 per cent of Jordan's population is of Palestinian origin and various refugee camps are scattered around the Arab states, in Jordan, Lebanon and Syria. In 1994 there were 2.4 million Palestinian refugees registered with the United Nations Relief and Works Agency (UNWRA). Although, the Arab/Israeli conflict was not the only reason for high levels of military spending in the region it was an important factor. (see Table 6.4)

Table 6.4 Military expenditure as a percentage of Gross National Product

	1960	*1986*
Israel	2.9	19.2
Syria	7.9	14.7
Iran	4.5	20.0
Iraq	8.7	32.0

Source: Keesings Record of World Events 1991

The Palestinian struggle gained considerable support within African states, as did the cause of the disenfranchised blacks living under the system of apartheid in South Africa. These two very separate issues became linked as part of a campaign against oppression and colonialism and, as such, partially legitimised the violence expressed in their causes. Freedom fighters, bombers, assassins, terrorists could be partly excused their crimes largely because the societies they represented were denied appropriate political channels to articulate their views. Violence ultimately became their only means of demonstrating their cause. For many years it was predicted that conflict would continue simply because there seemed to be no political solutions available to which all parties would agree.

However, since the end of the Gulf War in 1991 and the commencement of the international peace talks in Madrid later that year, the possibilities of some form of settlement began to appear on the political agenda. A 'Declaration of Principles', known as the 'Oslo Accord', was signed by Yassir Arafat, leader of the Palestine Liberation Organisation and the Israeli Foreign Minister, Shimon Peres on 13 September 1993 in Washington with US President Bill Clinton in attendance (See Appendix 4 for the text of the 'Declaration of Principles'). The Accord stated:

> The government of the State of Israel and the Palestinian delegation, representing the Palestinian people, agree that it is time to put an end to decades of confrontation and conflict, recognise their mutual legitimate and political rights and strive to live in peaceful coexistence and mutual dignity and security and achieve a just, lasting and comprehensive peace settlement and historic reconciliation through the agreed political process.
> (*Middle East International* 24 September 1993)

The signing of an agreement between Israel and the Palestine Liberation Organisation on 4 May 1994 which finalised plans for Israel to hand over the administration of Gaza and Jericho (the West Bank) to a Palestinian autonomous authority has raised the possibility of an end to the Arab/Israeli conflict and the chance of regional political renewal, although the assassination of the Prime Minister, Yitsak Rabin, in November 1995 by a Jewish opponent of the peace process has cast a shadow over events. Article V of the Declaration allows for a transitional period of five years during which time authority would be transferred to Palestinians in economic, welfare, social, education and taxation spheres. In order to guarantee public order and internal security for the Palestinians of the West Bank and Gaza Strip the interim self-government authority, the Council for the Palestinian People, has established a police force in place of a military alternative. A portion of British aid to the Palestinian territories takes the form of management and technical skill training and programmes aimed at making the civil forces more responsive to local communities (Chalker 1995; meeting). The withdrawal of Israeli military forces from the Gaza Strip and Jericho areas of the West Bank enhances the role of the Palestinian police force.

Disputes arising out of the application or interpretation of the Declaration of Principles or any subsequent agreements regarding the interim period will be resolved by negotiations through the Joint Israeli–Palestinian Liaison Committee. If negotiations fail, a process of conciliation will be attempted through the instittution of an arbitration committee. The management of formulas and processes to be employed in the event of disagreement, is an area of particular importance because of the necessity to prevent any irreversible slide into violence. A senior Israeli diplomat asserted that in order for security to be upheld, the Palestinian entities must have a centralised response to violence on the grounds that only one organisation can control 'state' violence. If private and separate militias exist, a state of anarchy prevails. Any clashes between anti-peace forces and the PLO in Gaza have to be seen within the context of regional pressures. It is important, however, for the PLO to have 'the upper hand' in security matters and to pursue policies appropriate to Palestinians rather than because of Israeli demands. The Middle East peace process remains unpredictable and there are certainly elements within both societies that are opposed to peace. However, in the final analysis 'peace will be secured only when it takes root in the everyday lives of the people of the region' (Fischer *et al.* 1994 p. 1). Accordingly, both societies must understand and be exposed to each other's culture and the young should be taught about equality and understanding. Whilst a political will for peace exists in the region, progress can take place.

SOUTH AFRICA

Political events changed in South Africa when ex-President de Klerk, leader of the former white minority government of South Africa, agreed in union with other principal political parties to change to a principle of one-person-one-vote. As a precursor to the elections it was agreed that a Commonwealth Observer Mission to South Africa (COMSA) should go to the country in order to 'provide practical assistance to arrest the ongoing violence' (*Violence in South Africa*, Report of the Commonwealth Observer Mission to South Africa (COMSA) February-May 1993). The work of the Mission ran from October 1992 through to June 1993 and its remit was to 'act impartially in all dealings across the political spectrum' (ibid.). COMSA recognised that violence in South Africa could not be divorced from the political context in which it occurred and that it would be naive to assume that all violence would automatically end with the installation of a democratically elected government. However, there existed clear linkages between the inequity and basic unjustness of the apartheid system of government and the outbursts of violence and resistance. COMSA, then, sought to broaden and deepen contacts with all political parties and to attempt a process of reconciliation. Much of the time, the international observers monitored marches and demonstrations. These were seen as crucial to free political expression but very often they also were flashpoints for violence, especially given the tense relations between marchers and law enforcement agencies. Commemoration rallies, for example, the Sharpeville Day Rallies held on 21 March 1993 in memory of the killing of 69 demonstrators by the South African Police on 21 March 1960, were traditionally emotive occasions simply because they reflected both past and, at that time, continuing injustices.

The policing of public events was considered inappropriate in that the police faced participants as though they were the enemy. As the COMSA report stated: 'Few physical structures provide more graphic monuments to the era of apartheid than South Africa's police stations, court houses and prisons' (ibid. p. 55). Over decades millions of black South Africans passed through these institutions convicted of breaches of the pass laws and other apartheid legislation. Those considered most dangerous, including the current President, Nelson Mandela, were incarcerated in places like Robben Island, a few kilometres off the coast near Cape Town or on Death Row in Pretoria's Central Prison.

COMSA also found that violence could be escalated by the anger, disillusionment and frustration of thousands of young black South Africans. Without schooling, jobs, or any real hope for the future many of the youths sought radical solutions to their problems. The Commission felt that future political leaders would have to find ways of defusing and containing such rage. Also they found that South African women, who constitute 53 per cent of the population, were among the worst victims of apartheid and violence:

1 According to 1991 figures, almost half the female population is likely to be raped within her lifetime.
2 It is estimated that one in six women is battered by her male partner (ibid.).

Empowering women was seen by COMSA to be essential in combating the particular effects of violence directed against females. Apart from socio-economic improvements, which are discussed in another chapter, COMSA recommended the recruitment of women into law enforcement agencies. Policing approaches would have to reflect the new democratic political order of South Africa and reflect the diversity of the communities they served with appropriate levels of accountability and consultation.

On 19 April 1994, Nelson Mandela of the African National Congress, F.W. De Klerk of the National Party and Mangosuthu G. Buthelezi, Chief Minister of KwaZulu Government and President of the Inkatha Freedom Party signed a Memorandum of Agreement for Reconciliation and Peace between the three parties. Section 2 of the Agreement stated that all parties 'reject violence'. Equally, Clause XXXI of South Africa's Constitution states

> Every member of the security forces – police, military and intelligence – and the security forces as a whole, shall be required to perform their functions and exercise their powers in the national interest and shall be prohibited from furthering or prejudicing party political interest.
> (Act no.200 of 1993: Constitution of the Republic of South Africa 1993 (as amended) Schedule 4) (For Full Constitution see Appendix 1.)

Booth and Vale, however, feel a certain ambiguity exists concerning South Africa's future regional role which largely rests on suspicions about its past behaviour (Booth and Vale 1995). They question whether a regional community, which they believe is the only guarantee of long-term security, can grow in a region steeped in considerable enmity and violence. The new Southern Africa requires a different approach, one which 'conceives of security holistically and sees regional security in terms of the extension of the notion of community' (ibid.).

The Southern African Development Community (SADC) demonstrates the desirability of adopting a regional approach but difficulties exist because polities must change. Booth and Vale see security in the form of 'peace, order and justice' which in order to be permanent, 'must be owned by the people' (ibid.). Security issues, then, can no longer only be concerned with military solutions and arsenals of weaponry; security now must be linked with accountable government, the rule of law and the development of civil society. States should now involve their populations in the process of security, rather than marginalising them. Yet certain elements in society continue to challenge the government of Nelson Mandela. A campaign against a gun-free South Africa was launched by the South African Health and Public Service Workers' Union, (SAHPSWU) in 1995. The union accused the government of planning its destruction and called on the black community not to surrender arms and ammunition which 'may be needed to defend the union'. SAHPSWU also maintained that it was planning to get assistance from the Palestinian Islamic group, Hamas, and from other Middle Eastern countries, in order to fight the government (SWB AL/2247 9 March 1995).

However, the fundamental political changes which have taken place in South Africa have, inevitably, raised hopes of real and meaningful change in the Continent as a whole. Similarly, the political agreements reached in the Middle East have charged parts of the region with the possibilities of peaceful security.

HUMAN RIGHTS

The seventeenth session of the African Human and People's Rights Commission held in 1995 submitted a proposal to be considered by heads of state for the creation of an African Human Rights Court. The Commission believed the institution of a human rights court would afford greater protection for human rights within the continent. The Commission itself was inaugurated in 1987 with a mandate set out in the African Charter on human and people's rights which was adopted by the OAU in 1981. The Charter emphasised economic, social and cultural rights of individuals as well as the duties of states in the promotion and defence of these rights. It also defined a new category of rights: the rights of peoples. These rights include freedom from discrimination, oppression and exploitation, and the right to self-determination, to national and international peace and security and to a satisfactory environment for economic and social development. In countries where rulers, often with external support, have used the state machinery to undermine the basic rights of individuals and peoples, a need for a more comprehensive view of human rights violations is seen as necessary (Nzongola-Ntalaja 1983). Generally, exclusive attention is paid to political and civil rights: acts of brutal violence, detention without charge, trial of dissident politicians, torture, detention camps, repression and interrogation. Algeria's Foreign Minister referred to the country's establishment, in 1994, of a National Conference of Consensus, the aim of which is to introduce a reform programme based on political consensus which will guarantee civil rights, especially the right to life (Dembri 1995; meeting). The right to life is viewed as the most important human right, especially in countries which have witnessed periods of political crisis. Populations desperately need to be reassured in order to regain their trust in political institutions (ibid.).

The functions of the African Commission are:

1   To promote human and people's rights and in particular:
    (a) To collect documents, undertake studies and researches on African problems in the field of human and people's rights, organise meetings and disseminate information, encourage national and local institutions concerned with human and people's rights and give its views or make recommendations to governments.
    (b) To formulate and lay down principles and rules aimed at solving legal problems relating to human and people's rights and fundamental freedoms upon which African governments may base their legislations.
    (c) To co-operate with other African and international institutions concerned with the promotion and protection of human and people's rights.
2   Ensure the protection of human and people's rights under conditions laid down by the Charter.
3   Interpret all the provisions of the present Charter at the request of a state party, an institution of the OAU or an African organisation recognised by the OAU.

The varied definition of human rights can, however, be problematic especially when the political, religious or ideological complexion of a state is felt to be undermined. A critical report by a Special Rapporteur of the UN Commission on Human Rights on Sudan

(1994) was condemned by the Sudanese government and judged: 'A vicious attack on fundamental principles of Islamic Penal Legislation and against Islamic faith in general.' Yet the report referred to certain practices which could be regarded as universal human rights abuses: 'large numbers of extrajudicial killings, summary executions, enforced or involuntary disappearances, systematic torture and widespread arbitrary arrest of suspected opponents' (ibid.). These actions are not, however, confined to African nations, nor indeed, are they necessarily associated with Islamic states. A reading of Hanna Batatu's descriptions of the torture chambers of Qasr al-Nihayah in Baghdad, a palace which became a centre for detention and interrogation during the struggle for Ba'th Party supremacy, creates grim and sobering images (Batatu 1978). Equally, the Syrian Ba'th Party's formidable suppression of oppositionist demonstrations in Hama in 1982 indicate that human rights abuses are not the preserve of one country or one continent (Hammade 1993; interview).

Some analysts and practitioners maintain that grinding poverty in developing countries remains a primary cause of human rights abuses, whilst others see violence and oppression manufactured and utilised as instruments of power (Cohen et al. 1994; El-Affendi; interview). Certainly, competition for scarce resources, economic underdevelopment and unaccountable political rule all contribute to a climate of tension and potential volatility. Equally, the African Commission on Human and People's Rights is partly subscribed by the composition of its commissioners, many of whom are chosen because of their loyalty and at times involvement with the government of a particular state. These affinities can sometimes affect the judgements the Commission makes about a country's human rights abuses. According to Laurie S. Wiseberg, an Executive Director of Human Rights Internet, this 'goes some way towards explaining the extreme timidity of Commission members in publicly challenging state parties' (Wiseberg 1994). He cites the case of Tunisia where human rights abuses were raised by Amnesty International, who called on the African Commission to investigate. The Commission drafted a general resolution on freedom of association but the Chair of the Commission, Dr Ibrahim Ali Badawi El Sheikh, actually praised Tunisia's human rights record (ibid.). The difficulties with a regional organisation of this nature is, as the OAU pinpointed: the existence of 'destructive differences between and within African countries', which result in the 'shedding of blood of millions of

Africans and the movement of hundreds of thousands of refugees and displaced people across borders' (SWB AL/2264 29 March 1995).

Yet under Article 62 of the African Charter, state parties are obliged to submit every two years 'a report on legislative or other measures taken with a view to giving effect to the rights and freedoms recognised and guaranteed' (Wiseberg 1994 p. 36). Wiseberg believes: 'monitoring the behaviour of states by reviewing their periodic reports can be an effective means of subjecting states to public scrutiny and encouraging them to bring their laws and practices into line with international standards' (ibid.). The potential for action exists and is recognised by the Commission who asserted in 1995 that African states must set their own example by protecting human rights (SWB AL/2261 25 March 1995). The problem in defining human rights broadly, commendable though it may be, is that classifications embracing: 'political, economic, social, cultural and people's rights, women's and children's rights as well as the rights of the elderly and the disabled', are especially difficult to uphold and may lead to stultification and impotence. Wiseberg complains of the apathy of the African Commissioners, fearful of offending governmental representatives and 'tip-toeing politely around gross human rights violators' but too wide a remit may lead to indifference and accusations that 'human rights' is just another, and more fashionable form of Western 'intellectual imperialism' (Wisberg 1994 p. 38). As Wiseberg himself cites, initially there was little response from the African Commission to Amnesty International's call for the appointment of an expert in international human rights law, to monitor continuing violations of the right to life. Some commissioners believed that poverty, the debt burden and other issues were more deserving of such attention (ibid.). Clearly, there has to exist a general consensus about human rights. The OAU Foreign Ministers meeting in 1995 called for political and financial support for a Conflict Management Mechanism which would attempt to prevent and settle disputes and thus provide a semblance of security and stability for the peoples of the continent (SWB AL/2265 30 March 1995).

In 1992, a new organisation was established, the Commission on Global Governance, which laid down a set of principles which represented 'global neighbourhood'. Global neighbourhood includes: respect for life, humanity, justice and human rights, and would interlink societies in major areas of concern such as: security, economic unity, the rule of law and the United Nations. The security of the people is now the priority rather than the security of states. Frank Judd, the former Director of Oxfam, asserted that with 80 per cent of African states suffering conflict there had to be a 'build up of global responsibility' (Judd 1995; meeting). As people become more insecure, through civil strife, catastrophe and domestic problems, the United Nations must become more responsive and act to prevent injustices. The UN could deploy peacekeeping forces but the UN Charter would have to be amended. A more accountable and democratic Security Council would be acceptable globally and there would have to be a clear legal system represented by the rule of law. An International Court of Justice should be re-invigorated and all UN members must acknowledge and accept the jurisdiction of such a Court. Terrorism and cross-border disputes would be dealt with within that arena. Table 6.5 shows the UN peacekeeping forces and observer missions still in effect on 31 December 1994. Forty

Table 6.5 UN peacekeeping forces and observer missions still in effect on 31 December 1994

Date estab- lished	Name and Place	Acronym
1948	UN Truce Supervision Organization (Middle East)	UNTSO
1949	UN Military Observer Group in India and Pakistan	UNMOGIP
1964	UN Peacekeeping Force in Cyprus	UNFICYP
1974	UN Disengagement Observer Force (Syria)	UNDOF
1978	UN Interim Force in Lebanon	UNIFIL
1991	UN Angola Verification Mission II	UNAVEM II
1991	UN Mission for the Referendum in Western Sahara	MINURSO
1991	UN Iraq-Kuwait Observation Mission	UNIKOM
1991	UN Observer Mission in El Salvador	ONUSAL
1992	UN Protective Forces (former Yugoslavia, mainly Bosnia)	UNPROFOR
1992	UN Operation in Mozambique	ONUMOZ
1993	UN Mission in Haiti	UNMIH
1993	UN Operation in Somalia II	UNOSOM II
1993	UN Observer Mission in Georgia	UNOMIG
1993	UN Observer Mission in Liberia	UNOMIL
1993	UN Observer Mission in Uganda-Rwanda	UNOMUR
1993	UN Assistance Mission in Rwanda	UNAMIR

Source: Council for Education in World Citizenship, London, February 1995

per cent of the UN's peacekeeping efforts are in Africa, and this figure approaches around 70 per cent if the Middle East is included (Chalker March 1995; meeting) Peacekeeping forces are military and sufficiently armed in order to defend themselves. Their main role is to provide a form of buffer zone in order to keep aggressors apart. Observers and truce supervisors are unarmed and report those who do not keep to agreed frontiers or cease-fire arrangements. However, there are UN-supported wars, one such being in the Gulf in 1991 and between 1948 and 1994 more than 1000 UN peacekeepers were killed (Council for Education in World Citizenship, London, January–February 1995). The Secretary-General of the UN, Boutros Boutros-Ghali proposed the establishment of new UN peace-enforcing units. These would be more heavily armed than peacekeepers and special volunteers would be trained for this work. A more modest arrangement has been started: a rapid-reaction standby force which can have 100,000 troops on a two-week standby. By the end of 1994, over 20 countries had pledged a total of 70,000 (ibid.).

Some NGOs, however, are uncertain about the role the UN is playing. The Director-General of the International Committee of the Red Cross (ICRC), Peter Fuchs, asserted that different ideas of 'humanitarian aid' already exist, sometimes implying military intervention, sometimes a military presence, but invariably politicians and generals are becoming increasingly involved. In a sense, this politicisation of humanitarian aid compromises the ICRC, who has a permanent presence in around 30 countries and can be immediately mobilised when conflict breaks out. If NGOs become identified as biased, partial and political, their own positions become difficult when left alone in countries in crisis. The ICRC alerted the international community about Somalia in 1991 and according to Peter Fuchs it is often the only agency operating in the field (Fuchs 1994; meeting). With the ending of the Cold War when certain structures of command were followed, there has been increasing anarchy, no respect for law and an increase in violent outbursts. The ICRC now negotiates with bands of fighters and militias with no clear points of reference. There must be an 'objective, unbiased, neutral, impartial organisation to carry out real 'humanitarian' tasks and reach deep into society without any political objectives' (ibid.). UN-protected agencies are often seen as biased and then become involved as party to the conflict with the consequence that the security and effectiveness of NGOs become jeopardised. As ICRC is often involved in the evolution of a conflict, information must be kept secret and divisions must be drawn between military, political and humanitarian policies.

GLOBAL CONFERENCE ON NATIONAL YOUTH SERVICES

The second Global Conference on National Youth Services took place in Nigeria in 1994. The organisation emphasises the role of the young in building a peaceful future. The phenomena of human conflict, ignorance, illiteracy and unemployment poses a challenge to social security and stability. These dangers had to be combated by mobilising the young for positive purposes (*West Africa* 31 October–6 November 1994). Youth service could be institutionalised through an exchange which would eventually develop into a global world scheme with an organisational framework. It was important that young people should not be exploited. They should be introduced to and trained in leadership, organisational and management attributes as well as vocational and entrepreneurial skills. Opportunities have to be aimed at creating employment chances for demobilised ex-combatants, most of whom are youths.

The relationship between the young, political activity and military action is becoming an increasingly important one. One writer has considered the role played by youth in South Africa and asserts: 'Those who confronted one another across the barricades were youth, whether on the side of the ANC, Inkatha, AXAPO, the South African Police or the South African Defence Force' (Cooper 1994 p. 27). Black and white youth had been socialised by Apartheid and responded to it with a 'singleness and zealousness of purpose which only youth can afford to sustain' (ibid.). Saths Cooper believes it is the environment to which youth are exposed that conditions their use of violence as a political expression. Moving away from South Africa to other African and Middle East states, the young have been trained in militias or as revolutionaries. More recently, it is the young who are becoming increasingly attracted by and involved in Islamic groups. With unemployment figures among those under 30 across North and sub-Saharan Africa estimated to be in the region of between 50 per cent and 60 per cent, the young provide a critical agency of potential change (*West Africa* 31 October–6 November 1994). It would be erroneous to underestimate the degree to which conflict continues to be a feature of African states and some analysts now point to the 'transnationalisation of conflict' in that domestic disputes are spilling over into the region as a whole (Keller 1995; meeting). Yet Goran Hyden believes that the role of the military will not be as important or significant as it once was (Hyden 1995; meeting) The extent to which competing Islamic forces will exacerbate tensions within the weaker nation states of Africa remains to be monitored.

Part V
CONCLUSION

7

THIRD WORLDS?

INTRODUCTION

The relationship between the Middle East and sub-Saharan Africa is a complex one and can be examined from a number of perspectives: it may be considered on a cultural level given the intertwining of historical association, settlement and religion between populations over the '*longue dureé*'; conventionally it may be viewed within the context of colonialism and neo-imperialism set against the backdrop of Western domination and control; alternatively, the relationship may be seen in terms of patron–client states operating in an unequal differentiated economic environment highlighted by escalating oil prices and rising indebtedness; contemporaneously, it may be viewed in terms of postmodernism and heterogeneity with a mixing and blurring set of changing relationships or within the umbrella term the 'Third World' in order to exact a firmer understanding of the meaning of what increasingly is becoming a catch-all phrase; ulti- mately, the relationship may be examined within the context of a maturing alternative Islamic development agenda which intends to be established and nurtured in the countries of sub-Saharan Africa. Islamic influences in sub-Saharan Africa, then, can be defined as political, religious and economic and it is necessary to examine these factors before placing the relationship within a wider discourse.

THIRD WORLD

The term 'Third World' is 'probably no more illuminating than the terms which preceded it, such as 'developing countries', 'under- developed countries' or 'emergent countries', but it has come into common usage for want of anything better' (Pinkney 1993 p. 1).

Robert Pinkney believes that the Third World was broadly delineated at the point at which the First and Second Worlds ended. Nigel Harris agrees: 'It (the Third World) identified not just a group of new states joined later by the older states of Latin America, nor the majority of the world's poor, but a political alternative other than that presented by Washington and Moscow, the First and Second Worlds' (Harris 1990 p. 18). Certainly, the Third World's identification with difficult social and economic circumstances, an unequal relationship with the 'developed' world and often a recent emergence from colonial rule, determined and defined the term more clearly' (Pinkney 1993 p. 2) Yet from the beginning, the term always included nations with very different cultures, religions, societies and economies. The Third World embraced and grouped together regions and individual countries of Africa, Asia, the Caribbean, Latin America and the Middle East under the assumption that they shared a common predicament: 'Directly or indirectly they suffered the after-effects of colonisation and they came late and on disadvantageous terms into the competitive world economy' (Randall in Pinkney p. vii). Although even this interpretation is not directly applicable to the oil-rich Arab states. For Mark Berger 'the idea of a Third World now serves an important function in terms of the 'management' of the global political economy and allows for the homogenisation of the history of diverse parts of the world' (Berger 1994). Whilst Mehran Kamrava calls for a 'new conception of Third World politics': one that can be 'conceptualised via a typology of state-society relationships' (Kamrava 1993a).

The recent dissolution of the so-called 'second world', the emergence of newly industrialising countries and the popular debate about the end of the Third World inevitably arouses discussion. Nigel Harris's assertion that the Third World is disappearing is based not on the countries or their inhabitants but on the argument itself (Harris 1990 p. 200). A new set of economic determinants have created a complex global economy and supersedes the old simplicities of 'First and Third worlds, rich and poor, haves and have-nots, industrialised and non-industrialised' (ibid.). Whereas in the past the Third World debate informed and instructed us of the differentials between the categories of First, Second and Third Worlds it is now time to change our perspective. In some senses, the Third World has been seen as a static debilitating category: countries economically impoverished and politically unstable, harnessed to a world economy on a detrimental basis, often dependent on aid, unable to sustain civil society and often linked together on the theoretical justification of Marxist/Leninist analysis. Some features are still apparent but manifestly not in every country as World Bank figures attest. It is the intention of this study to understand how far the relationship between the Middle East and Africa continues to be relevant within a Third World context and whether the amalgamation of the two regions into this category masks the complexities of a changing association.

When Mehran Kamrava speaks of the 'painful reverberations' of Third World dramas it is possible to find echoes in the countries of both the Middle East and sub-Saharan Africa. The images of politics played out within an arena 'plagued by violence and instability, greed and corruption, avarice and malice' with 'imbedded ethnic and tribal nuances' tearing societies and dividing peoples along 'lines of racial, tribal and linguistic differences' are powerful and disturbing' (Kamrava 1993b pp. 221–222). Yet as James Manor states 'the scope of politics in Third World settings is usually broader than in the West and our modes of analysis must accommodate themselves to that reality more effectively than the familiar paradigms have done' (Manor 1991 p. 5). In many ways, the Third World has always occasioned a convoluted response from the West, in part confessional, a *mea culpa* for past colonial misdemeanours and in part a notion of 'otherness', to be pitied and patronised, aided and armed and expected to contort to Western interests or indifference. Modernisation and Dependency theories, Marxist and liberal analysis have failed to fully understand the 'contradictory elements' and complexities of other societies.

The inappropriateness of the Western intellectually based Marxist or Liberal Democratic models of development has given rise to a general mood that not only is the category of the Third World problematic but also that patterns of political life should be reexamined. In this context, the *'longue durée'* approach has been used in attempting to understand change over a longer period of time. Jean-François Bayart has successfully brought these views to the fore (Bayart 1992). It may be that the post-colonial African state is 'not dissimilar from its colonial and precolonial predecessors', in that it functions on the basis of 'personal networks' (ibid. p. 261). Islamic leaders identify the comtemporary 'insecurity and mistrust' within Africa to be in part the result of 'protracted historical animosities and bitterness between various African tribes'. These tensions were then exacerbated by the colonial division of the continent.

Therefore, only a 'divine power', Islam, can resolve the situation peacefully' (Hazrat Mirza Tahir Ahmad, Friday Sermon 9 November 1990).

Attention has also focused on the theatrical and imaginary dimensions of politics (Wagner (1991) and Mbembe (1991)) and the ways in which states can politically create their 'own world of meanings' through various procedures of ceremonial and symbolic significance' (Mbembe 1991 p. 166). Myths and imaginings can be appropriated for political purposes and can be employed to justify conflict and war. War, in turn, can provide 'an ideology, including an exaltation of martial values and recourse to witchcraft' (Bayart 1992 p. xiii) Michel Foucault maintains that history which determines people has 'the form of a war rather than of a language: relations of power, not relations of meaning'. Of itself history has no 'meaning', though this neither diminishes it as 'absurd or incoherent' (Foucault 1995 p. 68). Power, however, is not necessarily linked to the state but to a range of power associations: family, kinship, knowledge, technology and so on. But according to Foucault each society has a 'regime of truth', that is a body of ideas or 'types of discourse which it accepts and makes function as true' (ibid. p. 75). Religion, mysticism and story-telling, especially in regions where literacy levels are low and oral traditions exist, are all processes which contribute to perceptions and interpretations of truth and falsehood. Most post-revolutionary states have been accompanied by a cultural revolution and such examples of this tendency can be found in the cases of Syria and Egypt. Egypt under Nasser introduced a 'Project for the Revision of Modern Historical Writing' and the Ba'th Party takeover in Syria inspired a decision to 'rewrite Arab history' (Freitag 1994).

In attempting to understand more clearly the relationship between Africa and the Middle East we must acknowledge that the historicity of African societies contains forms of political identity and expression associated with Muslim leadership (Constantin 1993 p. 46). In some instances, e.g. the Yao Muslims of Malawi, the adoption of Islamic practices, at times in response to Portuguese and British colonisation, transformed identities: 'Islam, which once assisted the Yao to sustain a tribal identity, has now furnished them with an entirely new identity' (Thorold 1993 p. 90). The coastal Swahili Muslims, as Louis Brenner points out, see themselves as the 'rightful guardians of the true Islamic heritage in East Africa', whilst Islamists in Sudan claim their policies represent a return to 'Afro-Islamic authenticity' (ibid., O'Fahey 1993 p. 7–9). For some analysts the degree to which many immigrants from Arabia were assimilated into Swahili society from the twelfth century has been under-estimated by Europeans (Frankl 1993). There is considerable strength and depth to the Islamic heritage of sub-Saharan Africa and permutations in the manner in which Islamic beliefs spread and manifested themselves within different tribal settings. These patterns of dissemination support Bayart's views that a 'holistic' interpretation of the character of African societies is misleading (Bayart 1992 p. 267). The very strong cultural links between Africa and the Arab world are enhanced by North African influences (El-Affendi 1995; interview). However, in searching for an Afro-Arab identity some novelists have attempted to refute the prevalent notion, assumed to be largely based on myth, of two conflicting identities, one Arab the other African, with each attempting to impose its hegemony on the other' (Yosuf Deng 1978 cited in Shoush 1991). But problems emerge in detaching and identifying a mythical past from past hostilities. Francis Deng writes of Sudan: 'Divisiveness has tended to over-emphasize the profundity of racial and cultural dichotomy, the depth of animosity and mistrust resulting from an embittering history, and impediments to any hopes for solidarity in nation building. So predominant did the adverse view resulting from the presumed racial and cultural divisions become, that myth over-shadowed reality' (ibid. p. 1). The bitter experience of Arab slavery, however, cannot be ignored and continues to be a 'historical truth' for many Africans in large swathes of the continent as are the painful experiences of European colonial rule. But it is the extent to which these grievances are stirred and fanned in order to inflame current hostilities and the pursuit of power which is important (El-Affendi 1995; interview). Interestingly, an examination of the work of an Islamic Arab writer of the late eighth, early ninth Century, al-Jahiz, reveals a piece devoted to black people. Although the work is regarded as 'strongly Islamic in flavour' it does include a selection from what is regarded as 'Arab secular tradition', including accounts of 'eloquent sayings of pre-Islamic blacks, various black poets, black warriors and a black uprising in Iraq' (McDonald 1992). The 'good qualities of the Zanj, the blacks of East Africa' are especially commended and blacks are regarded as 'highly civilised in the interior of their lands, where Arab trading vessels do not penetrate'. Perhaps, of greater significance is al-Jahiz's assertion that 'pre-Islamic Arabs had no prejudice against blacks; yet despite the coming of Islam such a prejudice is now found' (ibid.).

THE ISLAMIC AGENDA

From the statements of the Islamic Conference Organisation and the Islamic Development Bank to the sermons of religious leaders to the writings of Hasan Turabi and al-Ghazali there is a general consensus that Islam must unify Muslims over and beyond the confines of the nation state. 'Islam has no territorial boundaries' asserts one religious leader at a Friday sermon and Hasan Turabi states: 'The ideal of Islam is one of freely associating social groups united by common descent, custom, domicile, interest or moral purpose' (Hazrat Mirza Tahir Ahmad 1991; *Islamica* 15 March 1993). The political form such a structure could take is one in which the Caliphate is re-established and restored, upholding one centre of authority and uniting the Muslim community. In other words, the creation of a unified Islamic order under a political system which conforms to *sharia*. The Caliphate would serve as the central institution of the Islamic *umma* (community), preserving the deeply entrenched Islamic tradition of free migration and reminiscent of classical Caliphates (*Islamica* 15 March 1993). According to Mohammed Arkoun, however, notions of ideal communities are partly unreal. Mythical visions are presented and sustained by an idealised transmission of all events and words by a privileged generation: the disciples and companions who define and condition the spiritual quality of the ideal community (Arkoun 1994 p. 53).

Mythical ideas, however, need to connect with contemporary political realities and imperatives and it is within this framework that Islamist intellectuals have engaged with the question of democracy. As we have seen there is much debate about the relationship of Islam to democracy. Put simply, the discussion seems two-pronged: on the one hand, Islam is regarded as an obstacle to the establishment of democracy mainly because of the incompatibility between the absolute rule of God (Allah) and secular forms of political expression that rest on representation and accountability. One strand of Islamic thought associates democracy with secularism, with the consequence that democracy becomes a deliberate violation of God's law. Islam's total view contains social, political and economic creeds enshrined in Islamic law and based on interpretations of the Qur'an. This view precludes the need for other political movements and militates against the full participation of Islamic groups in competitive multi-party politics. The other dimension of the debate focuses on whether there exists an Islamic agenda for democracy. These ideas centre on the notion of the wider Muslim community, the *umma*, and the need for consultation, *shura*. In large states, *shura* takes place in a form of national assembly, *majlis*. In this context, Islamic parties may stand for election to national assemblies, and they can deliberate, advise, discuss and consult with individual leaders.

The issue, however, can be more complex. Indeed, some Islamists view the debate as a whole to be determined and framed in a Western context. Although others recognise the significance of the discussion to the Muslim world (Al-Azm 1995; meeting; Akbar Ahmed 1992; meeting; Ayubi 1991). Hasan Turabi believes the Islamic *al-shura* to be superior to Western representative democracy which is inhibited by social and economic inequalities. He maintains there is no place for secular governments in Islam and has referred to the need for social bias to be eliminated (El-Solh 1993; *Light and Hope for Sudan* 1994). Although al-Ghazali and Muhammad Amara agree that some aspects of representative democracy might be appropriate in an Islamic state, they maintain that *al-shura* does not apply to matters which are dealt with in the Qur'an (El-Sohl 1993). The political framework, then, is defined by the *Sharia* whilst day-to-day policy-making is formulated by an assembly whose representatives are chosen by the *umma*. Amara asserts: 'Western democracy has generally laid down proper principles for political life. We need to take much from these states in order to fill shortcomings due to the paralysis which has afflicted our jurisprudence for many centuries' (El-Sohl 1993).

Clearly, the debate about democracy is wide ranging and difficult to resolve, although it must be acknowledged that Islamic political parties exist, political programmes are presented, elections are contested and Islamic groups co-operate with secular parties in government. Hasan Turabi, on the other hand, continually asserts that representative democracy is of a degenerate form and that political parties are in direct contravention of ethical Islam (*Light and Hope for Sudan* 1995). Although maintaining that Islam is 'missionary and universalist in vocation' he believes there must be no coercion in religion. Non-believers must be persuaded to convert to Islam by argument, dialogue and example but central to his basic argument is that all people must adhere to the tenets of Islam (*Islamica* 1993). The National Islamic Front of Sudan, of which Turabi is leader, promotes Islam as the basis for national life. It does not allow any organised political opposition and would like to see Islam propagated

225

throughout the whole of Africa. Some non-Muslims feel themselves to be disadvantaged and other reports speak of a brutal campaign of forced Islamisation in southern Sudan (Rodgers, *Light and Hope for Sudan* 1995; *The Tablet* 18 February 1995). Edward Said dismisses Turabi's potential authority and maintains his 'decisive disability' and fundamental drawback stem from the fact that he is a political leader in Sudan, a nation which is one of the 'poorest and least influential of any country anywhere' (Said 1994 p. 407). Although it is widely acknowledged that the Arab world is not generally preoccupied with news about non-Arab Africa it would be wrong to assume that Sudan was an insignificant country within the continent as a whole (El-Affendi 1995; interview; *Sudan Update* April 1994). In fact, the weakness and vulnerability of some sub-Saharan African states make Turabi's ideas seem more applicable and feasible.

The fact that the Islam in Africa Organisation has been established at the behest of the Islamic Conference Organisation with the stated objective of ensuring the appointment of Muslims to strategic posts and the ultimate replacement of Western legal systems with the *sharia* is significant. The countries included are Nigeria, Gambia and Tanzania. It may be that the adoption of the *longue durée* perspective justifies the institution of *sharia* in sub-Saharan African states. Islam has certainly been part of Africa's historicity for a much longer period than European colonialism. More recently Islam has assumed a liberating posture, presenting itself as a religion that will rest countries from their neo-colonial dependencies and largely ignoring the fact that it too was a conquering and colonising force in Africa over the *longue durée*. In a sense, all societies are victims of domination but the farther back in time, the deeper the cultural impact. Pre-colonial Africa was for some time, and in part, Islamic Africa.

Yet the varied nature of what might be termed the recent Islamic resurgence creates tensions and contradictions within the religion. Abubaker Bagader maintains that historically during 'periods of political decline the ideals of Islam have been stressed in order to combat the threat of change, irrespective of whether this came from inside or outside' (Bagader 1994 p. 115). He cites four factors which he believes partly explain the rise in significance of Islam in the 1980s and 1990s: the success of the Muslim Brothers and the Islamic Revolution in Iran which confronted the modern world with a new set of ideas; the decline of Arab nationalism, continuous social and economic crisis and the diminishing legitimacy of the ruling elites; the modernisation process in the Arab world which dislocated traditional groups and created new social classes; and the increasing spread of secularisation among the elites of most Arab Muslim societies (ibid. p. 118). The Islamic responses to these challenges, however, manifested themselves in different groupings, some revolutionary, some spiritual, some ritualistic, some intellectual. Bagader sees a distinction between traditionalist groups which emphasise religious faith, piety and codes of dress; the Muslim Brotherhood groups which present an overtly political view, and the radical groups which reject gradual change in favour of extreme confrontation, at times with other Muslim groups, in order to establish an Islamic society' (ibid.). Some intellectuals and writers refer to Islam as dynamic and malleable, open to interpretation and carrying a propensity for conflict between traditionalists and reformers within the religion itself' (Bagader 1994; Arkoun 1994; Goytisolo 1994). Yet behind these pluralist elements lies the belief that to a greater or lesser extent, Muslim societies have forgotten *Taqwa* (fear of Allah and righteousness) (Hazrat Mirza Tahir Ahmad, Seventh Friday Sermon, 23 November 1990). Once *Taqwa* is lost, a condition of disobedience and transgression appears within societies. The great problematic for Islam is how to conduct the return to a state of *Taqwa*. Nazih Ayubi believes that political Islam, that which conjoins religion and state, appears to be a 'reponse movement to regimes that are avowedly more 'modernist' and secularising' (Ayubi 1991 p. 119). Militant Islamists do not simply refer to a traditional set of values and beliefs, rather, they largely improvise a 'novel religio-political body' of views based on specific readings and interpretations of the Qur'an' (ibid.).

How do these views fit into a development framework for less-developed countries? According to Hasan el-Turabi, Islam may provide 'the most powerful engine for development' (*Liberation* 5 August 1994). It may be that if the economies of sub-Saharan Africa are regarded as pre-capitalist, Islamic enterprises may be the 'spearhead for an emerging native capitalism, using its own cultural idiom and following its own behavioural patterns' (Ayubi 1991 p. 237). The appalling plight of impoverished developing nations has led some commentators to suggest that Islam could inflict no further damage on those countries than they have already suffered under the impact of neo-colonialism and capitalist marginalisation. In such circumstances Islam may assist them (Ahmed Rhiat 1995). Ayubi

believes there could be a gradualism in the spread of Islamic practices, and cites the examples of dress (*al-zayy al-Islami*) and non-usury
business, which may be adopted initially by some traditionalists then
'in a milder ameliorated form, by larger social segements', until it
is routinised as part of a general trend towards 'cultural nativisation'
(Ayubi 1991 p. 237). Perhaps, Islamic concepts relating to the establishment of an Islamic order are being 'gradually absorbed into a
broader intellectual discourse that is partly traditional and partly
communitarian' (ibid.). Nazih Ayubi refers to a possible emergence
of a process of 'cultural nativism' which situates Islam within a locale
and takes account of particular cultural patterns. Turabi, in outlining
the iniquities of the nation state touches on this aspect, but in a
very different way, when he refers to the ideal of Islam as being
one of 'freely associating social groups united by common descent,
custom, domicile, interest or moral purpose'. These groups,
however, should be united and balanced between the 'immediate
local community, the intermediate regional composite and the
distant universal collectivity' (Turabi in *Islamica* 15 March 1993).
Some intellectuals see Islam as a receding force in the industrial life
of secular countries in the Middle East, especially Iraq and Syria.
Islam is then largely reduced to a form of symbolism, illustrated in
calendars of religious celebration, and manifested in the Fast, the
Pilgrimage (*al-hajj*) and the Arms-Giving (*zakat*) (Al-Azm; meeting
1995; Goytisolo 1994). However, the particularist qualities of Islam
are already evident within the Middle East and in Africa as a whole
and can be glimpsed in countries as diverse as Iran, Sudan and
Saudi Arabia.

PATRON/CLIENT RELATIONS

In the recent relationship between the Middle East and Africa one
major catalyst for unity has been the economic and political linkage
forged in the early post-colonial years. However, it would be
misleading to judge that association to be untroubled and preserved
in the aspic of anti-imperialist nationalism. These sentiments may
have united disparate nation states in a common struggle against
external control in the 1950s and 1960s but the economic realism
forged in the 1970s has, at times, revealed unity to possess a shadowy
and chimerical quality. During that period academic studies
suggested that post-colonial affinities notwithstanding, a new and
more exacting relationship had developed, that of patron and client,

forged by an association between oil and aid and carrying the potential of a New Economic Order. In providing aid to poorer nations the relationship between the non-oil producing countries in the Third World and the oil-producing Arab states profoundly changed. As Le Vine and Luke put it:

> The Arab shift has left erstwhile African friends much worse off than they were before the new era dawned, turning them into clients and/or dependents ... and leaving them doubly vulnerable to political and economic changes in the international environment.
>
> (LeVine and Luke 1979 p. 97)

According to Tareq Y. Ismael, the exact direct or indirect effect of oil price fluctuations on non-oil producing African states is immaterial, the important point being that African oil consumers see the rise of the world oil prices as a serious threat to their development plans (Ismael 1986 p. 246–247). The difficulty with aid is that it has constantly to be re-negotiated and may, as Ismael points out, become an organ of foreign policy in so far as preferential treatment can be meted out to countries considered political correct or sympathetic. Choucri saw the political context of Arab OPEC aid as such: 'The predominance of petroleum in the economies of Middle Eastern states made the disbursement of oil revenues, that is, foreign aid, the major issue of economic policy. Surplus revenues gave the rich states a privilege' (Choucri 1976 p. 117). Certainly, Saudi Arabia has been criticised for missing opportunities and failing to use oil wealth more radically (Aburish 1994).

The Kingdom of Saudi Arabia provides the bulk of aid for Arab development projects. Dr Yousof Nimatullah, the Arab League's Assistant Secretary for Economic Affairs reported the statistics for the year 1992–1993 revealed that the Gulf Co-operation Council (GCC) gave development aid to other Arab states valued at 4.5 billion pounds. The GCC states account for 99 per cent of all development aid rendered by the Arab countries and of this total, Saudi Arabia provides almost 60 per cent. Saudi provides assistance to sub-Saharan African countries, through bilateral channels, grants and donations and economic and social development plans as well as through agencies such as the Islamic Development Bank, the International Islamic Relief Organisation and other agencies (The Kingdom of Saudi Arabia Relief Efforts, Riyadh, 1986). It established the Arabian Gulf Programe to support UN humanitarian development particularly in African states which earmarked around 40 per cent of its resources to the United Nations Children's Fund (UNICEF). Other agencies also benefited: World Health Organization (WHO), Food and Agriculture Organization (FAO), World Food Programme (WFP), the Environmental Programme, UNESCO and the Handicapped Programme.

Saudi development assistance for non-Arab African states totalled US$3, 500 million during the 1980s: irrecoverable grants and donations valued at over $US1, 000 million were extended to African states for various social, human, economic and developmental purposes; $US1,640 million in unconditional, concessionary development loans and $US725 million concessional cash loans to help execute reform plans and economic adjustments (ibid.). The predicted process of economic development in Saudi Arabia is, however, raising some fundamental political and economic issues: how long can the Kingdom resist political reform and the need to switch from public to private sector activity (Presley, *et al.* 1992; Ditchley Foundation Conference 1995). A recovery in oil revenues would be necessary to maintain old spending patterns and keep the existing political system afloat. The difficulty with Saudi Arabia, and more especially for countries depending on its donations, is that the country is a *rentier* state: the Monarchy's legitimacy depends upon the availability of money which the Kingdom then spreads as public *largesse*. Sufficient quantities of money are needed to secure the continued position and pre-eminence of Saudi Arabia within the Middle East as a whole, and also to finance its various donations to Islamic and development projects. With a population growth rate increasing by 3.8–3.9 per cent per annum, the likelihood of rising unemployment, deficiencies in the Qur'anic-based educational system and doubts as to whether alternative private sector utility companies will be allowed to emerge and compete with state firms, the fears are that these factors will be potentially destabilising. These worries are acknowledged by the government in Sudan who recognise the deficiencies of the Gulf states, fuelled by oil money but lacking industrial development. Clearly, the Gulf states cannot continually and indefinitely afford to give money to African states (El-Affendi 1995; interview)

ISLAMIC ECONOMICS

The difficulties with development aid from the Middle East to Africa leads to the wider question of Islamic economics. The Qur'an prohibits *riba*, which is generally taken to include all forms of interest payment. In this, Islam has much in common with a number of other pre-capitalist views, including mediaeval Christianity and Judaism. The first modern Islamic bank was established in Egypt in 1963 and as we have discussed in a previous chapter, an Islamic economic agenda is being presented as an alternative development strategy. Looking at the economic impact and possible application of the Islamic ban on interest on the economies of developing countries, David Cobham finds that Islamic banks need to have more information about the firms to which they lend (Cobham 1992). Such a system also requires substantial fixed-interest credits from banks to firms as well as equity participation. Islamic banking, therefore, is likely to be less flexible and potentially less conducive to economic development. It can also lead to much closer bank–firm relationships. In considering the case of Iran, Cobham finds that the proportion of Islamic bank lending remains low, partly conditioned by the weakness and lack of confidence of the private sector generally. Pakistan, on the other hand, experiences the effects of extreme caution among bankers in sharing ownership and control of businesses (ibid.). The most serious problem of Islamic banking, which has been identified in countries such as Sudan, Jordan and Saudi Arabia, is the failure to provide finance for industry (Wilson 1990). The permissible modes of Islamic partnership are short-term, which tend to inhibit long-term financing. Moreover, if banks finance imports without facing any risk themselves, which is contrary to the Islamic principle that they must not seek risk-free gain, they would not be conforming to religious requirements.

Looked at from this perspective Islamic economics may not automatically increase the development potential of sub-Saharan African states but, in a sense, Choudhury is right in his assertion that the economic systems of those countries are largely based on the 'Western free-enterprise or socialist paradigm' (Choudhury 1989 p. 389). He sees their overdependence on the export of raw materials to the industrial economies of the north as a major obstacle to the establishment of an Islamic economic programme. Equally, however, south-to-south trade has been hampered by a lack of co-operation between states. The goals, policies and strategies pursued by Islamic countries and their development finance institutions are far removed from Choudhury's theoretical foundation of Islamic ethico-economic development (ibid. p. 418). The Islamic Development Bank and other Islamic banks may provide examples of institutions working constructively in the direction of 'institutional reform and capital market development' (ibid.). But an inspection of IDB's accounts highlights the important role Saudi Arabia plays in resourcing Islamic financial institutions. Additionally, as Choudhury admits, the Islamic Conference Organisation is 'not sufficient' in forging an Islamic economic community, largely because it has no executive powers and all summit decisions and agreements can only come into effect after their ratification by individual member states. ICO decisions, therefore, are not binding on any member state (ibid. pp. 362–366). Individual countries become preoccupied with their particular national interests thereby working against the interest of the *umma*, the community of Muslim peoples. Islamic solidarity and by implication the pursuit of Islamic ethico-economics depends on the willingness of states to put aside their own national interests, economic or otherwise, in favour of the wider Islamic world community, which has certainly not been a general feature of recent economic behaviour in the Middle East. Admittedly, Choudhury, in developing his theory, has recognised the significance of potential conflicts of interest between the nation and the *umma*: decisions about locations for industries; regional allocation of funds for infrastructure projects; preferences for commodities, etc. (ibid.). If desperately impoverished sub-Saharan states were to be included in this procedure, with weak institutions and organisational frameworks and high levels of dependency, the propensity for economic discord and possible breakdown could be high. Also, around 60 per cent of the Islamic Development Bank's subscriptions come from only four countries: Saudi Arabia, Libya, Kuwait and Iran, all nations with varied patterns of Islamic political expression (see Table 7.1).

More generally, there exists a widespread public perception in parts of the Arab world that their economies are not really advancing as quickly as they could and that economic management could be better (Hammade 1993; interview; Wilson 1994). Although economic change and a degree of diversification has taken place in the last few decades, Rodney Wilson believes that development processes have been severely distorted. This situation partly results from the national boundaries inherited from the colonial era which to some extent perpetuate wealth and income inequalities. Migrant workers and remittance labour has been a feature of the region, exacerbating differences between the Gulf states and their poorer and more populated neighbours. According to Wilson most of the

Table 7.1 Subscription to IDB share capital on 30 June 1992 (ID Million)

Country	Subscribed amount	Percentage
1 Afghanistan	2.50	0.12
2 Algeria	63.10	3.11
3 Bahrain	7.00	0.35
4 Bangladesh	25.00	1.23
5 Benin	2.50	0.12
6 Brunei	6.30	0.31
7 Burkina Faso	6.30	0.31
8 Cameroon	6.30	0.31
9 Chad	2.50	0.12
10 Comoros	2.50	0.12
11 Djibouti	2.50	0.12
12 Egypt	25.00	1.23
13 Gabon	7.50	0.37
14 Gambia	2.50	0.12
15 Guinea	6.30	0.31
16 Guinea-Bissau	2.50	0.12
17 Indonesia	63.10	3.11
18 Iraq	13.05	0.64
19 Iran	177.50	8.75
20 Jordan	10.10	0.50
21 Kuwait	252.20	12.43
22 Lebanon	2.50	0.12
23 Libya	315.30	15.54
24 Malaysia	40.40	1.99
25 Maldives	2.50	0.12
26 Mali	2.50	0.12
27 Mauritania	2.50	0.12
28 Morocco	12.60	0.62
29 Niger	6.30	0.31
30 Oman	7.00	0.35
31 Pakistan	63.10	3.11
32 Palestine	5.00	0.25
33 Qatar	25.00	1.23
34 Saudi Arabia	506.37	24.96
35 Senegal	6.30	0.31
36 Sierra Leone	2.50	0.12
37 Somalia	2.50	0.12
38 Sudan	10.00	0.49
39 Syria	2.50	0.12
40 Tunisia	5.00	0.25
41 Turkey	160.00	7.89
42 Uganda	6.30	0.31
43 U.A.E.	143.72	7.08
44 Yemen	12.60	0.62
Total	2,028.74	100.00

Source: Islamic Development Bank 1993

Gulf oil wealth has been invested in the West not recycled within the Arab world, or indeed, the wider developing world (Wilson 1994 p. 141). The Arab Gulf countries assert that money invested in the northern Arab countries has largely been wasted in uncommercial, expensive state-owned industries and inefficient agricultural practices. Inevitably this criticism has been deeply resented by the non-oil producing states. Wilson sees the fostering of a new regional economic order based on economic co-operation to be 'more difficult than ever to achieve' (ibid.).

The extent to which Islamic approaches to development will be successful is open to question. M.A. Choudhury (1989) believes the existence of wide divergences in economic development, which socialist and capitalist practices have failed to resolve, demands an Islamic response but the extent to which joint venture projects and general economic programmes can be evaluated from a community rather than a national point of view without incurring conflict is problematic. This is not to argue, however, that an increase in south–south trade is undesirable. El-Affendi believes poor communications and transport networks combined with low levels of commercial expertise are contributory factors in the disappointing amount of trade between Africa and the Middle East (El-Affendi 1995; interview). Yet, Islamic economics is not only concerned with financial operations but includes social welfare services and education. The funding of these activities may come in part from donations and profits of Islamic ventures but they also result from religious payments or dues (*zakat*), which are given to voluntary societies.

POSTMODERNISM

Recently, the increased importance of religion in global politics has been partly explained by the intellectual discourse surrounding the concept of postmodernism and the decline of the 'Grand Narrative'. So is the Islamic development agenda for sub-Saharan Africa a postmodern phenomenon? In order to clarify the debate, distinctions must be drawn between three kinds of discourse: premodern, modern and postmodern. Premodern discourse can be characterised by the 'absence of a self-critical approach to one's understanding of the world which is structured by the language of the community to which one belongs' (Degenaar 1995). Often preliterate cultures fall into this category as do tensions between ethnic communities, largely because of the lack of a common ground. By contrast, modernism strives towards a rational explanation of the world by assuming that rationality has a universal validity which enables us to develop a 'Grand Theory' about reality and a 'Grand Narrative' of human progress. Premodern discourse is disqualified as backward, mythic, outdated, irrational. Postmodernism, on the other hand, assumes a plurality of ways of understanding and as Johan Degenaar explains: 'the mere existence of premodern, modern and postmodern discourses already illustrates the availability of alternative ways of structuring and articulating human experience' (ibid.).

Although these accounts seem straightforward, postmodernism at its most complex resists a single defining label. As a perpetual critique it seeks out areas which have been dismissed or forgotten, areas such as: 'the irrational, the sacred, the sublimated, the classical, the rejected, the peripheral, the tenuous, the silenced' (Rosenau 1992 p. 8). Tolerance of a multiplicity of forms, increasing societal fragmentation and representation, cultural heterogeneity, challenges to the sovereignty and centralising power of the nation state can all be identified as characteristics of postmodern politics.

According to Bryan Turner, Islamisation challenges the idea of a 'Grand Narrative', of a single national homogeneous identity. It undermines assumptions concerning the integration and ethnic coherence of the nation state (Turner 1993 p. 200). Certainly, Islamic intellectuals, political leaders and economic agencies all refer to the need to override the nation state in pursuit of Muslim solidarity and in this respect might be interpreted as postmodern. However, Islamic conversion follows a general process of homogenisation of religious belief and social practice. In fact, there are few dynamics more homogenising than the concept of the *umma*. But, it is the continuing discourse surrounding the traditional versus dynamic dimensions of Islam which rests at the core of where to situate Islam in the postmodern debate. If Islam adapts to changing global politics, adopts strands of other ideologies and straddles the private and public sphere in its ability to inform an understanding of how society is run on social, economic and behavioural levels, it surely must become a new 'modernism' or neo-modernist movement with its own 'Grand Narrative'. It will also provide a formidable development strategy for sub-Saharan Africa. However, if it assumes a retrogressive stance, continually seeking to re-enact past patterns of political organisation, it will become increasingly fragmented, intolerant and incoherent; a movement driven by its own divisions

235

and constantly challenged by its 'nervous discourses' (Sadik Al-Azm 1995; meeting). And, therefore, a premodern entity.

In order to firmly place an Islamic agenda into a postmodern category it would need to assume certain features. As Kearney asserts, it would have to 'enter into a dialogue with what is different and Other, and to welcome the difference' (Kearney 1988 p. 460). Pluralism and tolerance of the cultural or religious Other would be necessary. Historically, tolerance of other faiths was a distinctive quality of Islam but as Turner reminds us 'strong globalising tendencies have always existed within Islamic and Christian cultures' (Turner 1993 p. 201). Postmodernism is not concerned with a collision or levelling of differences but rather a negotiation of differences' (Degenaar 1995). A development agenda necessarily implies that countries within a region are moving forwards economically, politically, socially and to a degree that movement will detach those societies from previous patterns of political and economic exchange. The Namibian intellectual J. Diescho calls for more 'Africanness' and greater 'dignity' to be put back into Africa, with whatever consequences (Diescho 1995). Islam may provide a greater degree of 'Africanness' but only if it represents cultural and religious significance and identity. Forced religious conversion or Islam disseminated through economic power and control will merely reflect another form of domination.

COMPETING REGIONS

The question was raised earlier in this chapter: how far does the relationship between the Middle East and Africa continue to be relevant within a Third World context? This study suggests that the amalgamation of the two regions into this category hides the complexities of a changing association. In a sense, neither region is part of a Third World, the Middle East is moving to claim a Second World position whilst Africa slides into an impoverished Fourth World. Indeed, an alternative view may be that the whole system of numerical categories is redundant in a world which has changed radically since the terms were introduced. As states assert their identities and attempt to determine their own development procedures, politico-religious priorities and cultural/societal affinities, uniform notions of a 'Third World' are challenged. Other different categories emerge: the Islamic World, the Democratising World, the Arab/African World.

The importance of these developments, however, is not their emergence but the changing power relationships which are formed. And this is the key to understanding the contemporary relationship between the Middle East and sub-Saharan Africa. Remove anti-imperialist sentiments highlighted by the plights of Palestinians and South African Blacks which united the regions and their respective associations, the ICO and OAU, and a completely different picture emerges: one of dominance and subserviance, of aid and development strategies, of economic programmes and packages, of religious aggrandisement and revivalism, of tensions and conflict, of cultural and religious affinities. As Salim Ahmed Salim, General Secretary of the OAU asserts: 'terror and violence within Africa goes beyond simply political and ethnic differences' (Salim 1995; meeting). If we are to comprehend changes in the polities of sub-Saharan African states we must first acknowledge that Islam is a major influence.

APPENDICES

APPENDIX 1

CONSTITUTION OF THE REPUBLIC OF SOUTH AFRICA 1993

Constitutional principles

I. The Constitution of South Africa shall provide for the establishment of one sovereign state, a common South African citizenship and a democratic system of government committed to achieving equality between men and women and people of all races.

II. Everyone shall enjoy all universally accepted fundamental rights, freedoms and civil liberties, which shall be provided for and protected by entrenched and justiciable provisions in the Constitution, which shall be drafted after having given due consideration to *inter alia* the fundamental rights contained in Chapter 3 of this Constitution.

III. The Constitution shall prohibit racial, gender and all other forms of discrimination and shall promote racial and gender equality and national unity.

IV. The Constitution shall be the supreme law of the land. It shall be binding on all organs of state at all levels of government.

V. The legal system shall ensure the equality of all before the law and an equitable legal process. Equality before the law includes laws, programmes or activities that have as their object the amelioration of the conditions of the disadvantaged, including those disadvantaged on the grounds of race, colour or creed.

VI. There shall be a separation of powers between the legislature, executive and judiciary, with appropriate checks and balances to ensure accountability, responsiveness and openness.

VII. The judiciary shall be appropriately qualified, independent and impartial and shall have the power and jurisdiction to safeguard and enforce the Constitution and all fundamental rights.

VIII. There shall be representative government embracing multi-party democracy, regular elections, universal adult suffrage, a common voters' roll and, in general, proportional representation.

IX. Provision shall be made for freedom of information so that there can be open and accountable administration at all levels of government.

X. Formal legislative procedures shall be adhered to by legislative organs at all levels of government.

XI. The diversity of language and culture shall be acknowledged and protected and conditions for their promotion shall be encouraged.

XII. Collective rights of self-determination in forming, joining and maintaining organs of civil society, including linguistic, cultural and religious associations, shall, on the basis of non-discrimination and free association, be recognised and protected.

XIII. The institution, status and role of traditional leadership, according to indigenous law, shall be recognised and protected in the Constitution. Indigenous law, like common law, shall be recognised and applied by the courts, subject to the fundamental rights contained in the Constitution and to legislation dealing specifically therewith.

Provisions in a provincial constitution relating to the institution, role, authority and status of a traditional monarch shall be recognised and protected in the Constitution.

XIV. Provision shall be made for participation of minority political parties in the legislative process in a manner consistent with democracy.

XV. Amendments to the Constitution shall require special procedures involving special majorities.

XVI. Government shall be structured at national, provincial and local levels.

XVII. At each level of government there shall be democratic representation. This principle shall not derogate from the provisions of Principle XIII.

XVII:

1. The powers and functions of the national government and provincial governments and the boundaries of the provinces shall be defined in the Constitution.

2. The powers and functions of the provinces defined in the Constitution, including the competence of a provincial legislature to adopt a constitution for its province, shall not be substantially less than or substantially inferior to those provided for in this Constitution.

3. The boundaries of the provinces shall be the same as those established in terms of this Constitution.

4. Amendments to the Constitution which alter the powers, boundaries, functions or institutions or provinces shall in addition to any other procedures specified in the Constitution for constitutional amendments, require the approval of a special majority of the legislatures of the provinces, alternatively, if there is such a chamber, a two-thirds majority of a chamber of Parliament composed of provincial representatives, and if the amendment concerns specific provinces only, the approval of the legislatures of such provinces will also be needed.

5. Provision shall be made for obtaining the views of a provincial legislature concerning all constitutional amendments regarding its powers, boundaries and functions.

The powers, boundaries and functions of the national government and provincial governments shall be defined in the Constitution. Amendments to the Constitution which alter the powers, boundaries, functions or institutions of provinces shall in addition to any other procedures specified in the Constitution for constitutional amendments, require the approval of a special majority of the legislatures of the provinces, alternatively, if there is such a chamber, a two-thirds majority of a chamber of Parliament composed of provincial representatives, and if the amendment concerns specific provinces only, the approval of the legislatures of provinces will also be needed. Provision shall be made for obtaining the views of a provincial legislature concerning all constitutional amendments regarding its powers, boundaries and functions.

XIX. The powers and functions at the national and provincial levels of government shall include exclusive and concurrent powers as well as the power to perform functions for other levels of government on an agency or delegation basis.

XX. Each level of government shall have appropriate and adequate legislative and executive powers and functions that will enable each level to function effectively. The allocation of powers between different levels of government shall be made on a basis which is conducive to financial viability at each level of government and to effective public administration, and which recognises the need for and promotes national unity and legitimate provincial autonomy and acknowledges cultural diversity.

XXI. The following criteria shall be applied in the allocation of powers to the national government and the provincial governments:

1. The level at which decisions can be taken most effectively in respect of the quality and rendering of services, shall be the level responsible and accountable for the quality and the rendering of the services and such level shall accordingly be empowered by the Constitution to do so.

2. Where it is necessary for the maintenance of essential national standards, for the establishment of minimum standards required for the rendering of services, the maintenance of economic unity, the maintenance of national security or the prevention of unreasonable action taken by one province which is prejudicial to the interest of another province or the country as a whole, the Constitution shall empower the national government to intervene through legislation or such other steps as may be defined in the Constitution.

3. Where there is necessity for South Africa to speak with one voice, or to act as a single entity – in particular in relation to other states – powers should be allocated to the national government.

4. Where uniformity across the nation is required for a particular function, the legislative power over that function should be allocated predominantly, if not wholly, to the national government.

5. The determination of national economic policies, and the power to promote interprovincial commerce and to protect the common market in respect of the mobility of goods, services, capital and labour, should be allocated to the national government.

6. Provincial governments shall have powers, either exclusively or concurrently with the national government, *inter alia*:

(a) for the purposes of provincial planning and development and the rendering of services; and

(b) in respect of aspects of government dealing with specific socio-economic and cultural needs and the general well-being of the inhabitants of the province.

7. Where mutual co-operation is essential or desirable or where it is required to guarantee equality of opportunity or access to a government service, the powers should be allocated concurrently to the national government and the provincial governments.

8. The Constitution shall specify how powers which are not specifically allocated in the Constitution to the national government or to a provincial government, shall be dealt with as necessary ancillary powers pertaining to the powers and functions allocated either to the national government or provincial governments.

XXII. The national government shall not exercise its powers (exclusive or concurrent) so as to encroach upon the geographical, functional or institutional integrity of the provinces.

XXIII. In the event of a dispute concerning the legislative powers allocated by the Constitution concurrently to the national government and provincial governments which cannot be resolved by a court on a construction of the Constitution, precedence shall be given to the legislative powers of the national government.

XXIV. A framework for local government powers, functions and structures shall be set out in the Constitution. The comprehensive powers, functions and other features of local government shall be set out in parliamentary statutes or in provincial legislation or in both.

XXV. The national government and provincial governments shall have fiscal powers and functions which will be defined in the Constitution. The framework for local government referred to in Principle XXIV shall make provision for appropriate fiscal powers and functions for different categories of local government.

XXVI. Each level of government shall have a constitutional right to an equitable share of revenue collected nationally so as to ensure that provinces and local governments are able to provide basic services and execute the functions allocated to them.

XXVII. A Financial and Fiscal Commission, in which each province shall be represented, shall recommend equitable fiscal and financial allocations to the provincial and local governments from revenue collected nationally, after taking into account the national interest, economic disparities between the provinces as well as the population and developmental needs, administrative responsibilities and other legitimate interests of each of the provinces.

XXVIII. Notwithstanding the provisions of Principle XII, the right of employers and employees to join and form employer organisations and trade unions and to engage in collective bargaining shall be recognised and protected. Provision shall be made that every person shall have the right to fair labour practices.

XXIX. The independence and impartiality of a Public Service Commission, a Reserve Bank, an Auditor-General and a Public Protector shall be provided for and safeguarded by the Constitution in the interests of the maintenance of effective public service.

XXX. 1. There shall be an efficient, non-partisan, career-orientated public service broadly representative of the South Africa community, functioning on a basis of fairness and which shall serve all members or the public in an unbiased and impartial manner, and shall, in the exercise of its powers and in compliance with its duties, loyally execute the lawful policies of the government of the day in the performance of its administrative functions. The structures and functioning of the public service, as well as the terms and conditions of service of its members, shall be regulated by law.

2. Every member of the public service shall be entitled to a fair pension.

XXXI. Every member of the security forces (police, military and intelligence) and the security forces as a whole, shall be required to perform their functions and exercise their powers in the national interest and shall be prohibited from furthering or prejudicing party political interest.

XXXII. The Constitution shall provide that until 30 April 1999 the national executive shall be composed and shall function substantially in the manner provided for in Chapter 6 of this Constitution.

XXXIII. The Constitution shall provide that, unless Parliament is dissolved on account of its passing a vote of no-confidence in the Cabinet, no national election shall be held before 30 April 1999.

XXXIV. 1. This Schedule and the recognition therein of the right of the South African people as a whole to self-determination, shall not be construed as precluding, within the framework of the said right, constitutional provision for a notion of the right to self-determination by any community sharing a common cultural and language heritage, whether in a territorial entity within the Republic or in any other recognised way.

2. The Constitution may give expression to any particular form of self-determination provided there is substantial proven support within the community concerned for such a form of self-determination.

245

APPENDIX 2

THE WORLD BANK INFORMATION BRIEF
(C.02.4–93)

The debt crisis

Between 1972 and 1981 the external debt of developing countries increased sixfold to $500 billion. At the end of 1991, total external debt of these countries, including the hard-currency liabilities of the former Soviet Union – stood at $1608 billion.

The Mexican Payment Suspension 1982

With the 1982 decision by Mexico to suspend its debt repayment, the world became aware of the serious financial burden that accumulated debt can impose on developing countries. There were fears that a failure to pay back debt would lead to a complete breakdown of the international banking system. To avoid that outcome, banks and creditor governments responded with several measures, including rescheduling of payments and new loans.

The Baker Plan 1985

Many indebted countries had trouble attracting fresh loans from commercial banks. To overcome this impasse the then US Secretary of the Treasury, James Baker, put forward a three-year plan to stimulate new bank lending by fostering economic growth in indebted countries. This growth would result from a combination of trade liberalisation, increased foreign investment and privatisation of state enterprises.

Baker proposed that commercial banks lend up to $7 billion a year to a total of 17 countries. The multilateral development banks were to increase their lending to these countries by $3 billion. The industrialised countries were asked to augment these measures with greater trade and investment.

The Baker Plan envisioned the debt crisis as a long-term, structural problem whose ultimate solution would lie in better overall economic performance by the indebted countries. But the Baker Plan was not able to meet its main objectives. Commercial banks did not increase their loans as expected and indebted countries continued to pay more back to the banks in interest and principal than they received in new money. Foreign investors were slow to act and privatisation was not introduced in some of the major indebted nations.

The Brazilian Moratorium 1987

The decision by Brazil to suspend interests payments in 1987 led to a drop in the value of much Latin American debt, and so made holding such debt much less attractive to commercial banks. Many wished to sell their debt once and for all. In response, Secretary Baker proposed as an addition to his plan that several solutions be offered to debtors and creditors. This 'menu' approach included measures to convert debt into equity (debt/equity swaps), or bonds (exit bonds), which would allow banks to be free of their problem loans without resorting to outright cancellation.

The African Initiative

Meanwhile the World Bank launched its Special Programe of Assistance for poor, debt-distressed African countries. This programme quickly channelled loans to countries to support adjustment programmes in conjunction with debt relief measures and help from the International Monetary Fund (IMF). Most of the debt was owed to official sources (national and international aid and credit agencies), not commercial banks, and so debt reduction in these cases did not present a threat to the international banking system. Though the amount of money owed was not great compared with other developing countries, the debt was a major obstacle to economic growth.

The Toronto Terms 1988

Attention continued to focus on the problems of the poorest indebted countries, mostly in sub-Saharan Africa. At the June 1988 Toronto Economic Summit meeting of the Group of Seven industrialised countries, a set of rescheduling terms was proposed to the Paris Club to ease the debt burden of qualifying countries, both for concessional (at below-market interest rates) and for non-concessional loans.

IDA Lending 1989

The World Bank, through its concessional lending arm, the International Development Association, began a programme to support commercial debt reduction for the poorest countries. The IDA Debt Reduction Facility is one of the few efforts to ease the burden of the commmercial debt of poorer countries. Though commercial debt in IDA countries is a small part of total debt owed by developing countries, the high market interest rates of this debt make the burden of repayment greater.

The Brady Initiative 1989

The most important step to ease the debt burdens of middle-income developing countries was the intitiative of the then the US Secretary of the Treasury, Nicholas Brady, and was announced in March 1989. The assumption underlying Brady's idea was that banks would not provide new lending to less developed countries, and foreign investors would not return to them, until old debt had been reduced. Under this plan, the World Bank, the IMF, the Inter-American Development Bank and governments have provided loans to indebted countries to help finance debt buy-back or debt swaps. Mexico, the same country that precipitated the debt crisis in 1982, was the first country to benefit from the Brady measures in 1990. Through the Brady Plan, old debt began to be retired. Repayment prospects rose for the remaining developing country debt, reducing the risk for the banks holding such debt and prospects brightened for new loans and greater foreign investment.

Polish and Egyptian debt reduction 1991

In 1991 the Paris Club of government creditors announced a 50 per cent reduction in Poland's official debt and offered a similar write-off to Egypt. The decision to reduce Poland's debt was based on its severe economic difficulties and its reform programme, which is likely to cause additional temporary hardships for its people. Egypt's debt was reduced because of its role during the Gulf War, and its new economic reform programme sponsored by the IMF.

The Argentina Debt Reduction 1992

In 1992 Argentina signed an agreement that will greatly reduce its debt and debt service obligations to commercial banks. The arrangement, agreed to by Argentina's commercial bank lenders, permitted a restructuring of the country's $29 billion public debt, including $8 billion in interest arrears. Overall, debt and debt service to the commercial banks will be reduced by the equivalent of about $11 billion. The programme was supported with loans from the World Bank, the IMF, the Inter-American Development Bank and the Export–Import Bank of Japan.

APPENDIX 3

WORLD BANK INFORMATION BRIEF (C.03.4-93)

Glossary of debt terms

Commercial debt Debt owed to commercial banks. Most commercial debt in developing countries is owed to banks in the industrialised countries. Commercial loans are normally made at higher interest rates and carry shorter maturities than World Bank loans.

Debt/Equity swap Reducing a country's debt by exchanging it (sometimes at less than its face value) for shares in domestic private enterprises. A bank with an outstanding loan can exchange it for company shares or sell it to other investors who then exchange it for shares. Sometimes auctions are held where investors bid for the right to engage in debt/equity conversions.

Debt-for-nature swap A debt-reduction measure that has a positive environmental impact. A private conservation organisation, for example, purchases a country's commercial-bank debt (usually at a discount) and then exchanges it for that country's commitment to protect an environmentally sensitive area like a tropical rain forest.

Debt stock reduction The amount of decrease in net debt principal owed by a country through the use of debt/equity swaps, debt-for-nature swaps, buybacks or the issuance of bonds in exchange for outstanding debt.

Debt service The sum of principal repayments and interest payments actually made.

Debt service ratio Total debt service compared to exports of goods and services, including remittances sent by workers based overseas to home-country bank accounts.

IDA debt-reduction facility A $100 million fund established by the International Development Association, the arm of the World Bank which lends money to the poorest countries at below-market or 'concessional' rates. The money in this fund goes to help severely indebted, low-income countries reduce their commercial debt.

Official debt Debt owed by governments to other governments, usually to their development or export credit agencies, or to international financial institutions.

Offical development assistance Financial aid to developing countries and multilateral institutions provided by official agencies, including state and local governments, or by their executive agencies. ODA is administered with the promotion of the economic development and welfare of developing countries as its main objective, is concessional in character, and contains a grant element of a least 25 per cent.

Paris Club The name given to the *ad hoc* meetings of creditor governments that, since 1956, have arranged, when necessary, for the renegotiation of debt owed to official creditors or guaranteed by them. Neither the World Bank nor the IMF is a member of the Paris Club, although the IMF has played an increasingly important role in putting together debt-restructuring packages with commercial banks. To reschedule debt, both the Paris Club and commercial banks required the debtor country to have agreed on an economic stabilisation programme with the IMF.

Rescheduling Changing the terms of payment of interest or repayment of principal. Debt that is rescheduled may be paid back at higher or lower interst rates, or over a shorter or longer period of time. Countries seek rescheduling when economic problems limit their ability to service their debt according to the original terms.

Secondary market The market where buyers and sellers can trade sovereign debt, usually previously drawn commercial-bank loans. Currently the debt of many developing countries sells at below its face value on the secondary market, the discount reflecting the risk associated with holding such debt.

Severely indebted low-income countries The poorest developing countries, with heavy debt-burdens, mostly in sub-Saharan Africa. Their debt is owed mostly to governments and international financial institutions.

Severely indebted middle-income countries Better-off developing countries with serious debt burdens, most located in Latin America. These countries are prime candidates for Brady Initiative measures.

Special Program of Assistance A World Bank operation launched in 1987 and aimed at debt-distressed African countries. Under this programme, qualifying countries receive financial support for economic adjustment programmes and debt relief from official creditors.

Trinidad Terms A debt-reduction initiative advanced by the then Chancellor of the Exchequer of Britain, John Major, at a meeting in Trinidad of the Commonwealth countries in 1990. These proposals call for, among other things, the write-off of two-thirds of the debt of low-income developing countries.

APPENDIX 4

THE 'OSLO ACCORD'

Text of the Declaration of Principles

The government of the State of Israel and the Palestinian delegation, representing the Palestinian people, agree that it is time to put an end to decades of confrontation and conflict, recognise their mutual legitimate and political rights, and strive to live in peaceful coexistence and mutual dignity and security and achieve a just, lasting and comprehensive peace settlement and historic reconciliation through the agreed political process. Accordingly, the two sides agree to the following principles:

Article 1: Aim of the negotiations

The aim of the Israeli–Palestinian negotiations within the current Middle East peace process is, among other things, to establish a Palestinian Interim Self-Government Authority, the elected Council for the Palestinian people in the West Bank and the Gaza Strip, for a transitional period not exceeding five years, leading to a permanent settlement based on Security Council Resolutions 242 and 338.

Article II: Framework for the interim period

The agreed framework for the interim period is set forth in this Declaration of Principles.

Article III: Elections

1. In order that the Palestinian people in the West Bank and Gaza Strip may govern themselves according to democratic principles, direct, free and general political elections will be held for the Council under agreed supervision and international observation, while the Palestinian police will ensure public order.

252

2. An agreement will be conducted on the exact mode and conditions of the elections in accordance with the protocol attached as Annex I, with the goal of holding the elections no later than nine months after the entry into force of this Declaration of Principles.

3. Those elections will constitute a significant interim preparatory step toward the realisation of the legitimate rights of the Palestinian people and their just requirements.

Article IV: Jurisdiction

Jurisdiction of the Council will cover West Bank and Gaza Strip territory, except for issues that will be negotiated in the permanent status negotiations. The two sides view the West Bank and Gaza Strip as a single territorial unit, whose integrity will be preserved during the interim period.

Article V: Transitional period and permanent status negotiations

1. The five-year transitional period will begin upon the withdrawal from the Gaza Strip and Jericho area.

2. Permanent status negotiations will commence as soon as possible, but not later than the beginning of the third year of the interim period, between the government of Israel and the Palestinian people's representatives.

3. It is understood that these negotiations shall cover remaining issues, including: Jerusalem, refugees, settlements, security arrangements, borders, relations and co-operation with other neighbours, and other issues of common interest.

4. The two parties agree that the outcome of the permanent status negotiations should not be prejudiced or pre-empted by agreements reached for the interim period.

Article VI: Preparatory transfer of powers and responsibilities

1. Upon the entry into force of this Declaration of Principles and the withdrawal from the Gaza Strip and the Jericho area, a transfer of authority from the Israeli military government and its Civil Administration to the authorised Palestinians for this task as detailed herein, will commence. This transfer of authority will be of a preparatory nature until the inauguration of the Council.

2. Immediately after the entry into force of this Declaration of Principles and the withdrawal from the Gaza Strip and Jericho area, with the view to promoting economic development in the West Bank and Gaza Strip, authority will be transferred to the Palestinians on the following spheres: education and culture, heath, social welfare, direct taxation, and tourism. The Palestinian side will commence building the Palestinian police force, as agreed upon. Pending the inauguration of the Council, the two parties may negotiate the transfer of additional powers and responsibilities, as agreed upon.

Article VII: Interim agreement

1. The Israeli and Palestinian delegations will negotiate an agreement on the interim period.

2. The Interim Agreement shall specify, among other things, the structure of the Council, the number of its members, and the transfer of powers and responsibilities from the Israeli military government and its Civil Administration to the Council. The Interim Agreement shall also specify the Council's executive authority, legislative authority in accordance with Article IX below, and the independent Palestinian judicial organs.

3. The Interim Agreement shall include arrangements, to be implemented upon the inauguration of the Council, for the assumption by the Council of all of the powers and responsibilities tranferred previously in accordance with Article VI above.

4. In order to enable the Council to promote economic growth, upon its inauguration the Council will establish, among other things, a Palestinian Electricity Authority, a Gaza Sea Port Authority, a Palestinian Development Bank, a Palestinian Export Promotion Board, a Palestinian Environmental Authority, a Palestinian Land Authority and a Palestinian Water Administration Authority, and any other authorities agreed upon, in accordance with the Interim Agreement that will specify their powers and responsibilities.

5. After the inauguration of the Council, the Civil Administration will be dissolved, and the Israeli military government will be withdrawn.

Article VIII: Public order and security

In order to guarantee public order and internal security for the Palestinians of the West Bank and the Gaza Strip, the Council will establish a strong police force, while Israel will continue to carry the responsibility for defending against external threats, as well as the responsibility for overall security of Israelis for the purpose of safeguarding their internal security and public order.

Article IX: Laws and military orders

1. The Council will be empowered to legislate, in accordance with the Interim Agreement, within all authorities transferred to it.

2. Both parties will review jointly laws and military orders presently in force in remaining spheres.

Article X: Joint Israeli–Palestinian liaison committee

In order to provide for a smooth implementation of this Declaration of Principles and any subsequent agreements pertaining to the interim period, upon the entry into force of this Declaration of Principles, a joint Israeli–Palestinian Liaison Committee will be established in order to deal with issues requiring coordination, other issues of common interest, and disputes.

Article XI: Israeli–Palestinian cooperation in economic fields

Recognising the mutual benefit of cooperation in promoting the development of the West Bank, the Gaza Strip and Israel, upon the entry into force of this Declaration of Principles, an Israeli–Palestinian Economic Cooperation Committee will be established in order to develop and implement in a cooperative manner the programmes identified in the protocols attached as Annex III and Annex IV.

Article XII: Liaison and cooperation with Jordan and Egypt

The two parties will invite the governments of Jordan and Egypt to participate in establishing further liaison and cooperation arrangements between the government of Israel and the Palestinian representatives, on the one hand, and the government of Jordan and Egypt, on the other hand, to promote cooperation between them. The arrangements will include the constitution of a Standing Committee that will decide by agreement on the modalities of admission of persons displaced from the West Bank and Gaza Strip in 1967, together with necessary measures to prevent disruption and disorder. Other matters of common concern will be dealt with by this committee.

Article XIII: Redeployment of Israeli forces

1. After the entry into force of this Declaration of Principles and not later than the eve of elections for the Council, the redeployment of Israeli military forces in the West Bank and the Gaza Strip will take place, in addition to withdrawal of Israeli forces carried out in accordance with Article XIV.
2. In redeploying its military forces, Israel will be guided by the principle that its military forces should be redeployed outside populated areas.
3. Further redeployments to specified locations will be gradually implemented commensurate with the assumption of responsibility for public order and internal security by the Palestinian police force pursuant to Article VIII above.

Article XIV: Israeli withdrawal from Gaza and Jericho

Israel will withdraw from the Gaza Strip and Jericho area, as detailed in the protocol attached as Annex II.

Article XV: Resolution of disputes

1. Disputes arising out of the application interpretation of this Declaration of Principles, or any subsequent agreements pertaining to the interim period, shall be resolved by negotiations through the Joint Liaison Committee to be established pursuant to Article X above.
2. Disputes which cannot be settled by negotiations may be resolved by a mechanism of conciliation to be agreed upon by the parties.
3. The parties may agree to submit to arbitration disputes relating to the interim period which cannot be settled through conciliation. To this end,

upon the agreement of both parties, the parties will establish an Arbitration Committee.

Article XVI: Israeli-Palestinian cooperation concerning regional programmes

Both parties view the multilateral working groups as an appropriate instrument for promoting a 'Marshall Plan', the regional programmes and other programmes, including special programmes for the West Bank and Gaza Strip, as indicated in the protocol attached as Annex IV.

Article XVII: Miscellaneous provisions

1. This Declaration of Principles will enter into force one month after its signing.
2. All protocols annexed to this Declaration of Principles and Agreed Minutes pertaining thereto shall be regarded as an integral part thereof.

Excerpts from the annexes to the Declaration

Annex 1: Protocol on the mode and conditions of elections
Palestinians of Jerusalem who live there will have the right to participate in the election process, according to an agreement between the two sides.

Annex II: Protocol on withdrawal of Israeli forces from Gaza Strip and Jericho area.
1. The two sides will conclude and sign within two months from the date of entry into force of this Declaration of Principles an agreement on the withdrawal of Israeli military forces from the Gaza Strip and Jericho area. This agreement will include comprehensive arrangements to apply in the Gaza Strip and the Jericho area subsequent to the Israeli withdrawal.
2. Israel will implement an accelerated and scheduled withdrawal of Israeli military forces from the Gaza Strip and Jericho area, beginning immediately with the signing of the agreement on the Gaza Strip and Jericho area and to be completed within a period not exceeding four months after the signing of this agreement.
3. Other than these agreed arrangements, the status of the Gaza Strip and Jericho area will continue to be an integral part of the West Bank and Gaza Strip, and will not be changed in the interim period.

Annex III: This outlines fields on which an Israeli–Palestinian Standing Committee for Economic Co-operation will focus. These include water, electricity, energy, finance, transport, trade, industry, labour relations and social welfare, 'human resources', environmental protection, communication and media.

Annex IV: This is a protocol on regional development cooperation, within the context of the multilateral talks. The parties will seek the participation of the G-7 countries and other interested states in an Economic Development Programme for the West Bank and Gaza and a Regional Development Plan.

APPENDIX 5

ECONOMIC REFORM AND REGIONAL COOPERATION: A DEVELOPMENT AGENDA FOR THE MIDDLE EAST AND NORTH AFRICA

Partial text of speech given by Caio Koch-Weser, Vice-President, Middle East and North Africa region, World Bank in Washington 1992

There are five general themes and development challenges which apply to the region as a whole. Of these themes and challenges, the central and most pressing one is economic stagnation. The others may be seen as aspects, causes, or consequences of economic stagnation. They are:

population growth
unemployment
environment, especially water scarcity
economic management and governance

Economic stagnation/deterioration in the region Whereas the region performed relatively well in preceding decades, annual economic growth declined sharply in the 1980s to an average of 0.5 per cent per year. Over the same period, population growth averaged 3.1 per cent, well above increases in output. In this respect, the region, in spite of its good resource endowment, has failed to keep up with developments elsewhere in the world. Economic deterioration has been characterised by a sharp drop in the efficiency of the use of resources. The new capital required to produce a unit increase in output, a rough measure of economy-wide efficiency has increased significantly especially in countries with dominant public sectors e.g. Algeria, Syria and Egypt. Resources were also devoted to military rather than productive purposes.

At least six countries of the region devoted over 10 per cent of their GNP to military expenditures during the 1980s. In contrast, the same countries spent only 5 per cent on education and health combined. To this we must add the losses incurred during conflicts. The costs of reconstruction in Iran and Lebanon have been put at a staggering $US100 billion and

257

$US25 billion respectively. In addition, political stability, and the sense of insecurity associated with military activities have undermined the resolve of governments in the region to make difficult decisions necessary for long term economic development.

Population growth rapid population growth has complicated economic management and constrained overall progress. With annual growth rates exceeding 3 per cent many countries in the region have among the highest population growth rates in the world. Even under optimistic scenarios, none of the countries in the region is likely to reach a stationary population level until well into the next century. The resultant young age structure of the region's population – 44 per cent are under the age of 15, compared with 36 per cent for other comparable countries – poses unprecedented demands on the provision of education, health and housing. Already the region lags behind other comparable countries on all the basic indicators of education and health with some notable exceptions e.g. Tunisia.

Unemployment unemployment is a direct consequence of the inadequacy of growth in economic activity relative to population. It is now a serious problem throughout the region. Most countries have unemployment rates well over 15 per cent and the figures have risen to as high as 25 per cent. In addition, rapid population growth implies that increases in the labor force will continue to be felt over the next twenty years. Algeria's labor force, for example, will increase from less than 6 million to more than 20 million in the next twenty years. A large share of the urban unemployed in Algeria and Egypt, with a relatively high level of education are supporters of radical movements. The combination of high population growth and economic stagnation makes the unemployment problem particularly difficult and potentially explosive.

Environment and Water The region is rapidly moving to a water crisis with very few untapped sources of fresh water. The fact that most rivers cross national boundaries has been a source of increasing tension in the region. Rational management of the region's water resources will increasingly require agreements at national and trans-national levels. The region is also experiencing difficult environmental conditions due to urban migration and the concentration of population, industry and agriculture along the coast and in river valleys.

Economic management and governance Throughout the region, large but inefficient parastatal enterprises dominate the economy. One-half of Egypt's GDP is still produced by the public sector. The share of parastatals in industrial production in Algeria is over 80 per cent. Yet, the basic elements for economic and social progress also seem to be present:

> The region is and will continue to be relatively rich in resources. Almost two-thirds of the world total known oil and gas reserves are located within its boundaries.
> The location of the region, close to Europe and at the doorstep of Africa and the fast growing East, is strategic.
> The region has been a major exporter of capital to OECD countries.

258

The region has a large pool of skilled and relatively inexpensive manpower and a dynamic entrepreneurial and trading class.

So is there a case for optimism? The answer is a cautious yes. The success of the peace process in the Middle East can have an important role in accelerating the pace of reform. In all countries economic reform should take the form of macro-economic stabilization: liberalisation of exchange rates, interest rates and prices; the encouragement of private sector activity; increased trade; improvements in public sector management and the re-allocation of military expenditures to social sectors; an emphasis on education, training, health and population reduction. Regional investments in physical infrastructure can both strengthen regional integration and yield substantial economic benefits. Promising proposals in this category are:

> completion and improvement of the Highway Network 'M' linking the main urban and industrial centres in the Maghreb;
> reconstruction of the Eastern Mediterranean Coastal Highway linking Europe with North Africa through Turkey, Syria, Lebanon, Israel and Egypt;
> interconnection of the National Power Grids of Iraq, Jordan, Syria and Lebanon to benefit from significant differences in local demand patterns and cost of electricity generation.
> installation of the National Gas Pipeline System to supply Algerian gas to Europe through Morocco.

International Support

Because of the large demands on scarce international aid resources, country requests for external assistance will have to be exceptionally well substantiated and relatively modest in size. However, four principles underlie the basic international approach:

The first is the idea of 'burden sharing'. All parties both in the region and in the international community have an interest in stability in this part of the world. All should, therefore, share in the costs of securing that stability. For countries undertaking reforms, a significant part of the costs can be financed from reduced military spending. This is obviously a sensitive issue and easier said than done, but if the countries in the areas of tension could reduce their spending for military purposes to the average for all developing countries, they could release as much as 5 per cent of GDP for new investment. The capital-surplus countries of the region should also be expected to share the costs. The reopening of regional labour markets and private capital flows will certainly contribute significantly to the foreign exchange needs of the reforming countries and will make the contributions of the countries outside of the region relatively modest.

The second principle relates to the role of the private sector. To the greatest extent possible, private rather than official capital should be attracted to finance the development of the region. To restore the credit-worthiness of the countries of the region, debt and debt service reduction programmes will have to be pursued in some cases.

The third and fourth principles for international support are related: that international support be dependent on successful implementation of economic reform programmes and that this international support be provided in a way that contributes significantly to regional peace and reduces domestic tensions. Both principles can be pursued by using external support to fund specific programmes to help the unemployed or to finance some of the regional projects.

REFERENCES

INTERVIEWS/MEETINGS

Akbar, A. Royal Institute of International Affairs, Chatham House, London, May 1991.

Al-Azm, Professor S. St Antony's College, Oxford, May 1995.

Al-Azmuh, A. St Hugh's College Oxford, June 1991.

Aloui, S. Director Tunisian Information Bureau, London, July 1995.

Armanazi, G. League of Arab States, University of Durham, July 1995,

Bryer, Dr D. Director of Oxfam, London October 1993.

Carlsson, I. Prime Minister of Sweden and Ramphal, S. Secretary General of the Commonwealth 1975–1990 both Co-Chairpersons of the Commission on Global Governance, RIIA, London February 1995.

Chalker, Baroness L. UK Minister for Overseas Development, RIIA London, July 1994 and March 1995.

Cohn-Sherbok, Rabbi Professor D. London, June 1994.

Connolly, Father M. Holy Ghost Fathers, London, June 1994.

Decalo, Professor S. University of Durban, South Africa, July 1995.

Dembri, M. S. Foreign Minister of Algeria, RIIA, London, April 1995.

El-Affendi, Dr A. Former Cultural Attaché, Embassy of Sudan, January 1995.

Fuchs, P. Director General, International Committee of the Red Cross, Geneva, November 1994.

Hadjar, A. Highway Department, Damascus, November 1993.

Haines, Professor R. Executive Member, African Studies Association of South Africa, Port Elizabeth, South Africa July 1995.

Hammade, Dr H. Curator, Aleppo, Syria, November 1993.

Hamza, S. Cairo Museum, August 1994.

Hyden, Professor G. President of the American African Studies Association, Port Elizabeth, South Africa, July 1995.

Judd, F. Former Director of Oxfam, RIIA, Chatham House, London, 1995.

Kanoun, Mme H. Member of the Tunisian Chamber of Deputies, Conference of the British Society for Middle East Studies, University of Durham, July 1995.

Keller, E. Former President of the African Studies Association, University of Port Elizabeth, July 1995.

Klenk, Dr J. Staatlicher und Halbstaatlicher Unternehmen, University of Erlangen, Gesselschaft für Technische Zusammenarbeit, Germany, February 1994.
O'Leary, Father P. Society of African Missions, Nigeria, May 1994.
O'Toole, Father. V. Maryknoll Missionaries, London, June 1994.
Oumlil, Dr A. Arab Thought Forum, Amman. Jordan, November 1993.
Rodgers, Dr R. Light and Hope for Sudan, London, April 1995.
Sadik, Dr N. Secretary General of the United Nations Population and Development Conference, Cairo, Royal Institute for International Affairs, October 1994.
Salim, Dr S. A. Secretary-General of the Organisation of African Unity, Royal Institute of International Affairs May 1995.
Van Eeghen, W. Senior Economist, World Bank, Banz Castle, Germany, February 1994.
Venter, Dr D. Director of African Institute, Pretoria, South Africa, July 1995.
Walsh, Father J. Director of the Institute of Pastoral Affairs, Jos, Nigeria. August 1994.

TEXT REFERENCES

Africa Bulletin
Africa Contemporary Record
Africa Confidential
Africa Events
Africa South and East
African Business
Abdel Monem Said Aly (1992) Privatisation in Egypt: The Regional Dimensions, in I. Harik and D. Sullivan, *Privatisation and Liberalisation in the Middle East*, Indiana University Press, Bloomington.
Aburish S.K. (1994) *The Rise, Corruption and Coming Fall of the House of Saud*, Bloomsbury, London.
Ade Ajayi J.F. (1982) *Expectations of Independence*, Deadalus, London.
African Development Report (1993) African Development Bank Research Group, Cote D'Ivoire
Aidoo T.A. (1983) Ghana: Social Class the December Coup and the Prospects for Socialism, *Contemporary Marxism* no. 6
Ake C. (1990) *The Case for Democracy. African Governance in the 1990s*, Atlanta, Carter Centre.
Akintola S.L. and Balewa T. (1965) Nigeria Debates Self-government, in R. Emerson and M. Kilson (eds) *The Political Awakening of Africa*, Prentice-Hall, New Jersey.
Akbar A. (1992) *Postmodernism and Islam*, Routledge London.
Al-Hayat
Almond G. and Coleman J. (1960) *The Politics of the Developing Areas*, Princeton University Press, Princeton.
Almond G. and Verba S. (1963) *The Civic Culture*, Princeton University Press, Princeton NJ.
Al Saud Al-Sabah (1995) *Prospects for Kuwait*, Kuwait City, February.

REFERENCES

Al-Turabi, H. (1993) *Islamica*, London

Apter D. (1967) *The Politics of Modernisation*, University of Chicago Press, Chicago.

Arab Bank for Economic Development (BADEA) (1991, 1992, 1993, 1994) *Annual Reports*, Banque Arabe pour le Developpement en Afrique (BADEA), Khartoum.

Arkoun M. (1994) *Rethinking Islam*, Westview Press, Colorado.

Assaad R. (1994) *Structural Adjustment and Labor Market Reform in Egypt*, symposium on Privatisation and Economic Liberalisation in Socialist Countries of the Arab World, Centre for Regional Research University of Erlangen, Nuremberg Germany.

Awolowo O. (1965) Nigerian Nation and Federal Union, in R. Emerson and M. Kilson (eds) *The Political Awakening of Africa*, Prentice-Hall, New Jersey.

Ayubi N. (1991) *Political Islam*, Routledge, London.

BBC Summary of World Broadcasts (SWB)

Badie B. and Birnbaum P. (1983) *The Sociology of the State*, University of Chicago Press, Chicago.

Bagader A. (1994) Contemporary Islamic Movements in the Arab World, in Akbar S. Ahmed and H. Donnan, *Islam, Globalization and Postmodernity*, Routledge, London.

Balda J.L. (1993) The Role of Kiswahili in East African Islam, in L. Brenner (ed.) *Muslim Identity and Social Change in Sub-Saharan Africa*, Hurst and Co., London.

Batatu H. (1978) *The Old Social Classes and the Revolutionary Movements in Iraq*, Princeton University Press, Princeton, NJ.

Bayart J.-F. (1992) *The State in Africa*, Longman, Harlow.

Bendjelid A. (1994) *Algerian manufacturing: From Administered Economy to Market Economy*, Symposium on Privatisation and Economic Liberalisation in Socialist Countries of the Arab World, Centre for Regional Research, University of Erlangen, Nuremberg, Germany.

Berelson R, Lazarfeld P. and McPhee W. (1954) *Voting*, University of Chicago Press, Chicago.

Berger M.T. (1994) The End of the Third World. *Third World Quarterly* vol.15.

Bianchi R. (1986) The Corporatisation of the Egyptian Labor Movement, *The Middle East Journal* vol. 403.

Booth K. and Vale P. (1995) Security in South Africa: after Apartheid, beyond Realism. *International Affairs* vol.71, no. 2, April.

Bozeman A.B. (1976) *Conflict in Africa: Concepts and Realities*, Princeton University Press, Princeton, New Jersey.

Braudel F. (1969) *La Longue Dureé in Ecrits sur l'Histoire*, Flammarion, Paris.

Brenner L. (ed.) (1993) *Muslim Identity and Social Change in Sub-Saharan Africa*, Hurst and Co., London.

Bromley S. (1994) *Rethinking Middle East Politics*, Polity Press, Cambridge.

Brownlie I. (1983) *Basic Documents in International Law*, Oxford University Press, Oxford.

Bush R. (1983) The United States and South Africa in a Period of World Crisis, *Contemporary Marxism* no.6, pp. 36–43.

Callaway B. and Creevey L. (1994) *The Heritage of Islam*, Lynne Reinner Publishers, Boulder, Colorado.

Cammack P., Pool D. and Tordoff W. (1991) *Third World Politics*, Macmillan, Basingstoke.

Chabal P. (1992) *Power in Africa. An Essay in Political Interpretation*, Macmillan, Basingstoke.

Chazan N., Mortimer R., Ravenhill J. and Rothchild D. (1988) *Politics and Society in Contemporary Africa*, Lynne Rienner, Boulder, Colorado.

Childs S. (1994) .Women and Gender in South Africa, unpublished paper, University of Sussex.

Choucri B. (1976) *International Politics of Energy Interdependence*, Lexington Books, Lexington Massachusetts.

Choudhury G.W. (1990) *Islam and the Contemporary World*, Indus Thames, London.

Choudhury M.A. (ed.) (1989) *Islamic Economic Co-operation*, Macmillan, London.

Choueiri Y. (1990) *Islamic Fundamentalism*, Pinter, London.

Clapham, C. (1985) *Third World Politics*, Croom Helm, London.

Clarke W.N. (1891) *An Outline of Christian Theology*, Charles Scribners Sons, USA.

Cleary T. (1993) *The Essential Koran*, Harper, San Francisco.

Cobham D. (1992) *Finance for Development and Islamic Banking*, British Society for Middle Eastern Studies, Conference Proceedings, St Andrews.

Cohen R., Hyden G. and Nagan W. (ed.) (1994) *Human Rights and Governance in Africa*, University Press of Florida, Gainesville.

Coleman J. S. (1970) Sub-Saharan Africa, in G. Almond and J.S. Coleman (eds) *The Politics of the Developing Areas*, Princeton University Press, Princeton, NJ.

Commonwealth Observer Mission to South Africa (COMSA) (1993) *Violence in South Africa*, The Report of the Commonwealth Secretariat, Pall Mall, London.

Constantin F. (1993) Leadership, Muslim Identities and East African Politics: Tradition, Bureaucratisation and Communication, in L. Brenner (ed.) *Muslim Identity and Social Change in Sub Saharan Africa*, Hurst and Co., London.

Cooper S. (1994) Political Violence in South Africa: The Role of Youth, *Journal of Opinion* vol. XXII/2.

Coulon C. and D. Cruise O'Brien (1991) Senegal, in D. Cruise O'Brien, J. Dunn and R. Rathbone (eds)*Contemporary West African States*, Cambridge University Press, Cambridge.

Council for Education in World Citizenship (1995) London, January–February.

Crowder M.W. (1987) Whose Dream was it Anyway? Twenty-Five years of African Independence, *African Affairs* vol. 86 no. 342.

Dahl R.A. (1989) *Democracy and Its Critics*, Yale University Press, New Haven.

D'Arboussier G. (1965) The Theoretical Foundations of the RDA, in R. Emerson and M. Kilson, op. cit.

Decalo S. (1995) *Transitions to Democracy*, African Studies Association of South Africa, University of Port Elizabeth.

REFERENCES

Deegan H. (1993) *The Middle East and Problems of Democracy*, Open University Press, Milton Keynes.

Degenaar J. (1995) *The Concept of Politics in Postmodernism*, African Studies Association of South Africa, University of Port Elizabeth.

Diamond L., Linz J. and Lipset S.M. (1988) *Democracy in Developing Countries Africa*, Lynne Reinner, Boulder, Colorado.

Diescho J. (1995) *Democracy in Africa*, African Studies Association of South Africa, University of Port Elizabeth.

Ditchley Foundation Conference (1995) *The Gulf: Problems and Prospects*, Report.

Doumato E.A. (1992) Gender Monarchy and National Identity in Saudi Arabia, *British Journal of Middle Eastern Studies*, vol.19.

Durkheim E. (1976) *The Elementary Forms of Religious Life*, George Allen Unwin, Surrey.

Ehteshami A. (1994) *After Khomeini*, Routledge, London.

Ekechi F.K. (1971) Colonialism and Christianity in West Africa: The Igbo Case, *Journal of African History* vol. XII.

El-Solh R. (1993) Islamist Attitudes Towards Democracy, *British Journal of Middle Eastern Studies* vol. 20.

Emerson R. and Kilson M. (1965) *The Political Awakening of Africa*, Prentice-Hall, New Jersey.

Falola T. and Ihonvbere J. (1985) *The Rise and Fall of Nigeria's Second Republic 1979–1983*, Zed Books, London.

Fayek Mohamed (1985) *The July 23 Revolution and Africa* in Khair El-Din Haseeb, op cit.

Fetter G. (1964) A Comparative Study of Christian and Moslem Lebanese Villagers, *Journal for the Scientific Study of Religion* vol. 4, pp. 33–46.

Fieldhouse D.K. (1973) *Economics and Empire 1983–1914*, Weidenfeld & Nicolson, London.

Finer S. (1962) *The Man on Horseback*, Pall Mall Press, London.

Fischer S., Hausman L., Karasik A., and Schelling T. (1994) *Securing Peace in the Middle East*, MIT Press, Massachusetts.

Foucault M. (1995) Truth and Power, in D.Tallack (ed.) *Critical Theory*, Harvester, Wheatsheaf, Hertfordshire.

Frankl P. J .L. (1993) An Arabic Deed of Sale from Swahili Mombasa dated 1292/1875, *British Journal of Middle Eastern Studies* vol. 20.

Freitag U. (1994) Writing Arab History: the Search for the Nation, *British Journal of Middle Eastern Studies* vol. 21, pp. 22–45.

Frey F. (1963) Political Development, Power and Communication in Turkey, in L. Pye (ed.)*Communications and Political Development*, Princeton University Press, Princeton, NJ.

Fukuyama F. (1992) *The End of History and the Last Man*, Penguin Books, Harmondsworth.

Garnett J. (1991) The Role of Military Power, in R. Little and M. Smith (eds) *Perspectives on World Politics*, Routledge, London.

Geertz C. (1967) The Integrative Revolution: Primordial Sentiments & Civic Politics in the New States, in C. Welch (ed.) *Political Modernisation*, Wadworth Publishing Co. Inc., Belmont, California.

Gellner E. (1993) *Muslim Society*, Cambridge University Press, Cambridge.

Gellner E (1994) Introduction in Akbar Ahmed and H. Donnan Islam,

265

Globalisation and Postmodernity, Routledge, London.
Gerth H.H. and Wright Mills C. (1948) *From Max Weber*, Routledge, London.
Ghanaian Times.
Ghiles F. (1993) Shadow of the Sharia. *The Tablet* March.
Goldberg E. (1992) The Foundation of State–Labour Relations in Today's Egypt, *Comparative Politics* vol. 24 no. 2.
Goytisolo J. (1994) *El Pais* (trans. by P. Bush) 24 August.
Grove A.T. (1978) *Africa*, Oxford University Press, Oxford.
Habermas J. (1989) *The Structural Transformation of the Public Sphere*, parts III, IV, MIT Press, Cambridge, Mass.
Habermas J. (1995) Questions and Counterquestions, in D. Tallack (ed.) *Critical Theory*, Harvester Wheatsheaf, Hertfordshire.
Haddad Y. (1983) Sayyid Qutb: Ideologue of Islamic Revival, in J. Esposito (ed.) *Voices of Resurgent Islam*, Routledge, London.
Haines R. and Wood G. (1995) *Mozambique's Democratisation Process and its Developmental Implications*, South African Sociological Association, Grahamstown, South Africa.
Hallwood P. and Sinclair S. (1981) *Oil Debt and Development, OPEC in the Third World*, George Allen and Unwin, London.
Hardie A.R. and Rabooy M. (1991) Risk Piety and the Islamic Investor, *British Journal of Middle Eastern Studies* vol. 18
Harik I. (1994) Privatisation and Development in Tunisia, in I. Harik and D. Sullivan (ed.) *Privatisation and Liberalisation in the Middle East*, Indiana University Press, Bloomington.
Harris N. (1990) *The End of the Third World*, Penguin, Harmondsworth.
Hatem M. (1993) Post Islamist and Post Nationalist Feminist Discourses, in J. Tucker (ed.) *Arab Women*, Indiana University Press, Bloomington.
Haynes J. (1993) *Religion in the Third World*, Open University Press, Buckingham.
Hazrat Mirza Tahir Ahmad (1993) *The Crisis and the New World Order*, Unwin Brothers Ltd, Surrey.
Heal G. and Chichilnisky G. (1991) *Oil and the International Economy*, Oxford Univerity Press, Oxford.
Hess R. and Loewenberg G. (1966) The Ethiopia No-Party State: A Note on the Functions of Political Parties in Developing States, in J. Finkle and R. Gable *Political Development and Social Change*, John Wiley and Sons Inc., New York.
Hirschmann A.O. (1970) *Exit Voice and Loyalty: Responses to Decline in Firms, Organisations and States*, Harvard University Press, Cambridge.
Hughes A. (1992) *Marxism's Retreat from Africa*, Frank Cass, London.
Huntington S. (1967) Political Decay, in C. Welch *Political Modernisation*, Wadsworth Publ. Co., Belmont.
Hyden G. (1983) *No Shortcuts to Progress*, University of California Press, Berkeley.
International Islamic Relief Organisation, Jeddah, Saudi Arabia, May, July, December 1994, April 1995.
Islamic Development Bank (1991, 1992) *Annual Reports* Saudi Arabia.
Islamica
Ismael T. Y. (1969) Islam in sub-Saharan Africa, *Current History* no. 3. March.

Ismael T. Y. (1986) *International Relations of the Contemporary Middle East*, Praeger, New York.

Jalingo A.U. (1982–1985) Islam and Political Legitimacy in Northern Nigeria, *Kano Studies* vol. 2 no. 3.

Kainyah R. (1995) *The Trade and Environment Debate from the Perspective of Developing Countries in Africa*, ASASA Conference, South Africa.

Kamrava M. (1993a) Conceptualising Third World Politics: The State Society See-saw, *Third World Quarterly* vol. 14

Kamrava M. (1993b)*Politics and Society in the Third World*, Routledge, London.

Kayhan (1994) Vol. XV, 3 p. 917

Kearney R. (1988) *The Wake of Imagination*, Hutchinson, London.

Keesing's Record of World Events, CIRCA, Cambridge.

Kierkegaard S. (1974) in Brand Blanshard, *Reason and Belief*, George Allen & Unwin, London

Khair El-Din Haseeb (ed.) (1985) *The Arabs and Africa*, Croom Helm, London.

Kingdom of Saudi Arabia Relief Efforts (1986) *Saudi Arabian Government Report*, Riyadh, Saudi Arabia.

Klenk J. (1994) Experiences in the Design and Implementation of National Privatisation Programmes (Gesellschaft für Technisch Zusammenarbeit). Paper presented at Banz Castle, Germany, February.

Kokole A. and Mazrui Uganda (1988) in Diamond. Linz J. and Lipset S.M. (eds) *Democracy in Developing Countries, Africa*, op. cit.

Kornhauser W. (1957) *The Politics of Mass Society*, Free Press, New York.

Kukah M.H. (1993) *Religion, Politics and Power in Northern Nigeria*, Spectrum Books, London.

LaPalombara M. and Weiner M. (1966) *Political Parties and Political Development*, Princeton University Press, Princeton, NJ.

Lasswell H. and Kaplan M. (1950) *Power and Society*, Yale University Press, New Haven.

Lerner D. (1958) *The Passing of Traditional Society*, Free Press, Glencoe.

LeVine V.T. and Luke T.W. (1979) *The Arab–African Connection: Political and Economic Realities*, Westview, Boulder, Colorado.

Lewis I.M (1966) *Islam in Tropical Africa*, Cambridge University Press, Cambridge.

Liberation 1994

Light and Hope for Sudan (1995) Birmingham.

Lijphart A. (1977) *Democracy in Plural Societies: A Comparative Exploration*, Yale University Press, New Haven.

Luckham R. (1991) Militarism: Force Class and International Conflict, in R. Little and M. Smith (ed.) *Perspectives on World Politics*, Routledge, London.

McDonald M.V. (1992*) Al-Jihiz's Method of Composition: An Analysis of Risalat Fakhr al-Sudan ala al-Bidan*, British Society for Middle Eastern Studies, Conference Proceedings.

MacIntyre A. (1971) *Marxism and Christianity*, Pelican Books, London.

Magubane B. (1983) Imperialism and the Making of the South African Working Class, *Contemporary Marxism* no. 6, pp. 33–42.

Mandivenga E.C. (1991) Resurgence of Islam: Implications for African

Spirituality and Dialogue, *Religion in Malawi* no. 3 pp. 24–31.

Manor J. (ed.) (1991) *Rethinking Third World Politics*, Longman, Harlow.

Markakis J. (1992) cited in A.Hughes (ed.) *Marxism's Retreat from Africa*, Frank Cass, London.

Mbembe A. (1991) Power and Obscenity in the Post Colonial Period: The Case of Cameroon in J. Manor (ed.) *Rethinking Third World Politics*, Longman, Harlow.

Mboya T. (1970) in E. Kedourie (ed.) *The Mass Movement in Nationalism in Asia and Africa*, Weidenfeld and Nicolson, London.

Middle East International

Middle East and North Africa (1990) Europa, London.

Moinuddin H. (1987) *The Charter of the Islamic Conference*, Clarendon Press, Oxford.

Mosley P., Harrigan J. and Toye J. (1991) *Aid and Power*, vol. 1, Routledge, London.

Murphy E. (1994) Structural Inhibitions to Economic Liberalisation in Israel, *Middle East Journal* vol. 48 no. 1, pp. 35–49.

Musa, I.A. (1985) Islam and Africa, in Khair El-Din Haseeb (ed.) *The Arabs and Africa*, Croom Helm, London

Naim K. (1985) in Khair El-Din Haseeb (ed.) op cit.

Nwokedi E. (1994) *Violence and Democratisation in Africa*, Institut für Friedensforschung und Sicherheits Politik, Hamburg.

Nuar Adnan M. and Zainuddin M. (1989) Technical Programmes in M.A. Choudhury (ed.) *Islamic Economic Cooperation*, Macmillan, London.

Nzongola-Ntalaja T. (1983) Class Struggle and National Liberation in Zaire, *Contemporary Marxism* no.6

Oberschall A.R. (1969) Rising Expectations and Political Turmoil, *Journal of Development Studies* vol. 2, pp. 36–49.

O'Fahey R.S. (1993) Islamic Hegemonies in the Sudan: Sufism, Mahdism and Islamism in L.Brenner (ed.) *Muslim Identity and Social Change in Sub-Saharan Africa*, Hurst and Co, London.

Okuma W. (1963) *Lumumba's Congo: Roots of Conflict*, Ivan Obolensky, New York.

Omari C.K. (1984) Christian Muslim Relations in Tanzania; The Socio-Political Dimension *Journal of the Institute of Muslim Minority Affairs* vol. 5 no. 2, pp. 25–27.

Organisation of Arab Petroleum Exporting Countries (OAPEC) (1994) *General Secretariat Economic Report*, OAPEC, Kuwait.

Othman S. (1991) Nigeria: Power for Profit, in D. Cruise O'Brien, J. Dunn and R. Rathbone (eds) *Contemporary West African States*, University of Cambridge, Cambridge.

Ottaway, M. and Ottaway, D. (1986) *Afrocommunism*, Holmes and Meier, New York.

Overseas Development Institute (1994) *Political Liberalisation and Economic Reform*, ODI, London.

Peretz D. (1983) *The Middle East Today*, Praeger, New York.

Philips J.E. (1982–1985) *The Islamisation of Kano Before the Jihad*, Kano Studies vol. 2. no. 3, Nigeria.

Pinkney R. (1993) *Democracy in the Third World*, Open University Press,

Buckingham.

Pool D. (1991) *Democratisation and Its Limits in the Middle East*, Political Studies Association, Lancaster University.

Posusney M.P. (1994) *Labor and Privatisation in Egypt*, Symposium on Privatisation and Economic Liberalisation in Socialist Countries of the Arab World, Centre for Regional Research, University of Erlangen, Nuremberg, Germany.

Presley J., Westaway T. and Sessions J. (1992) *Saudi Arabia, Problems of Economic Development in the 1990s*, British Society for Middle Eastern Studies, Conference Proceedings, 1992.

Pye L. (1966) Concept of Political Development, in J. Finkle and R. Gable (eds) *Political Development and Social Change*, John Wiley & Sons, New York.

Randall V. (ed.) (1988) *Political Parties in the Third World*, Sage, London.

Roberts H. (1995) Algeria's Ruinous Impasse and the Honourable Way Out, *International Affairs* vol. 71 no. 2, pp. 247–268.

Rosenau P.M. (1992) *Postmodernism and the Social Sciences*, Princeton University Press, Princeton, NJ.

Said E. (1994) *The Politics of Disposssession*, Chatto & Windus, London.

St.Louis Sisters (1978) *The Contribution of the Society of African Missions*, Ambassador Publications, Nigeria.

Salim Ahmed (1985) *Arab Communities in Africa*, in Khair El-Din Haseeb (ed.) op. cit.

Seekings J. (1995) *Media Images of 'Youth' During the South African Transition*, South African Sociological Association, Grahamstown..

Seyyed Hossein Nasr (1975) *Islam and the Plight of Modern Man*, Longman, Harlow.

Shoush M.I. (1991) In Search of an Afro-Arab Idenity, *British Journal of Middle Eastern Studies* vol. 18, pp. 67–81.

Smith J.D. and Niedermeier E. (1995) *Health for All or Death for All – The Case of Southern Africa*, African Studies Association of South Africa (ASASA) South Africa.

South Africa's Elections and New Constitution (1994) International Affairs and Defence Section, research paper 94/60, House of Commons

Sudan Update (1994) vol. 5. no. 8

Summers L. (1992) *Scientific American* pp. 130–132.

Tetzlaff R. (1992) Politicised Ethnicity – An Underestimated Reality in Postcolonial Africa, *Law and State* vol. 46, pp. 35–46.

The Star, Amman, Jordan.

The Star International Weekly, Johannesburg.

The Tablet

Thisen J.K. (1994) *The Projection of Africa's External Debt by the Year 2000*, United National Conference on Trade and Development no. 82 Geneva.

Thompson G. (1995) *Ministering to the Oppressed: The Independent Charismatic Churches in Durban during the Early 1980s*, ASASA Conference, South Africa.

Thorold A. (1993) Metamorphoses of the Yao Muslims in L.Brenner (ed.) *Muslim Identity and Social Change in sub-Saharan Africa*, Hurst and Co, London.

269

Tordoff W. (1993) *Government and Politics in Africa* 2nd edn, Macmillan, Basingstoke.

Trimingham J.S. (1970) *A History of Islam in West Africa*, Oxford University Press, Oxford.

Turner B. (1994) *Orientalism, Postmodernism and Globalism*, Routledge, London.

Turner H.W. (1993) New Religious Movements in Islamic West Africa, *Islamic and Christian Muslim Relations* vol. 4. No. 1.

United Nations Commision on Human Rights on Sudan (1994) Report. *Opinion* Atlanta, US.

United Nations Development Programme (1993) *Human Development Report*, United Nations, New York.

United Nations Focus on the New Agenda for Africa (1993) United Nations, New York.

Uys S. (1994) *South Africa's Elections*, RIIA, Chatham House, London.

Van Dam N. (1979) *The Struggle for Power in Syria*, Croom Helm, London.

van Hoek F. and Bossuyt G (1993) *Democracy in Sub-Saharan Africa: The Search for a New Institutional Set Up*, Revue Africaine de Developpement, African Development Bank.

Vogt E. and O'Dea T. (1953) A Comparative Study of the Role of Values in Social Action in Two Southwestern Communities, *American Sociological Review* vol. 18, pp. 55–65.

Voll J. (1989) Islamic Fundamentalism, in H. Maull and O. Pick (eds) *The Gulf War*, Pinter, London

Wagner M.D. (1993) Trade and Commercial Attitudes in Burundi Before the 19th Century, *International Journal of African Historical Studies* vol. 26 no. 1.

Wagner R. (1991) Political Institutions, Discourse and Imagination in China at Tiananmen, in J. Manor (ed.) *Rethinking Third World Politics*, Longman, Harlow.

Wai D. (1985) African–Arab Relations in a Universe of Conflict: An African Perspective, in Khair El-Din Haseeb (ed.) Op. cit.

Wallerstein I. (1983) The Integration of the National Liberation Movement in the Field of International Liberation, *Contemporary Marxism* no. 6, pp. 17–25.

Warburg G.R. (1991) The *Sharia* in Sudan, in J. Voll (ed.) *Sudan State and Society in Crisis*, Indiana University Press, Bloomington.

Weber M. (1974) *The Protestant Ethic and the Spirit of Capitalism*, Unwin University Books, London.

Welsh, D. (1994) The South African Elections, RIIA, London

West Africa.

Westerminster Interfaith (1995) London.

Williams D. and Young T. (1993) *Civil Society and Democratisation*, British International Studies Association, Warwick University.

Wilson R. (1990) *Islamic Financial Markets*, Routledge, London.

Wilson R. (1994) *The Middle East after the Gulf War: The Regional Economic Impact*, Macmillan, Basingstoke.

Wiseberg L.S. (1994) The African Commission on Human and People's *Rights. A* Journal of Opinion, *Africa Studies*, Association vol. XXII/2.

Woods D. (1992) Civil Society in Europe and Africa: Limited State Power through a Public Sphere, *African Studies Review* vol. 35 no. 2, pp. 32–45.

REFERENCES

World Bank (1992) *Algeria: Labour Market Overview Study: Population and Human Resources Division*, Washington.

World Bank (1992) *Governance and Development*, Washington.

World Bank (1993) *Economic Development and Cooperation in the MiddleEast and North Africa*, no. 9, Washington.

World Bank (1993) *Environment and Development*, E.01.4.93, Washington

World Bank (1993) *Global Environment Facility*, E.02.4.93 Washington

World Bank (1993) *The IDA and Economic Reform*, B.06.4.93 Washington.

World Bank (1993) *The IDA and Infrastructure*, B.05.4.93 Washington.

World Bank (1993) *The IDA's Contribution to Poverty Reduction*, B.04.4.93 Washington.

World Bank (1993) *IDA and the Environment*, B.07.4.93 Washington.

World Bank (1993) *The IDA and the Tenth Replenishment*, B.02.4.93 Washington.

World Bank (1993) *The International Development Association*, A.01.4.93 Washington.

World Bank (1993) *The World Bank and the IMF*, A.02.4.93 Washington.

World Bank (1993) *The World Bank Group*, A.01.4.93. Washington.

World Bank (1993) *Toward a Market Economy*, D.01.4.93 Washington.

World Bank (1993) *War and Development*, L.01.4.93.Washington.

World Bank (1994) *World Development Report, Infrastructure for Development*, Oxford University Press, New York.

Wright M. (1989) *Iran, The Khomeini Revolution*, Longman, Harlow.

Yinger M.J. (1970) *The Scientific Study of Religion*, Macmillan, New York.

Young C. (1980) *Ideology and Development*, Yale University Press, New Haven.

Yousuf H.S. (1986) *African Arab Relations*, Amana Books, Vermont.

Zebasia, A. (1985) Islam, in Khair El-Din Haseeb (ed.) op. cit.

Zeinelabdin A. (1993) Technology Sustainable Development and Environment: OIC/UN Cooperation. *Journal of Economic Cooperation Among Islamic Countries* vol. 14 no. 2.

Zubaida S. (1990) The Politics of the Islamic Investment Companies in Egypt, *British Society for Middle Eastern Studies* vol. 17.

INDEX

272

INDEX

Awolowo, O. 19
Ayubi, Nazih 26, 225, 227–8
Azaouad Arab Islamic Front 119

Ba'th Party 42, 188, 190, 211, 222
Badie, B. 194
Bagader, Abubaker 226–7
Baker, James 246, 247
Baker Plan (1985) 179, 246–7
Balala, Sheikh Khalid 50
Balda, Justo Lacunza 199–200
Balewa, T. 21
Banda, Hastings Kamuzu 44
bank finance 231
Banque Arabe pour le Développement Economique en
  Afrique 96–106, 116, 131, 133
Barghash, Sultan 13
Basotholand Congress Party 43
Basotholand National Party 43
Batatu, Hanna 211
Bayart, Jean-François 7, 13, 18, 23, 25, 27, 72–3, 221–3
Ben Ali, President (Tunisia) 190
Bendjelid, Abed 161
Benin 59
Ben Masaoud Institute 120
Berelson, R. 35
Berger, Mark 220
Berlin Conference (1884) 14, 19
Bianchi, R. 160
Birnbaum, P. 194
Booth, K. 208–9
Bossuyt, G. 40, 58–9, 61, 62–3
Botswana Development Corporation 150
Boutros-Ghali, Boutros 32, 60, 134, 165, 214
Bozeman, Adda B. 193–4
Brady Initiative 179, 248, 250
Brady, Nicholas 248
Braudel, Fernand 7
Brazilian Moratorium (1987) 247
Brenner, Louis 11, 114, 222
Bretton Wood Conference 125
Bromley, S. 69
Brownlie, I. 115
Bryer, D. 40
Bugaje, Usman 52, 60
Burkina Faso 63, 164
Burundi 74, 187, 198, 199–200
Bush, R. 195
Buthelezi, Mangosuthu G. 208

Cairo 145
Cairo Summit (1977) 106–8
Caliphates 224
Call to Islam 52, 120
Callaway, B. 61, 74, 83
Calvinism 68–9, 135
Cammack, P. 12, 14
capitalism 195, 234
Catholicism 68–9, 71–5, 88–9
Chabal, Patrick 198
Chad 59, 74–5, 88, 119
Chalker, L. 3, 40, 47, 62, 149, 187, 206, 214
Chazan, N. 17, 18, 23, 24–5
Chichilnisky, G. 108–9
Chihana, Chakufwa 58
Chiluba, President (Zambia) 147
China 195
Choucri, B. 229
Choudhury, G.W. 52
Choudhury, M.A. 135, 139, 142, 167, 171, 231–2, 234

Chouciri, Y. 52
Christian–Islamic divide 8–11, 26
Christian Association of Nigeria 112
Christianity 65–6, 231; Catholicism 68–9, 71–5, 88–9;
  Protestantism 68–71; state and 72–5
civic culture 37–8
civil disorder *see* violent conflict
civil society 2, 38–40, 154, 209, 221
Clapham, C. 14, 19, 41
Clarke, W.N. 65
class struggle 195
Cleary, Thomas 65
clientelism 1, 42; patron/client relations 57, 95, 219,
  228–30
Clinton, Bill 205
Cobham, David 231
Cohen, Hermann 192, 211
Cohn-Sherbok, D. 65
Cold War 22, 37, 214
Coleman, J.S. 10, 51, 73
colonialism 11–18, 27, 73
COMCEC 169
COMESA 164
commercial debt 249
Commission on Global Governance 212
Common Market for Eastern and Southern African
  States (COMESA) 164
Commonwealth Observer Mission to South Africa
  (COMSA) 207–8
communism 37, 196; *see also* Marxism
competing regions (Third World Conference on
  Environment and Development (1992)) 176, 177
Conference of Southern African Maize Producers 167
conflict *see* violent conflict
Conflict Management Mechanism 212
Congo 19, 22, 56, 150
Connolly, Father M. 50, 60, 68, 71, 72, 73, 88, 116, 133
consociational democracy 49, 56–9
Constantin, F. 222
Constitution Amendment Bill (Malawi) 32–3
Constitution of South Africa 208, 241–5
Constitutional Conference 44–5
Convention People's Party (Ghana) 18–19, 21
Cooper, S. 215
Côte d'Ivoire 145
Coulon, C. 17
Council of Arab Ministers Responsible for Environment
  (CAMRE) 177
Council for Education in World Citizenship 213–14
Council for the Palestinian People 206
Council for the Protection of the Constitution (Iran)
  76
Creevey, L. 61, 74, 83
Crowder, M.W. 194
Cruise O'Brien, D. 17
cults 71–2
Cultural and Islamic Association of Mauritania 120
cultural nativism 228
cultural revolution 222
culture: Islam and democratisation 31–63;
  theocratic/secular states and societies 64–91

Dahl, Robert A. 34–5
D'Arboussier, G. 20
deaths (in wartime) 201, 202
debt: Baker Plan 179, 246–7; Brady Initiative 179, 248,
  250; crisis 109, 163, 179, 246–8; equity swaps 249;
  rescheduling 179, 250; service ratio 249; stock
  reduction 249; terms (glossary) 249–51
Decalo, Sam 197

273

274

INDEX

Overseas Development Administration 149, 187
Overseas Development Institute 59

Pakistan 231
Palestine: Israel conflict 114, 156, 204–6; Oslo Accord 205–6, 252–6
Palestine Liberation Organisation 111, 114, 117, 205, 206
Pan-African Telecommunications Union Conference 167
pan-Africanism 11, 192
pan-Arabism 21, 42
Paris Club 247, 248, 250
Patasse, Ange-Felix 119
patron-client relations 57, 95, 219, 228–30
peacekeeping forces (UN) 213–14
Peres, Shimon 205
Peretz, D. 77
Philips, John E. 9, 11, 24, 26
Pinkney, Robert 219–20
Poland (debt reduction) 248
political agendas 59–61
political change (in 1990s) 32–4
political leaders (power longevity) 203
political parties 40–1; African 42–6; South African 46–50, 206–7
political progress 36–8
politics 222; Islam and democratisation 31–63; theocratic/secular states and societies 64–91
polyarchy 34, 35
Poole, D. 57
Popular Movement for the Liberation of Angola 185, 195
population 258; conferences 88–9, 154
postmodernism 70, 219, 234–6
Posusney, M.P. 159, 160, 162
poverty 130–3
power 2, 203, 222
Preferential Trade Area 164
Presley, J. 230
privatisation 149–54
Programme of Targeted Interventions 133
Protestantism 68–71
Pye, Lucien 36–7, 187–8, 190

Qadhafi, Moammar al- 200–1
Qu'ran 8, 22, 53–4, 65–6, 77, 81, 119–20, 224, 227, 230–1
Qutb, Sayyib 54

Rabin, Yitsak 205
Rabooy, M. 139, 174
Radio-Television Libre Mille 198–9
Rafsanjani, Hashemi 80, 115, 123, 199
Randall, V. 43, 220
Rassemblement Démocratique Africain 20
regional influences see international and regional influences
regional co-operation (Middle East and North Africa) 154–9, 257–60
regional trade 162–7
regions, competing (Third World) 236–7
religion: beliefs 24–6, 64–8, 236; Christian-Islamic divide 8–11, 26; cults and magic 71–2; Protestantism 68–71; and the state 72–5; theocratic state 76–82; see also Christianity; Islam
Renamo 45, 192
rescheduling debt 179, 250
Rhiat, Ahmed 227
riba (prohibition of interest) 135, 231
Roberts, H. 203
Rosenau, P.M. 235

Rutomorangingo Radio 198
Rwanda 64, 73–5, 185–6, 198–9, 201
Rwandese Patriotic Army 185

Sadik, Nafis 88–9
Said, Edward 226
St Louis Sisters 73
Salim Ahmed 8, 17
Salim Ahmed Salim 32, 116, 166, 201, 237
Saudi Arabia 81–2, 117, 120, 229–32
Saudi Arabian Monetary Agency 174
Sauti ya Umma 199
SAVAK 77
SAVAMA 77
Savimbi, Jonas 185
Savir, Uriel 156
Schumpeter, Joseph 34
scientific socialism 196; see also Marxism
secondary market (debt) 250
sectoral adjustment loan (SECAL) 147–8, 152
secular/theocratic states and societies: beliefs 64–8; Protestantism 68–71; religion and the state 72–5; religious cults and magic 71–2; theocratic state 76–82; women and Islam 82–91
secular humanism 54
Senegal 25, 83, 90, 121, 122
Seyyed Hossein Nasr 76
Shah of Iran 77
sharia 60, 75–8, 81–2, 89–90, 119, 173, 194, 224, 226
Sharpeville Day Rallies 207
Shi'ism 54–5, 76–9, 122
Shoush, M.I. 223
Shura (consultancy) 52–3, 55, 60, 61, 225
Sierra Leone 188
Sinclair, S. 109
slave trade 7, 10, 11, 13, 24, 26, 223
Smith, J.D. 89
social and economic data: Africa 36–9; Middle East and Arab World 140–1
socialism 195–6, 197, 234; Ba'th Party 42, 188, 190, 211, 222; scientific see Marxism
'socialist nationalism' 42
societies, see theocratic/secular states and societies
Society of African Missions 74
Somalia 119–20, 186–7, 193, 197, 214
South Africa: constitution 208, 241–5; parties and elections 46–50, 61–2, 206–7; violent conflict 206–9
South African Health and Public Service Workers' Union 209
Southern Africa Development Community 164–5, 193, 209
Southern Africa Research and Documentation Centre 45
Soviet Union 22, 37, 151, 195, 197
Special Programme of Assistance 131, 247, 251
states see theocratic/secular states and societies
structural adjustment loans 58–9, 89, 105, 130, 146–9, 161–3, 165, 250
sub-Saharan Africa and Middle East (Third World perspective) 219–37
Sudan 81–3, 90, 119–20, 125, 167, 185, 186, 200, 210–11, 222; National Islamic Front 53–5, 117, 122, 225
Sudan Update 226
Summers, L. 83, 88
Sun Ray (newspaper) 44
Sunna 77, 81, 122
Supreme Assembly of the Islamic Revolution in Iraq 55
Supreme Council for Islamic Affairs 21, 119
Surat al-Ma'idah 120
Swahili 199–200, 222–3

277

INDEX